COLONIALISM IN INDIA

Ram Chandra Pradhan

Published by
PRABHAT PRAKASHAN PVT. LTD.
4/19 Asaf Ali Road,
New Delhi-110 002 (INDIA)
e-mail: prabhatbooks@gmail.com

ISBN 978-93-5266-434-4
COLONIALISM IN INDIA
by Ram Chandra Pradhan

Edition
2025

Price
₹ 400.00 (Rupees Four Hundred only)

Printed at
Narula Printers, Delhi

COLONIALISM IN INDIA

To the sacred memories of Acharya Dada Dharmadhikari: A seminal Gandhian thinker and a front-ranking freedom fighter

&

Shrimati Damayanti Dharmadhikari: A symbol of life-togetherness and a freedom fighter in her own right.

वन्दे मातरम्

सुजलां सुफलां मलयज शीतलां
शस्यश्यामलां मातरम्।
शुभ्र ज्योत्स्ना-पुलकित यामिनीम्,
फुलकुसुमित-द्रुमदलशोभिनीम्,
सुहासिनी सुमधुर भाषिणीम्
सुखदां वरदां मातरम्॥
सप्तकोटिकण्ठ-कलकल-निनाद कराले
द्विसप्तकोटिभुजैर्धृतखरकरवाले,
अबला केन मा एत बले।
बहुबलधारिणी नमामि तारिणीम्
रिपुदल वारिणीं मातरम्॥
तुमि विद्या तुमि धर्म,
तुमि हृदि तुमि मर्म,
त्वं हि प्राणाः शरीरे।
बाहुते तुमि मा शक्ति,
हृदये तुमि मा भक्ति,
तोमार प्रतिमा गंडि मन्दिर मन्दिरे।
त्वं हिं दुर्गा दशप्रहरणधारिणी
कमला कमल-दल-विहारिणी
वाणी विद्यादायिनी नमामि त्वां
नमामि कमलां अमलां अतुलाम्
सुजलां सुफलां मातरम्,
वन्दे मातरम्
श्यामलां सरलां सुस्मितां भूषिताम्
धरणीं भरणीम् मातरम्॥

Preface

I taught a course on 'Colonialism and Nationalism' in India for several decades at Ramjas College, University of Delhi. The idea of writing an authentic and standard textbook on the subject cropped up during my teaching years. The primary reason for such a felt-need was the absence of a standard textbook on the themes covered by the course. True, there are several history books. But they suffer from two major limitations. One, they are too heavy on facts and somewhat short on political developments and their analyses. Two, they appear to have fallen between two stools of research and textbook writings.

Prompted by all these reasons, I penned, *Raj to Swaraj : A Textbook on, Colonialism and Nationalism in India* which is being used by a large section of the teaching and student community. It has run through several reprints and has a Hindi version also. There is a plan to get it translated in several regional languages of India. I followed up with another book *Reading and Reappraising Ganthi*. Both these books present a comprehensive picture of our national movement.

However, on account of the introduction of the semester system in several Indian universities, including the Delhi University, there has been a separation of colonialism and nathionalism on semester basis. Hence, there has been a felt-need for a separate volume on colonialism as several new themes including the concepts like capitalism, colonialism, post-colonialism etc., have been included in the new syllabus. The present work attempts to cover all these themes between the two covers of the book.

I have retained my basic approach of an inclusive presentation of all viewpoints in this work as I have done in my earlier works. Such an approach is based on my conviction that any doctrinaire approach violates the basic norms of the textbook writings. Besides, it alone could enable the readers to see through the smokescreens created by the passionate argumentation and counter argumentation of the rival schools.

So far the arrangement of the material is concerned, I have adopted a thematic instead of a chronological order. Besides, several other reader-friendly measures have been taken viz. lucid and facile style, a fine balance between factual presentation and interpretative evaluation; interweaving each chapter with its historical context, so that each of them could be read independently. The book is divided in three parts. Part I deals with major theoretical concepts like capitalism, colonialism, imperialism, post-colonialism and nationalism. Part II deals with the issue of the British occupation of India and its overall impact on the several aspects of our national life. The major theme of Part III of the book is how India responded to the British challenge in thrce different ways: armed rebellion, socio-religious reform movement and through the emergence of national movement.

I owe a lot of intellectual debt to a number of scholars whose books I have used in the preparation of the present work. The list of such scholars includes historians like R. C. Majumdar, Tara Chand, B. R. Nanda, Bipin Chandra, Sumit Sarkar and Partha Chatterjee, and sociologists like T. N. Madan, D. L. Seth and political scientists like Rajani Kothari and Ramashray Roy. Macmillan Publishers India Ltd has been more than supportive of all my works.

In a book like this, it is quite natural for a few errors to have crept in both in terms of facts and interpretations. I invite my readers to join me in identifying them. However, presently, I alone should be taking the responsiblity for any error on these counts.

Ram Chandra Pradhan

Contents

Part I

Some Theoretical Concepts

When imperialism feels weak, it resorts to brute force.

Hugo Chavez

Every empire, however, tells itself and the world that it is unlike all other empires, that its mission is not to plunder and control but to educate and liberate.

Edward W. Said

What do nations care about the cost of war, if by spending a few hundred millions in steel and gunpowder they can gain a thousand millions in diamonds and cocoa.

W.E.B. Dubois

1 Capitalism: An Introduction

Capitalism is the astounding belief that the most wickedest of men will do the most wickedest of things for the greatest good of everyone.

J.M. KEYNES

Capitalism/liberalism and socialism/Marxism have been two major ideologies offering two different socio-economic political order in our times. However, after the collapse and disintegration of the Soviet Union and the communist China too taking to the capitalist road, Marxism as a working system has been on the decline, though purely at an ideological level, it still continues to be popular among a section of intelligentsia and even among the common masses. We know from the study of the world history that socialism/Marxism came up with a vibrant promise to remedy and remove the infirmities and iniquities afflicting the capitalist system of production. But in the course of its historical developments, it led to the emergence of a totalitarian system headed by a 'new' class which indulged in self-promotion putting aside the real interests of the common masses. All these developments ultimately led to its collapse in 1991.

Capitalism, on the other hand, is still going strong as a system, though at times, it appears to be on a life-support system. But from every crisis, it reappears in a new 'avatar' with a renewed determination to meet the challenges confronting it. Naturally, it raises an interesting question: What is the source of its enormous adaptability to the new challenges and new situations? Such an enquiry would also enable us to peep into its future and that in turn would require a close look at its historical developments. But first of all, one must have a view of its various definitions offered by different scholars.

True, there is no single definition of capitalism which is acceptable to all scholars. The primary reason for such divergence of views lies in its multi-dimensional character, which is why different scholars define it differently by underlining one or other of its dimensions. Besides, there is another reason for its not being defined in a precise and unanimous form. In the course of its historical developments, it has been assuming different colours and complexions. For instance, today's capitalism is entirely different from one that prevailed during the eighteenth century. Not only that, the kind of socialist capitalism prevailing in the ex-communist countries like China, hardly has any resemblance to the kind of capitalism prevailing in the Western countries. For all these reasons, it is difficult to arrive at a widely acceptable definition of capitalism. Many scholars attempt to define it by emphasing it as a system of production. Some other scholars prefer to look at it as a system in which the bulk of the means of the production is in the private hands. Still other scholars know it as a system which is primarily organised for optimising the profit-making. Another group of scholars underline its chief characteristics in terms of division of labour as its life-force which keeps it going; overcoming its numerous crises. At times, a mixed economy marked by the absence of all pervasive State ownership of the means of production is also taken as a capitalist system of production. Interestingly, even the Soviet system, with its all pervasive system of State ownership, was also characterized by some scholars as being nothing other than State capitalism. In a word, different scholars have attempted to define capitalism by stressing one or the other of its aspectual characteristics. It also goes without saying that its one or the other characteristics have been predominately associated with different stages of its historical developments.

Taking a synoptic view of all these, one could safely conclude that the capitalist system is marked by the following characteristics: profit making is the primary motive-force of production; market forces play the most crucial role in the entire system; the means of production primarily remain in the private hands and it is primarily marked by the system of division of labour and free labour.

However, it is interesting to note that even the above mentioned diverse characteristics are not exhaustive. In fact, a number of crucial questions still remain to be tackled and answered. Some of these questions are:

> What is the political system most suited to the capitalist system of production? What should be the relative role of the State, the civil society and market forces in the entire process? What kind of division of powers among the different organs of the government would be the most suitable for its smooth and effective working? What kind of party system would smoothen its working? What kind of institutional and ideological set up would enable it to meet the challenges of social justice on the one hand and the liberty of its citizens on the other? These and a number of other questions still remain in a realm of speculation, as it is difficult to find the exact and precise answers to all these questions. It is precisely for the above reasons that in the following pages an attempt would be made to understand and delineate the capitalist system by describing its major characteristics, instead of offering its exact definition in a few words.

Chief Characteristics of Capitalism

1. Capital: The concept of capital is the soul and quintessence of the capitalist system of production. It may be noted that there is a radical difference between the concept of capital and that of wealth. Wealth is a much wider concept. It could be used to meet the needs of accumulation, acquisition, consumption, self-indulgence and even for charity and other social purposes. On the other hand, capital is that part of wealth which gets invested to drive and promote the system of production. Capital could be owned by the private individuals or even by a State. But capitalism underlines the fact of the capital remaining primarily in the private hands though it does not completely rule our State ownership as a part of the entire system.

It needs to be stressed that the concept of capital is very complex. It is not that simple as it appears at the first instance. A number of questions get irretrievably associated with it. Some of these questions are: How does the primitive accumulation of capital take place? What kind of social system is congenial for its promotion? Is exploitation inherent in the very womb of capital? These and similar other questions have been subject of fierce debate among scholars. We do not have to deal with all these questions as they are beyond the purview of the present study. But it is clear from the above discussion that capital is that portion of wealth which remains surplus after meeting the needs of consumption. How that surplus is generated is again a controversial question. For surplus could be genuinely generated or could be forcibly taken by the powers-that-be. And again that surplus could be used for self-indulgence by the powers-that-be or it could be used to fire and promote the production system. For instance, the State could take away the surplus by using its enormous force at its disposal. Zamindars did extract surplus from tenants by keeping them at subsistence level. Broadly speaking, one could conclude that under the capitalist system, surplus wealth/capital mostly remains in the private hands and is used for making profit, though apparently working under a system of free labours.

2. Profiteering: It is taken to be the primary motive force of capitalist system of production. It needs to be mentioned that some kind of production as a means of livelihood has been in vogue since time immemorial, i.e., even during the days of primitive communism and feudalism. However, the capitalist system of production makes a departure, as it is not done purely for personal consumption. Rather, it is primarily done for the market with a basic motive for profit-making. In the process, a part of profit is turned into capital and gets invested in trade and industry. Market plays a crucial role in the entire process, as goods and services are circulated through it even to the far-flung areas. Not only that, even prices of goods and services are fixed through market based on the sovereign law of demand and supply.

3. Wage Labour/Free Labour and Division of Labour: Capitalism is also featured by a system of wage labour/free labour and division of labours. On account of the factory system, a very complex system of production develops under capitalism. In fact, the process of production of a particular product is not completed at a particular place or by a single individual. In other words, production is spread both in terms of labour as well as a place. Some workers produce some parts of a particular product, while other workers produce its other parts. Not only that, production of different parts may take place at different places and locations. For instance, in a case of shoe-making, it is quite likely that its sole could be produced at a particular place, while the other parts could be produced at different places and by different people.

So far as the labour is concerned, it could be procured from a market. In the process, workers could very well bargain about their wages and related facilities. This is what is called the system of wage labour or free labour as workers are free to move from one factory to another or one place to another in search of a better bargain. However, in actual life, the free labour may not enjoy absolute freedom to choose his job or his wage structure, as he may face many constraints on account of non-availability of better bargain. It also depends on the level of his skill available in the market – its scarcity or abundance. Accordingly, he could avail a bad or a good bargain. As stated earlier, the entire process of production is not completed at a single place or by a single individual. Hence, there develops a system of division of labour. No single worker could get the satisfaction for being the sole producer of a particular product. As a consequence, many scholars including Karl Marx have diagnosed the system of division of labour as being the chief villain of the piece for the intractable problem of the workers alienation arising out of distance between a worker and the final product he is associated with.

But let us not forget that a worker is not just a producer of goods, he is also a consumer of goods and other services. Hence, his economic condition also plays a role in the expansion of economic activities. If his economic condition is good and thus he has enough surplus resources, he could play an important role in the expansion of economic activities. If his economic condition is not good, it may adversely affect the economic activities of the society.

4. Economic Competitiveness: Competitiveness is one of the major characteristics of the capitalist system of production. At every stage, a system is marked by competition. A capitalist competes for a good bargain for raising the required capital from the market. He has also to compete with his peer groups for producing his goods at competitive rates. He competes for capturing the optimal size of the market for his goods. He has also to compete for the acquisition of labour and the raw materials at the cheapest possible rates. Not only that, he has to take work from the labour with maximum efficiency, and acquire new instruments and machines to maximize the production. In simple words, it can be said that the entire process of competition is always on and it never comes to an end. The fact of the matter is that if the entrepreneur fails to compete in any of the above mentioned fields, he may be forced to close his shop. But it also needs to be mentioned that the scope and opportunity of perfect competition is more imaginary than real. In actual life, it is the imperfect competition that rules the roost. This is so because the group of entrepreneurs engaged in a particular field more often than not enter into an agreement among themselves instituting some kind of a cartel. As a result, they succeed in taking some kind of collective decisions in respect of the quantum of production of a particular product as well as its pricing. Thus, it becomes difficult for other entrepreneurs to enter into the field and compete with the already existing cartel successfully. In actual practice, a kind of monopolistic control is created. What is more, such a development does not remain confined within the national boundaries of a particular country. In fact, it also covers the international field. And this is how a number of multinational companies come up playing such a crucial role both in the national and international market.

5. Financial Institutions and the Banking System: Money plays a crucial role in commerce, trade and exchange and distribution of goods through the market. In a capitalist system, sale and purchase of goods takes place virtually at impersonal level. Hence, a sound monetary system is required for all kinds of business transactions including for making and receiving payments. Not only that, as Max Weber rightly observes that a sound monetary system is also required for calculating the cost of production as well as for calculating the quantum of profit. Besides, it is also a well-known fact that a capitalist system could not be made fully functional under the old pattern of a small time private entrepreneur with his small private capital. Hence, a very good financial system is required for making all kinds of financial calculations including the quantum of capital and labour required. Hence, a sound financial system is required which could efficiently and effectively handle all these requirements. A good banking system handles and meets all these requirements. Thus, it is the bank that extends credits to the entrepreneur for all kinds of his financial requirements, be it for trade, commerce and capital investment. And that is why an economist like Schumpeter asserts that banking is the main feature of capitalist system, as most of its financial requirements are met by the banks. According to Schumpeter, it is the banking system that has become a hallmark of the modern capitalist system. In a word, capital has assumed two major forms – (a) as one of the major means of production, and (b) as different forms of financial assets in the capital market.

To sum up, the above mentioned characteristics of capitalism provide a fairly good and comprehensive view of the system. It goes without saying that their nature, structure, quantum and their respective role may differ in spatio-temporal terms. Nevertheless, they do constitute the main characteristics of the capitalist system.

Capitalism and the Political System

Historically speaking, there has been a close relationship between capitalism and the institution of State and the system of governance. In the initial stages of capitalism, there came to exist a virtual alliance between the kings and the merchants. Kings got the right to rule and collect taxes whereas the merchants had ample opportunities for profit-making. Thus, a bipolar authority system emerged under the capitalist system: kings were endowed with political power and merchants with economic power. Subsequently, this relationship between the king and the merchants became much more complex. Modern State plays a very crucial role in creating a congenial environment for economic activities. Some of these ways are:

(i) It promotes a social system which facilitates economic activities.
(ii) It builds up an institutional and legal framework which promotes competitiveness on the one hand and facilitates the exchange of goods on the other.
(iii) It takes major initiatives in building up different kinds of infrastructure which could not be handled by the private sector and which is required for the smooth functioning of the capitalist system. Thus, the State takes major steps in the field of education, public health, monetary matters, communications, etc., which could keep both material and the human capital in the working and productive condition.
(iv) The State undertakes such projects of public welfare essential for tackling emergency situations like economic depression and high incidence of unemployment.

In fact, there are several perspectives on the relationship between the State and the market forces. On the one hand, liberal thinkers inspired originally by Locke and Adam Smith, strongly believe that the market has great potentiality for self-regulation. Therefore, the State should play only the minimal role in the economic field. On the other hand, socialist thinkers, inspired by Karl Marx and his followers, do believe that the State should not only play a major role in the economic field, but it should also have the sole control over the means of production. There is also a third school of thought which believes that both State and the market could play equally important roles in the economic life of the people. However, in the present age of globalization and liberalization, the role of the State vis-a-vis the market forces is getting diminished in the economic life of the people. In the course of historical development, a very close and intimate relationship developed between the capitalist system and liberal democracy particularly in the areas like Western Europe and North America. However, of late some form of capitalist system is becoming popular even on the universal scale. In the process, some kind of disconnect is taking place between capitalism and liberal democracy particularly in the areas like Islamic World,

Latin American countries and ex-communist countries like China and Russia. Thus, one could hardly surmise whether the liberalized and globalized phase of capitalism would ultimately lead to some form of liberal democracy on a universal scale. But recent people's upheaval including in the Arab World, does hold robust hope towards a new dawn of democratic polity.

Different Forms of Capitalism

Capitalism has assumed different forms at different stages of its historical development. Besides, it has also taken to different hues while based in different socio-economic situation. Any detailed discussion on all these forms of capitalism is beyond the scope of our present study. It has covered a vast ground while transforming itself from *laissez-faire* stage to that of welfarism. But it was Lenin who traced the historical evolution of capitalism underlining its three stages of mercantile capitalism, industrial capitalism and financial capitalism. Incidentally, it continues to dominate the Marxist thinking even in our times.

Mercantile Capitalism

The historical period of mercantile capitalism is considered to fall between fifteenth and sixteenth century to the eighteenth century. It was a vibrant working system in some of the countries of the Western Europe. Trade and commerce was the primary characterstic of the mercantile capitalism. In others words, the main source of profit-making was trade and commerce–purchasing goods from South Asian and the East Asian countries at the cheapest possible rates and selling them in the European market at the highest possible rates. In the process, they made huge profits. The East India Company founded in 1600 could be cited as an illustrative example. Initially, the East India Company came into being by the energetic initiatives of some private traders and entrepreneurs. Subsequently, it was turned into a joint stock company after it had raised enormous resources for its working. In the course of time, it succeeded in garnering the State support which strengthened its position on a massive scale. Prior to that, Portugal had also an important role in the commercial market of India after Vasco da Gama had landed on the Indian coast in Calicut in 1498. Netherland was another country which also entered into the fray for a while. France was another country which competed with the British in the Indian market. However, on account of various reasons the British succeeded in driving out all these European powers from India and came to dominate the Indian market for many years. Germany, Belgium and Spain were some of the other European countries which launched similar ventures in Africa and Latin American countries, most of these commercial ventures ultimately resulted in colonial possessions. It is also believed that it was the loot of this phase of capitalism by the metropolitan countries which ultimately led to the ushering of the industrial revolution in most of the West European countries particularly in England.

Industrial Capitalism

Once the industrial revolution overtook the countries of the Western Europe, capitalism entered into its second phase which Lenin described as industrial capitalism. The distinguishing mark of industrial capitalism was that industrial goods started being sold to the colonial countries and the latter were turned into the producer and supplier of raw materials. Thus, there was a paradigm shift from trade to industry and major capital investments were started being made in industrial production, instead of trade and commerce. Not that trade and commerce were totally forgotten, but the industry became the main repository of the capital investment. Some of the West European countries, including Great Britain became major centres for industrial production. In the process, some of the characteristics of capitalism, which we have discussed earlier, started taking concrete shape. A large number of factories and industries were set up and capital investment assumed humongous form. In the process, labour market marked by the system of free labour and division of labour also came up in a big way. In the subsequent period, there emerged a conflict of interest situation between the labour and the capitalist class. The capitalist class was trying to retain the maximum amount of surplus value on the one hand and the working class was trying to maximise its wages and other working facilities. Capitalism faced tussel at every stage of its development. Here it needs to be pointed that the working class had a great deal of social role to play. They played a crucial role in the production system. At the same time, they were also playing the role of consumers of goods and services leading to the expansion of market in various fields. But the capitalist class was also looking for an assured market for their finished goods, as well as for acquiring raw materials. This accelerated the process of colonial possessions. Such a development further boosted the pace of industrial capitalism in the metropolitan countries.

Financial Capitalism

As stated earlier, during the days of industrial capitalism, banks and other financial institutions had started playing major roles in the entire process. On account of humongous expansion of trade and industry, enormous amount of surplus capital came in the hands of banks and other financial institutions. However, it was becoming less and less profitable to invest all the surplus capital within the boundaries of their respective countries. Such an investment could lead to several problems including that of overproduction. And such a situation could result in radical reduction of prices of goods creating a major crisis situation. Besides, in most of the metropolitan countries, trade unionism was gaining strength putting different kinds of demands in respect of their wage structure and other working conditions. Moreover, procuring raw materials from far-flung countries was raising the cost of production. Added to that was the transportation cost for taking out the finished goods to the different parts of the world. All these related problems were adversely affecting the market. Thus, it became obvious that the capital should be invested in the areas where it could yield the maximum profits; the areas where cheap labour and raw materials were available in abundance. Thus, metropolitan countries started investing their capital in their colonies as that would enhance the margin of profit which could be easily ploughed back on account of colonial control. This new form of capitalism, marked by export of capital rather than finished goods, came to be described by Lenin as finance capitalism. Different kinds of financial institutions including banks played crucial role in the entire process. Subsequently, all these led to the emergence of multinational companies (MNCs) which became important institutions in the international economic order.

Apart from Lenin's categorization of different system of capitalism as discussed above, there has been other types of its categorization based on the relative role of the State and market forces in the process of capitalist production which range from *laissez-faire* to State capitalism. *Laissez-faire* stands for the system of capitalism in which the State plays the minimum role and the market forces play the most dominant role. On the other extreme is the system of the State capitalism in which the State owns all the means of production and also plays a crucial role in the entire process of production. In this system, the State is also inspired by the profit motive, though it continues to clamour for the social good. In actual practice, the economic orders of some of the communist countries came to be characterised as State capitalism. Between these extremes, there lie different categories of capitalist system, viz. mixed economy, corporate capitalism, social market capitalism. Social market capitalism is the system in which though the means of production remain in the private hands but the State plays a dominate role in respect of labour laws, social security, etc. In the capitalist system of mixed economy, the means of production are owned both by the State and private individuals. Corporate capitalism is the one in which the economic life of the society is dominated by big companies and multinational companies.

Reasons for the Emergence of Capitalism in West European Countries Particularly in England

A lot of literature has been generated to explain the emergence of the capitalist system in the West European areas in general and England in particular including the work by Max Weber. Keeping in mind the limitation of our study, we could be hardly doing anything more than offering some general comments. The quintessential view is that the roots of the capitalist system in the

European countries could be located in the nature and structure of the feudal order which existed in this area. We know from the study of the British history that during the fifteenth century, one-third of the British population was wiped out by the pandemic spread of the bubonic plague, which in turn led to the scarcity of the labourers in the British society and the demand went up virtually in geometric progression. As a result, the workers could easily move from one place to another in search of better bargain. In the process, the feudal stranglehold over the peasants and workers got loosened. As a consequence, the seeds of market based capitalism were sown during those days. The feudal lords owning huge land-tracts started leasing out their land to the peasants. They had to compete for the peasants in the market. In the process, land became a marketable commodity, i.e., available for sale and purchase. The Enclosure Movement also played a crucial role in the entire process. Thus, a wage labour system started emerging in the agrarian field. Attempts were also being made to increase the availability of food even for those sections which were outside the agricultural productive system. This led to the emergence of the grain market, wherein the peasants could sell their produce. But with the improvement of the agricultural system, less and less number of workers were being required for the agricultural sector. Hence, they were available for getting absorbed in non-agricultural sector including industry. All these factors cumulatively created the congenial atmosphere for the emergence of capitalism in England. Besides, as compared to other European countries, social order in England was much more liberal and law abiding. As such, the feudal lords of England did not have the kind of freedom enjoyed by the feudal lords of the other countries. They have to work within the legal boundaries. These factors also contributed significantly for laying the foundation of the capitalist system in England.

Subsequently, capitalism also emerged in other European countries. Several explanations have been offered for such a development. One explanation is that in some of the European countries, city States had emerged in a significant way. In such areas, feudal lords had hardly much role to play in the entire system. In fact, the areas under the city States were primarily dominated by the culture of trade and commerce, which ultimately led to the emergence of capitalism in these areas. Some other scholars have tried to locate such causal factors in the very nature of the European feudalism. In these areas, there was neither any developed slavery system nor were there fully independent peasant classes. The system fell between the two extremes. Peasant had greater freedom than slaves, but less freedom than the fully independent peasants. They had to work for the feudal lords, but they could be paid in cash by them. Thus, farmers could earn their wages by working for the feudal lords. Besides, they could also sell their produce in the market. On the other hand, feudal lords could spend their earnings on the acquisition and consumption of luxury goods. Thus, a nascent system of market mechanism emerged which ultimately led to the foundation of capitalism in the European subcontinent.

Some other scholars have tried to link-up the emergence of capitalism in the European subcontinent with the prevailing system of multi-State system there. Such a system facilitated the movement of entrepreneur classes from one State to another State. Thus, they could easily move and invest their capital in the area which offered them better facilities, and in this way, some kind of market competitiveness developed in these areas. Max Weber was the most prominent scholar who underlined the role of religion in the emergence of capitalism. In particular, he stressed the role of the Protestant ethics and Calvin's new social values for the emergence of capitalism in the West European countries. Thus, their simple and intoxicant free life played a crucial role in the process of primary accumulation of the capital – an essential requisite for the growth of capitalism. Besides, these new religious leaders also underlined the fact that the empirical world despite its problems and travails was not to be rejected. Rather, one has to play a crucial role in working for its betterment. Not only that, they went to the extent of saying that the true service of God was to serve His world and its creatures. Consequently, religion started playing a crucial role in the day-to-day life of the people. These groups migrated to the countries of North-Western Europe. Besides, there was also a major migration of Jews in these areas – a group which was well-versed in the matter of trade and commerce.

For all these reasons, these scholars aver that capitalism emerged in the West European countries.

Capitalism: A Critique

As stated earlier, capitalist system of production has been changing its colour and has been assuming different forms and formats in the different phases. Capitalism has had a long history starting from the days of mercantile capitalism to the present age of liberalized and globalized capitalism. It has faced various kinds of criticisms in the course of history. The challenges have come from the trade union movement, from national liberation movement and also from its rival system of communism. Thus, it has faced criticisms from different quarters. Some of these major criticisms have been as follows:

(i) Capitalism has led to the creation of steep inequality on account of its exploitative character of exploitation of man by man. So much so that it has come to be identified with the problem of marginalization of millions of people. In the process, it has, so its critics allege, served only the interests of small sections of the society – the capitalist class.

(ii) In search for market, it has assumed the form of colonialism and imperialism and even neo-colonialism. As such, primary blame of the mass pauperization of the people of Asia, Africa and Latin America has been laid at its door. The Marxist has been in the forefront of these criticisms. They have not only offered its bitter critique, but also have tried to offer alternatives. Besides, the criticisms of capitalism have come from other groups like anarchists, Gandhians and even from post-colonialist and post-modernist thinkers.

(iii) Its philosophy of the conquest of Nature has broken the symbiotic relationship between man and Nature creating problems like climate change, warming of the earth, hole in the ozone layer and a host of other ecological imbalances.

(iv) The entire system of capitalism, so the critics allege, is based on greed rather than the need of man. Hence, it lays too much emphasis on the material aspects of human life, making it lopsided as it overlooks the spiritual and other aspects of human existence.

Reasons for the Survival of Capitalism

One question which continues to be raised is in the respect of its persistent survival despite all the criticisms it has faced throughout its history. Perhaps the most reasonable explanation for its persistent survival has been located in its being very near to human nature. It has come to be identified with individualism, liberalism, democratic principles and human liberty and freedom. Besides, today people also look at individual liberty and individual property being inseparable. Thus, human need for freedom and initiative has been the driving force behind human action that has turned out to be irrepressible. And this has also been the main sustaining force behind capitalism.

Another factor that has contributed to its survival could be located in its immense capacity for adaptability and flexibility. Its life force has remained evergreen as it has been ever free from atrophy and rigidity. Whenever faced with a challenge, it goes to the enemy's ground to imbibe and integrate some of its strong points without compromising its fundamental principles. This is how it has fairly changed its role from the minimum State to welfare State. Today, it has entered into a new phase of liberalization and globalization. In the process, it has tried to emerge as a universal system with some changes based on local and regional variations. However, in its much celebrated phase of globalization and liberalization, millions of marginalized people have been left behind. The crucial question thus is whether in its present avatar, capitalism would be able to take them along on the road to human liberty and prosperity? That future alone will be able to tell, though at present, it seems quite improbable.

2 Imperialism and Coloniälism: An Overview

The West won the world not by the superiority of its ideas or values or religion but rather by its superiority in applying organized violence. Westerners often forget this fact, non-Westerns never do.

SAMUEL HUNTINGTON

Imperialism and colonialism are often used as interchangeable terms as there is a lot of common ground between them. In modern parlance, they symbolize, convey and underline the fact of the physical, intellectual and cultural domination of the Western capitalist countries over those of Asia, Africa and Latin America. However, there is a section of scholars who believe that even the socialist countries like Soviet Union and the People Republic of China had and continue to have their own areas of colonial domination. However, we are not making a detailed investigation into the historical and ideological evolution of these terms. Our primary purpose is limited: to familiarize our readers with the basic contours of these terms. Hence, a brief introduction to these concepts would be more than sufficient for our study.

Imperialism

Let us first look at the concept of imperialism as it is an old and wide concept. Etymologically, the term 'imperialism' is linked up with its parental term of empire. The term empire, on its turn, refers to the process of domination, control and occupation of one country by the other. Traditionally, it is also taken as a term symbolizing the extension of the rule of one country over the other. The most illustrative example is taken to be the case of the Roman Empire.

But in the course of historical development, its meaning got extended as it started being looked upon as direct or indirect control of one country over the other. Initially, some of the countries of Western Europe like, Britain, Portugal, Spain, France and others came to be identified with imperial and colonial possessions. Subsequently, USA, Soviet Union and even the People's Republic of China were also put in the same category. Thus, the term imperialism has been evolving and today it stands for all attempts by strong and powerful countries to control and dominate the socio-economic and political lives of the weaker countries. However, it goes without saying that generally imperialism stands for the attempt of the Western countries to control and dominate the weaker countries. With this brief introduction, let us move towards providing a broad definition of the term, imperialism.

Imperialism has been defined differently by different scholars. For instance, Eckhart explains it by saying that it symbolises that kind of politics in which a particular country going beyond its political boundary establishes its politico-economic domination over other countries. Similarly, the Oxford Dictionary looks at it as a policy and attempt of one particular country which helps it in extending its power and influence over other countries through colonialization, through use of military force or by any others means. According to the same dictionary, the term empire indicates that situation in which some country or countries come under the domination of some others countries. Thus, it could be safely said that whenever a strong and powerful country establishes a kind of relationship with any weaker country which is marked by exploitation, domination and dependence that could be reasonably described as being an imperialist relationship. In fact, this is what exactly happened in the post-war period when the old pattern of imperialist occupation virtually disappeared. It was replaced by a new and subtle form of indirect control, exploitation and domination. In the new era, military aid, trade and commerce, economic aid and diplomacy became the major instruments of the imperialist control. However, there was some resistence to the Western imperialist moves on account of the existence of bipolar world, non-aligned movement and the challenge of communism.

But, with the collapse of the Soviet Union in 1991 and the the emergence of the policy of liberalization and globalization, the world virtually became unipolar dominated by the Western countries led by the United States of America. Thus, under the leadership of the USA, the Western countries unleashed and ushered into a new era of the direct use of military power and even physical occupation. And all these are being done in the name of war against international terrorism or the protection and promotion of the democratic rights of the people. The military intervention of the Western countries led by the USA in Iraq, Afghanistan and Libya are the illustrative cases of the new policy.

Colonialism

For a fuller understanding of imperialism, a close look at the term 'colonialism' is also required, as both these terms are virtually like twins. One could not be fully grasped without a clear view of the other. However, like imperialism, the term 'colonialism' has also been defined differently by different scholars. For instance, the Russian dictionary defines colonialism as a system in which a powerful country subjugates the weaker country through economic or military means and indulges in an excessive exploitation of the people of the subjugated country. A number of other Marxist and progressive writers also view it in the same perspective. Scholars like Palmers and Parkinsons have defined it by saying that when a country establishes a relationship of domination and control with a weaker country through political and economic control, the situation which arises constitutes colonialism. The Oxford Dictionary also defines it in the similar vein. According to it, colonialism denotes a policy or political behaviour of a country which establishes full or partial control over the other country. Such a state of control is achieved through colonial settlement of its people in that country or by imposing a relationship of economic exploitation through any other means. According, to the same dictionary the term 'colony' stands for a particular region or country in which the people from the distant places and from different culture come and settle down or start exercising the control over that region. Thus, the literal meaning of the term 'colonialism' is quite clear. But in more specific terms, it is related to the political and economic domination of the Western capitalist countries over those of Asia, Africa and Latin America. Historically, it has assumed three major forms. One, when a particular country occupies another region or country physically and totally subjugates the people of that region or country. In the process, the original inhabitants of the occupied country/ region are physically eliminated and remaining ones are sent to 'reservations'. It also results in the large scale settlement of the people of the occupying country in that region/country. This is what exactly happened when the people from the European countries occupied the landmasses of America, Australia, New Zealand and Canada. In such a situation, physical occupation and domination is total and complete. Another form of such settlement occurs when the people of a more developed region/country go and settle in another country, occupy a major part of that land, and that the original inhabitants are pushed virtually to the level of slavery. The settlement and rule of the white people in South Africa with their policy of apartheid was a classical case in this category. In both these cases, the people coming from the far off countries and who settled down in a new country virtually did lose physical contact with the countries of their origin. There is a third category of colonialism in which the metropolitan countries established political and economic control over other countries but do not settle down in a big way in that country. The British occupation of India falls in this category of colonialism.

Distinction Between Imperialism and Colonialism

Though quite often the terms 'imperialism and colonialism' are used interchangeably, but in the terms of nuances, there are subtle differences between the two, which could be underlined as follows:

(i) Imperialism is a much wider concept than colonialism. It denotes the relationship of domination and dependence in various overt and covert forms.

(ii) Colonialism refers to the entire historical process of colonial domination from the mercantile stage to that of direct political rule. But according to a Marxist thinker like Lenin, imperialism denotes only the monopoly phase of capitalism.

(iii) In the formal sense, colonialism came to an end in the post-war period when the process of decolonization came to an end. But imperialism in various subtle forms still continues to dominate the international world. In fact, it is spreading its tentacles in different parts of the world. Quite often, it is being described as neo-imperialism or even neo-colonialism.

(iv) Colonialism is marked by its directness and its visibility. The features of imperialism are much more subtle and indirect.

In a word, it could be safely concluded that colonialism created the ground through its various institutional frameworks on which the edifice of imperialism was built. And that is why imperialism is flourishing and its challenge is much more stupendous than the erstwhile colonialism.

Historical Evolution of Colonialism

One knows from the study of world history that in the ancient times there were no well-defined national boundaries. Thus, there were not much obstacles to the migration of people from one region to another. Hence, people from many regions/countries migrated to other regions and occupied them permanently. They came to accept their new habitation as their own land and were even acceptable to the people already living there. But in modern parlance, colonialism could be traced to the act of daring navigator of Portugal who during the fifteenth century reached out to the west coast of Africa. Ultimately, Vasco da Gama succeeded in reaching out to India in 1498 crossing through the Atlantic Sea. Prior to that, Columbus had discovered new land of America in 1492 though initially he had started on a voyage to India. These voyages of Columbus and Vasco da Gama opened the floodgates of colonialism. Portugal and Spain played crucial role in the initial stages of colonialism, though ultimately they were left out in the course of the long race of the colonial occupation. In the course of time, the entire North America was occupied by the people of Europe. Simultaneously, the people of Great Britain moved towards India and Indo-China regions, for the purposes of the trade and commerce. The major blow to colonialism was delivered by the people of USA who became independent in 1776. In subsequent times, the bulk of the people of the South America became free and independent by throwing away the Spanish colonial yoke.

However, during the nineteenth century, the European countries expanded their areas of colonial occupation in a big way. Ultimately, Britain and France emerged as big colonial powers with their strong colonial foothold both in Asian and African regions. Britain succeeded in occupying the bulk of the Indian territories and France occupied Indo-Chinese regions and Algeria. Though the Western countries did reach out to the mainland China, but no serious attempts were made to extend colonial control over mainland China. In the entire process, the Great Britain emerged as the greatest colonial power.

A new impetus for colonial occupation came in the last quarter of the nineteenth century. The primary reason for such dramatic change was the coming of the industrial revolution in most of the countries of Europe which led to the need for cheap raw material and also captive markets for their finished goods. This opened the floodgates of colonial occupation and intense competition particularly in respect of African regions. Soon the whole of the African continent came under the occupation of the European countries. During this period, a number of wars like the Spanish-American war, the Boer War, and ultimately the the First World War occurred, all of which in some way or the other were related to the colonial competition. At the end of the First World War, some areas which were under Germany and Turkey came under the tutelage of the allied powers. In a way, colonial occupation got a further boost at the end of the war, though the allied powers had earlier insisted that the war was being fought to promote the principle of 'self-determination.'

Interestingly enough, the end of the First World War also released anti-colonial forces in a big way. But it needs to be mentioned that India was in the forefront of the anti-colonial movement. In fact, the Indian National Congress ever since its inception in 1885 was spearheading anti-colonial movement in its own way. In fact, in the wake of the partition of Bengal, concepts like swadeshi, swaraj, boycott and national education had been popularised on a very significant scale. Going back still earlier, a number of rebellions had taken place in India as a part of anti-colonial movement which ultimately resulted in the great Indian Rebellion of 1857. Mahatma Gandhi's movement in South Africa was also a part of the anti-colonial movement, though its primary purpose was not the end of the British rule in South Africa. But after coming back to India in 1915, Mahatma Gandhi gradually involved himself in the National Movement and in fact became its undisputed leader. A new momentum to the anti-colonial movement was given by the October Revolution of 1917 in the Czarist Russia under the leadership of Lenin. But the Indian National Movement under the leadership of Mahatma Gandhi became the most vociferous voice in the anti-colonial movement. In the inter war period, Italy tried to occupy Ethopia and Japan was active in the South East Asian region and even tried to occupy the mainland China. Then came the Second World War which also boosted the anti-colonial movement in its own way. It was in the midst of the War that India launched the Quit India Movement, which became one of the major sources of inspiration for the anti-colonial movement. However, the end of the War marked a new phase in the history of the anti-colonial movement. With the independence of India in 1947, the process of decolonization gathered new momentum. Thus, by the middle of 1960's, a large number of colonies of Asia and Africa became independent. Only the questions of Rhodesia and South Africa remained, which also got solved by the end of the century. Thus, colonialism in the form of physical occupation of one country by another came to an end.

Colonialism: An Assessment

Scholars have held long and heated debate both on the character and impact of colonialism. That debate is still on even today. Those who have been justifying it mostly comprise the protagonist of the colonial powers. They justify colonialism both on the basis of the original aims of the founding fathers as well as that for its subsequent historical impact. They argue that the original purpose of the colonial expansion was to take the torch of civilization to the lands of the uncivilized people. This was called the 'civilizing mission' by the colonial powers-that-be. In other words, it was said that it was the responsibility of the white people particularly from the West European countries to launch a 'civilising mission' for the people of Asia and Africa. They even looked at it as their Providential mission. In some sections, it was also being described as 'White Man's Burden Theory'. The spread of Christianity also became an integral part of their project, so that the light of true knowledge could be brought to the people living in the areas of darkness. Subsequently, a racial element was also added to it. It was said that the white people represent the best of the races and there was work cut out for them to spread culture and civilization among the coloured races of the world. All this was nothing but an attempt to justify colonial occupation on the basis of the professed intentions of the colonial powers.

Besides, an attempt was also made to justify colonialism based on the historic impact on the people of the colonies. It was said that on account of colonial occupation, the people of the colonies were able to enjoy many kinds of fruits of development like rail, road, post and telecommunication and other basic amenities of life. Besides, they had also their own training in democratic processes, modern education, socio-economic reforms and even in modern system of health care. In the process, these societies were put on the road to modernisation, individualism, rationalism and the modern ideas of human liberty and equality. Not only that, modern mode of production informed by scientific methods was also introduced in these societies marked by the traditional mode and methods of production. In other words, on account of colonial occupation, winds of modernity started blowing in these areas.

It is interesting to note that even a revolutionary thinker like Karl Marx could not escape the impact of such colonial mindset. His entire theory of historical materialism was based on the limited history of the European countries and that too on the selected facts and evidences of his choice. The history and experiences of the people of Asia and Africa were hardly taken into consideration in the course of the formulation of his major thesis. He offered his own line of thinking and put it as a major theoretical formulation. He argued that agriculture in the Asian region needed more water as the land was dry. Hence, big irrigation projects were needed in these areas. Developing such large scale irrigation system was not possible on the individual basis. Hence, the state started playing a big role in the entire process of water management and irrigational facilities. Thus, there emerged a system which Marx called 'Asiatic Mode of Production' which in turn resulted in the system of Asiatic Despotism.

It was on the basis of such theoretical perspective that Marx while writing about the 1857 Indian Rebellion, underlined both the destructive and constructive impact of the British rule on the lives of the people of India. He did admit that the people of India had suffered immensely in the course of the British colonial rule, but he also asserted that it had helped India in transiting from the feudal stage to the capitalist stage. Marx's arguments were overstretched and virtually justified the British occupation in India. The entire thesis was based on a society moving from a lower stage to a higher stage from primitive communions to feudalism and from feudalism to capitalism. Finally, the capitalist system was to be replaced by a socialist society. But India did not go through the kind of feudalism marked by the manorial system which Europe had experienced in the course of its historical development. Hence, Marx's entire thesis on the Indian society was based on an ill perceived theoretical perspective.

So far such outlandish theories like White Man's Burden or civilizing mission marked by a deep but ill-founded racial theory are concerned, they were nothing more than a part of the make belief of some sections of the Western people who used them as shibboleth for justifying their colonial occupation. All these theories had neither historical roots nor scientific basis. Nor could they be justified on the basis of the actual history of the colonial rule and their major initiatives at the ground. History is witness to the fact that all these justifications were offered mainly for subjugating the weaker races of the world in terms of military and physical prowess and technological development. The leaders of the Indian National Movement vividly brought out the insincerity of the British colonialist through their studies and writings. The Indian nationalist scholars like R.C. Dutt and Dadabhai Naoroji, to name just the two of them, squarely blamed the British colonial rule for the mass miseries and mass pauperization of the Indian people. Similarly, socio-religious reformers like Vivekananda, Dayanand, Aurobindo, Tilak, Mahatma Gandhi and others challenged all claims of superiority of the Western civilisation over the Indian culture. They successfully established the superiority of Indian culture over the modern European civilization.

Besides, a number of modern scholars have dismissed the major claims of the protagonists of colonialism by raising some of the most serious theoretical questions. One of the major theoretical questions raised by these scholars is why even in the post-colonial era, the people of ex-colonies have failed to build up a rapid pace of development? Answering their own questions, some of these scholars have propounded the theory of underdevelopment and dependency. The major thesis of the proponents of the underdevelopment theory is that in the days of colonial occupation the surplus wealth of these colonies was appropriated by the colonial powers. As a result, these areas are perennially deprived of surplus wealth, which could have been invested to kickstart the process and pace of development. Hence, it is the deprivation of surplus wealth during colonial days which is primarily responsible for their underdevelopment. Looking back, one could clearly see that the theory of underdevelopment has some theoretical connections with Lenin's theory of imperialism. We may recall that Lenin's major formulation was that metropolitan countries had developed at the cost of their colonies, as the latter had been used as captive market for procuring cheap raw material, as well as for selling their industrial goods. Not only that, the colonial powers were also able to establish an alliance with the reactionary and retrogressive forces of colonies in their desire for strengthening their stranglehold over them. On the basis of the above, the theorists of 'underdevelopment' assert that the process of development in the ex-colonies had been thwarted in a very fundamental way in their colonial days.

Subsequently, scholars like Paul Baran and Gunder Frank further fine-tuned some of these theoretical formulations. Their main contention is that the developed countries find it difficult to make profitable investment of their vast capital within the boundaries of their own country. Hence, they try to invest their capital in several profitable ways. They invest in armament industry through which they make huge profit. But the bulk of their capital they also invest in their colonies. In this way, they escape the problem of excessive production in their own country, which in turn might create various kinds of economic crisis. In the process, they also succeed in imposing their own model of development on their ex-colonies. They do make huge profits which they might share with the elite section of these areas, so that their stranglehold goes unchallenged. Hence, they invest their capital in the areas which provide a congenial environment for the maximization of their profits. Thus, the process of real development in these areas gets stunted and the people of these areas continue to be in the grip of poverty. Gunder Frank has put the entire thing in his own theoretical perspective.

Similarly, the proponents of dependency theory do contend that ex-colonies even in the post-colonial era keep on depending on their ex-metropolitan countries for capital investment as well as technological help. They further contend that the elite of these under developed countries entered into some kind of alliance with the capitalist class of the developed world. Both these groups join hands for exploitation of the people of these areas. Such a dependency is becoming more evident in the days of liberalization and globalization. In fact, the so called free trade has primarily helped the developed countries.

There are scholars who challenge the above theoretical formulation. They contend that these theorists have indulged in exaggeration both in terms of facts and arguments. They further argue that it is not true to say that these areas are not developing. In support of their argument they cite the examples of India and China and some of the countries of South East Asia. In fact, India and

China are emerging as great economic powers. All these facts go to prove that the theorist of 'dependency' and underdevelopment have overstated their case, though there might be some truth in their basic formulation. But the fact that the benefits of development are not reaching equitably to the weaker sections of the societies is too glaring to be ignored by any serious scholar.

Leaving aside these theoretical debates, it could be safely concluded that the colonial system greatly harmed the basic interests of the people of their colonies. They have profited much less than what they have lost in the process. And it goes without saying that metropolitan countries have been real beneficiaries in this relationship at every stage of historical development.

3 Theories of Imperialism: An Evaluation

If it were necessary to give the briefest possible definition of imperialism, we should have to say that imperialism is the monopoly stage of capitalism.

V.I. LENIN

Imperialism has been studied by a number of scholars and thinkers. It continues to attract the attention of scholars and social activists even today. Some of the activist theorists have made in-depth study of imperialism and its historical importance. They have dealt with a number of critical questions relating to imperialism – its origin, evolution and its role in the world history. Some of these questions are: Is imperialism the child of capitalism? Or does have it to do more with the relationship between the powerful and the weak nations irrespective of their ideological moorings? Will it last forever? Or will it collapse at the end of the colonial era? Or will it assume a more subtle and indirect form and continue even in the post-independent era? Could even a socialist country develop an imperialist design? These and similar other questions have been dealt with by a number of theorists and activists. However, in the present study we would be confining ourselves to examine four main thinkers, who have made significant contributions towards the study of imperialism. The reason for such selection is based on our understanding that most of the questions raised above have been dealt with by them in a comprehensive way. Four major theorists of imperialism under our study are J.A. Hobson, Rosa Luxemburg, V.I. Lenin and Joseph Schumpeter.

J.A. Hobson

J.A. Hobson, a well-known intellectual of the labour party, made a detailed investigation into the phenomenon of imperialism in his book, *Imperialism: A Study* written in 1902. Delving deep into the nature and structure of imperialism, he did concede that the imperialist expansion is inherent in the very womb of capitalism. However, simultaneously he also submitted that such an outgrowth need not be inevitable. For the easy understanding and convenience of our readers, we would sum-up Hobson's views on the origins and growth of imperialism along with his line of arguments as follows:

(1) Hobson is firmly of the opinion that the capitalist countries are out to capture the natural resources of the less developed countries. These capitalist countries even compete among themselves for such a profitable enterprise. According to him, the primary reason for such cut-throat competition is that they need captive markets both for selling their finished product, as well as for acquiring the needed raw materials at the cheapest possible rate. These capitalist countries also need these colonies for profitable investment of their abundant capital. For securing all these objectives, they try to mobilise public opinion inside their own country by arousing a deep feeling of nationalism, at times even verging on jingoism. Not only that, they even do not hesitate to resort to militarism to promote and secure their political and economic interests. To that end, they create a cartel and conglomeration of a number of vested interest groups like companies interested in import and export and armament production, Christian missionaries committed to the spread of Christianity and those sections of the capitalist classes who want to invest in those areas. Hobson is firmly of the opinion that there are both economic and non-economic reasons for the imperialist expansion. But he hastens to add that only the capitalist class and not the general public of the Great Britain has been real beneficiaries of such imperialist expansion. Thus, capitalism coupled with the imperialist expansion has resulted in the emergence of an iniquitous class structure both in the metropolitan countries as well as in the colonies.

(2) If the imperialist expansion has not done any good to the general masses of the metropolitan countries, then why is there fierce competition for the acquisition of the colonies? According to Hobson, the primary incentive for imperialist expansion is related to the greed for accumulation of capital which is made possible by the high margins of profit and saving on account of the colonial earnings. Another reason for competition for acquiring colonies is related to the problem of under consumption of goods at the level of the masses. Besides, the wages of the working class is deliberately kept at the minimum level resulting in their subsistence living and minimal purchasing power. The capitalist classes are guided by their ever increasing desire for more profit and production. But surplus goods could not be purchased and consumed by the general masses and the working classes on account of their low purchasing power and their subsistence level wages. In other words, the quantum of goods produced in excess could not be consumed within the boundaries of the metropolitan countries. Excess production leads to the problem of low prices which often results in the closing of the shops by small time entrepreneurs. In such a situation, there exists a situation of cut-throat competition only among the big capital classes. Consequently, big capital gets accumulated in possession of the major capitalist class which needs outlet for capital investment. This is so because these capitalists do not want to raise the wages of the working class which could have enhanced their purchasing power. Such a generous move could have solved the problem of excess production within the boundaries of the metropolitan countries. But in such a situation, the margins of their profit was bound to go down in a significant way, which they were not willing to accept. In fact, the scale and margins of their profit are so high that they could not end up by spending them on their luxurious living. Hence, they are forced to make excessive saving. The scale of saving becomes so enormous that banks are able to get huge amount of capital even on low interest rate. But the bulk of the capitalist class is not willing to park their capital in the bank account on such a low interest. They could not use another avenue of investing in a developed country as they also faced the similar problems of excess production and low consumption. Hence, only

profitable choice for them is to invest their capital in the colonies of Asia and Africa. As stated earlier, in such a venture, they are able to seek and receive the support of various sections of the vested interest of their own country. Thus, they are led to believe that the imperialist expansion resulting in the colonial possessions is the best bargain in the existing situation. Exclusive colonial possessions also free them from the problem of competition from the capitalist classes of the similar developed countries.

(3) Hobson asserts that such imperialist expansion does not benefit the common people of the metropolitan countries. In fact, they have to pay both direct and indirect taxes for meeting the expenses of such colonial expansion. Then why do people support such ventures, if they hardly derive any benefit from them? Hobson asserts that there are a number of non-economic reasons for such support including the feeling of extreme nationalism, the desire to conquer other people, the feeling of competition with other nations and even the desire for spreading one's own religion and moral values. The capitalist class deliberately plays on these sentiments of the people and succeeds in garnering their support through untruthful propaganda and manipulations. By giving several examples, Hobson comes to the conclusion that all talks of 'civilising' local people or working for their interest is meaningless. Similarly, any claim of promoting the national interests of their own country is equally bogus and without any basis. This is nothing more than a strategy for the manipulation of the public opinion by the vested interests.

(4) Interestingly enough, Hobson avers that capitalism need not be eliminated for ending the problem of the imperialist expansion. Rather, he firmly believes that this problem could be solved by bringing about radical changes in the very system of capitalism. He puts forward the thesis that there is need for reforms in the capitalist system to solve its problems of under consumption and excess production as they are the real maladies. As a remedial measure, he suggests that wages of the working classes would have to be increased in a substantial way. Another suggestion made by him is to increase the public taxation rates in respect of the richer sections of the society. The third remedial measure he suggests is

for considerable increase in the public/State expenditure. All these measures, he asserts, could easily solve the fundamental malady of capitalism, viz. the problem of under-consumption and excess production. As a result, the need for the imperialist expansion could be easily tackled.

Thus, Hobson does not find a direct and inevitable correlation between capitalism and the problem of imperialist expansion. According to him, if the above remedial measures are taken, the surplus capital could be profitably invested within the boundary of the metropolitan/capitalist countries and as such, the basic need and urge for the imperialist expansion would automatically go away.

It is true that Hobson was one of the earliest critics of the phenomenon of imperialism. But the critics do point out that he failed to offer any alternative system of capitalism. All that he did was to offer some remedial and reforming measures. He did not suggest which sections of the society would take the initiative to bring about these measures. He failed to understand that both the capitalist class and working classes have developed some kind of vested interest in the imperialist expansion. Even the common masses did derive some vicarious pleasure on account of false sense of national pride in the imperialist expansion. The basic failure of Hobson was that he never accepted the proposition that the only way to end the problem of the imperialist expansion was to cut it at the very roots – the capitalist system of production. However, it should not be forgotten that the capitalist countries in the subsequent years did take some of the measures like increasing the wages of the working class and high taxation on the richer sections of the society. These measures did not end the problem of the imperialist expansion but they did give a new lease of life to the capitalist system.

Rosa Luxemburg's Theory of Imperialism

Rosa Luxemburg, a Pole by birth, was a German socialist thinker and a popular leader. In her book, *Accumulation of Capital* published in 1913, she delineated her well considered views on imperialism. Quite contrary to Hobson's views on imperialism, Rosa finds a close linkage between capitalism and its progeny imperialism. She looks at imperialism as being inherent in the very system of capitalism. At the same time, she also believed that but for the support received from the imperialist expansion, it could have died its natural death. She strongly believes that capitalism would continue to flourish only so long as it is able to avail the captive markets outside the capitalist world. That is so because capitalist world needs such markets for selling its excess goods as they could not consume it fully in their own limited market. But she was also of the opinion that there is a limit to the imperialist expansion and hence capitalism could not go on endlessly. In fact, the areas of imperialist expansion are limited; hence it could soon come to an end. Not only that, those far-flung areas are bound to develop their own system of capitalism at some stage of their development. Hence, both capitalism and imperialism are bound to come to an end. But she was also of the opinion that before capitalism reaches the end of the road and meets its nemesis, it is bound to bring about a number of catastrophes. This is so because militarism is inherent in the very nature of capitalism. And it was through militarist ventures that the capitalist world was able to acquire and dominate colonies. Thus, competition for very acquisition of colonies would lead to a war among the capitalist countries.

Like Hobson, Rosa is also of the opinion that the common masses of the metropolitan countries have not benefitted from the imperialist expansion/possessions as they have to pay both direct and indirect taxes for colonial wars engaged in by these countries. Thus, imperialism has been of no benefit both for the people of the colonies as well as the metropolitan countries. Rosa also believes that the production of goods for human consumption and production for the market with profiteering motive are entirely two different things. In capitalism, the basic motive behind all production is profit making and that is its fundamental flaw and bane. Thus, Rosa comes to the conclusion that the capitalist/imperialist expansion is bound to adversely affect the living standards of the working classes of the metropolitan countries. All this would result in world wide economic crises which in turn would adversely affect the accumulation of capital preparing the ground for the end of both capitalism and imperialism.

Looking back, one can safely say that subsequent historical developments have falsified Rosa's basic prediction of demise of capitalism and imperialism. In fact, neither the development in the capitalist world nor in the erstwhile socialist world could be explained on the basis of Rosa's theoretical perspective. The demise of capitalism is nowhere in sight. On the contrary, in the present age of liberalization and globalization, capitalism is doing fairly well, despite some setback after the 2008 world economic slump. What is more, even the socialist roaders are taking to the capitalist road. All these major historical developments could not be explained on the basis of Rosa's formulation. However, that does not take away her basic premise that the people of the colonies immensely suffered in the days of colonialism and imperialism.

Lenin's Theory of Imperialism

It is true that a number of scholars have written about the close linkage between capitalism and imperialism giving their own perspective on the issue. However, it goes without saying that Lenin's theory of imperialism has been the most discussed and debated theory on the theme of imperialism. But for a better understanding of Lenin's theory of imperialism, it would be in the fitness of things to say a few words about Karl Marx's view on capitalism. Karl Marx was firmly of the opinion that capitalism would meet its end sooner or later. This is so because the concentration of wealth would take place in fewer and fewer hands and the bulk of the people would join the rank of proletariat. Thus, capitalism would be producing it own grave diggers in the form of the proletariat classes. But by the time Lenin took over the leadership of the Russian communist movement, Marx's prediction about capitalism had not come true. On the other hand, capitalism was dominating the world scene on its own acquired strength. The capitalist countries have divided the countries of Asia and Africa among themselves and were competing among themselves for retaining and even expanding their hold on these areas. What was more, Lenin could also see that even the working classes of the metropolitan countries have joined hands with their capitalist classes in the latter's nefarious game of the imperialist expansion. Thus, both these major development – history falsifying Marx's prediction of the demise of capitalism and close collaboration between the working classes and the capitalist classes of the Metropolitan countries posed serious intellectual challenge to Lenin. He was called upon to explain these major historical developments which were quite contrary to Marxist theoretical formulations. Moreover, Lenin wanted the crisis of the World War to be turned into a Godsend opportunity for the socialist revolution. He wanted the working classes of these countries not only not to support the capitalist class war effort but to lead towards a socialist revolution. This was the historical and intellectual background to Lenin choosing to propound his much celebrated theory of imperialism enunciated in his booklet, *Imperialism: The Highest Stage of Capitalism*. It needs to be mentioned that Lenin had both practical and intellectual compulsions for penning his basic ideas in respect of capitalism and imperialism. His practical consideration was to persuade the people of the Czarist Russia more particularly the working classes not to support the Czarist regime in its war efforts and rather use this opportunity to work for a socialist revolution. His theoretical consideration was to explain why capitalism has not collapsed as predicted by Marx and also to explain the real genesis of the World War which was a result of competitiveness among the world capitalist countries to divide the world under their respective domination and influence.

It also needs to be mentioned that in the propagation of his theory of imperialism, Lenin was greatly influenced by Ruddolph Hilferdig's book *The Finance Capital* published in the year 1910. Hilferdig was a German social democrat and an intellectual in his own right. He had made a penetrating analysis of 'finance capitalism'. Based on his in-depth study, he had concluded that capitalism had turned into finance capitalism. His main thesis was that in the prevailing system of capitalism, a close linkage between banks and other financial institutions and monopolistic industrial houses had turned traditional capitalism into finance capitalism. Thus, the export of capital and its investment in the colonies had become the mainstay of capitalism.

A close perusal of Lenin's book, *Imperialism: The Highest Phase of Capitalism* could easily reveal that Lenin heavily draws from Hilferdig's work. The main formulations of Lenin's theory of imperialism could be summed up as follows:

(i) Imperialism is nothing but a direct continuation of the fundamental properties of capitalism. Hence it suffers from all the limitations of capitalism.

(ii) Imperialism appears at a particular phase of capitalism, viz. phase of monopoly capitalism and finance capitalism. During such a phase of capitalism, export of capital to the colonies became more profitable than the export of the industrial goods.

(iii) Lenin explains the entire process through which capitalism is turned into monopoly capitalism. According to Lenin, in the initial stages, capitalism is primarily fueled by small entrepreneurs and their personal capital and skill. Gradually, however with more complex technological innovation and greater mechanization, the scale of capital needed for investment becomes huge and enormous. Besides the areas and scale of production also takes new heights. In such a cut-throat competition, small entrepreneurs have to close their shop as they fail to remain competitive. Thus, only a handful of big entrepreneurs survive and as such they succeed in establishing their monopolistic hold both in respect of production and marketing. They are also able to control and dominate the banking and other financial institutions. Thus emerges an alliance between monopoly capitalist class and the banking and other financial institutions. It is this alliance which gives birth to finance capitalism. Now the export of capital becomes more profitable than the export of industrial goods. In these colonial areas, even cheap labour and raw material is available in abundance. Hence, business becomes very profitable. In the process, capitalism gets a new lease of life by such imperialist expansions.

(iv) Lenin also could clearly see a close and direct relationship between monopoly capitalism, militarism and the imperialist expansion. All these ultimately lead to war among the capitalist countries competing for their hold over the colonies. Hence, he looked at the First World War as an imperialist war being fought among the capitalist countries for the control of their colonies. He gave a clarion call to the international working class not to lend any support to such capitalist ventures.

Five Main Features of Imperialism

Lenin summed up the entire process by enumerating the five main features of imperialism. They are:

(i) Monopolies develop on account of concentration of capital and production in a few hands. In every industrial sector, a small number of companies are able to achieve dominating position on account of their huge capital investment and technological innovations. This process is further strengthened by their mutual interlocking arrangement leading to the creation of cartels and joint monopoly.

(ii) In the process, banking capital and industrial capital join hands leading to the emergence of financial and industrial oligarchy. More often than not, the people controlling the banks and industries are one and the same persons. In fact, with the emergence of stock market and share bazar, the people owning and controlling the banks could also become the major shareholders of the company, by purchasing the bulk of their shares. On the other hand, even the big capitalists could purchase the shares of the banks and could easily establish their hold over them. In the process, a new class of banker capitalist is born resulting in its monopolistic control over various industrial sectors.

(iii) Towards the closing years of the nineteenth century,

various capitalist countries of Europe had reached a stage of monopoly capitalism. Huge investible capital had accumulated in these countries which could not be profitably invested within their national boundaries as such an investment could very well create the problem of over-production. Besides, the wage structure of the working class had also gone up in these countries. Moreover, importing raw materials from far-flung areas and exporting finished industrial goods to those areas was also turning out to be quite an expensive business. But the fact of the matter was that both cheap labour and raw material was available in abundance in these areas. Thus, capital investment in these areas was bound to be more profitable than similar investment in the metropolitan countries.

(iv) According to Lenin, monopolies do also emerge on the world scale and they invariably try to divide the world among themselves. Thus, there emerges a cartel of international monopoly houses and they successfully divide the world market among themselves. On account of their monopolistic control, they also control the pricing mechanism and thereby succeed in raising the margins of profit on a considerable scale.

(v) Lenin further asserted that by the end of the nineteenth century, the international division of the world had taken place on account of such monopolistic control of some of the concerns. However, by the way of his own conclusions, Lenin did believe that imperialism is nothing but a developed form of capitalism. Hence, it could not remain a life saviour for capitalism forever. According to Lenin, the main difference between capitalism and imperialism was that competition, a primary feature of capitalism at the earlier stage, had been replaced by monopolistic cartels at its new phase of imperialism. However, Lenin was quite firm in his belief that ultimately capitalism would meet its end, as the life-support system provided by imperialism could not continue forever.

> Capitalism has survived through assuming a new garb of imperialism. But, ultimately monopolistic control over the colonies which withheld the inner class contradiction within capitalist countries could not last forever. Once such monopolistic control goes off, the inner contradiction of capitalism between the bourgeoisie and the working class would emerge in a big way leading to its natural demise. Lenin also reached out to another conclusion that the international communist movement should strongly support the national liberation movement of the colonies as that would hasten the process the demise of capitalism.

However, critics have assailed Lenin's theory of imperialism on a number of counts. Some of these points are:

(i) Critics do assert that Lenin's theory of imperialism is based on the limited experiences and evidence from a small number of the capitalist countries. Some of his generalization are based on small amount of empirical evidence and statistical data. Besides, some of the scholars have gone to the extent of questioning the main theoretical proposition of Lenin that capitalism had survived on account of its imperialist phase and that capitalism would die its natural death once this life-support system goes off. Many of these scholars contest Lenin's main formulation that colonies had played such a decisive role in the survival of capitalism. They contend, contrary to Lenin's perception, that the bulk of the capital of the capitalist world was invested in European countries. Besides, the bulk of trades of these countries were among themselves rather than with the colonies. They further argue that Switzerland, despite not being a colonial power, had achieved high rate of growth. Hence, their contention is that Lenin was not right in linking the high economic growth of the capitalist countries with their economic relationship with their colonies. They further contend that support to imperialism was not always inspired by economic reasons. There could be equally valid political reasons including national pride. In fact, Lenin's assertion virtually sounds like economic determinism – not a very sound theoretical proposition. For all these reasons, they contend that the attempt by Lenin to link-up capitalism, colonialism, imperialism and finance capitalism, appears far off from the historical truth.

(ii) The second point of criticism is that war need not be necessarily fought for economic reasons. There could be other reasons equally valid for any kind of war mongering. Hence, Lenin's attempts to link-up war with capitalism is not a theoretically correct proposition, nor is it based on historical evidence. Wars were being fought much before capitalism emerged as a world economic system.

(iii) Lenin's assertion that imperialism is nothing but a child of capitalism has also been contested by a number of scholars. They further assert that even erstwhile Soviet Union and the People's Republic of China had their own kind of colonial relationship with the neighbouring countries. There was also a short-term war between these two socialist countries. In fact, most of the time imperialist relationship could be found between powerful countries and the weaker ones. In fact, imperialistic relationship had hardly anything to do with any ideological colouring. It depends more on power relationship than ideological foundation.

(iv) There is much historical evidence to prove that colonial and imperialist expansion took place much before capitalism reached its monopoly stage. British colonial expansion in India is an illustrative case. Dadabhai Naoroji through his 'drain of wealth' theory had proved that Industrial Revolution in England owed much for its origins to the plunder of wealth from India. Another Indian scholar, Rammanohar Lohia in his paper *Economics After Marx* tried to prove that Lenin's theory of imperialism was totally inapplicable to the Indian situation. He contended that in the case of England, capitalism and imperialism grew together and the latter did not come at the monopoly stage of the former as suggested by Lenin's theory.

However, despite these critical points levelled against Lenin's theory of imperialism, the fact remains that Lenin did expose the fact of exploitation indulged in by the Western capitalist countries. Besides, it goes to the credit of Lenin that he exposed the economic and political abuse of the western industrial States in respect of their colonies of Asia and Africa. Moreover, the debate which Lenin initiated continues to occupy a substantial part of political discourse even today. It has not subsided even with the completion of the process of decolonization in the post-war period. It has assumed a new form of debate on neo-colonialism and neo-imperialism. In fact, it has got intensified in this age of globalization and liberalization. The persistence of this debate is virtually a great tribute to Lenin.

Joseph Schumpeter's Views on Capitalism and Imperialism

As we have seen earlier that Marxist and socialist thinkers have been in the forefront of presenting a critique of capitalism and imperialism. But liberal thinkers look at that critique as being one-sided and devoid of historical evidence. These liberal thinkers have underlined the central role of the non-economic factors more than that of the economic factors (as believed by the Marxist thinkers) being responsible for the emergence of the phenomenon of imperialism as a system. They further assert that to look for a single and solitary cause for the emergence of imperialism is neither scientific nor a correct approach. They further assert that like other events in history, there could be more than one factor responsible for emergence and growth of imperialism. These liberal thinkers have offered various explanations, viz. psychological factor like aggressive nature of man, his willpower to dominate, invention of the new and effective weapons, better system of ship building and sea faring and so on and so forth. Among these liberal thinkers, Joseph Schumpeter stands out as a seminal thinker. He in his work,

Imperialism and Social Classes published in 1919 took up the theme of imperialism for detailed investigation. He dismissed the views of Hobson and Lenin on imperialism particularly their attempt to find its roots in the capitalist system of production. According to him, imperialism had hardly anything to do with capitalism. He further dismisses Lenin's view that imperialism has much to do with the monopoly stage of capitalism. Not only that, Schumpeter goes to the extent of asserting that capitalism has been opposed to imperialism.

Schumpeter's basic formulation is that one has to find the roots of imperialism in other historical factors. He traces its roots in psychological need of man, in the feudal structure of society and in the long tradition of war in human history. Referring to the human history, he asserts that since time immemorial war has been a part of human history. As such, in every society there emerges a group of battle hungry people who are gripped by the deep desire for war and violence. The feudal structure of the old society further boosted this process of such psychological need. On the whole, the commission of aggression and will to power has a long history in human affairs. Schumpeter avers that imperialism is the outgrowth and a by-product of this deep-seated psychological need of the human beings. Schumpeter further asserts that in the age of capitalism, on account of trade and commerce, and similar factors, a new society with a new social structure has emerged. Hence, man could utilize his inner urge for creative acquisition in a much better way. In fact, with the coming of capitalism and its new system of production, the possibility for such utilization of human creativity has much vaster and better opportunities. This is so because under capitalism, nature and structure and areas of expression of human proclivities, creativity and ingenuity have become much more wider, democratic and individual-centred. Hence, there is not much scope left for aggressive, violent imperialist tendencies under capitalism. So according to Schumpeter, capitalism promotes anti-war and anti-violence tendencies among men.

Schumpeter is of the opinion that if violent and imperialist tendencies do appear under capitalist system, they could be attributed to some other factors. According to him, these tendencies could be traced back to the stage of feudalism. In fact, they have emanated from the feudal order, and capitalism has failed to curb these tendencies. He believes that nationalism and militarism existed much before capitalism appeared on the scene. Both nationalism and militarism are opposed to the system of capitalism. But it is also a fact that presently they have derived their strength from capitalism. It would be even true that capitalism supports and promotes these tendencies both on political and economic fronts. They in turn also support capitalism. But Schumpeter asserts that in future capitalism would get rid of these aggressive tendencies. He was firmly of the opinion that monopolistic tendencies in import and export business would be curbed. Hence, capitalism would assume its pristine form by ridding itself of these imperialist tendencies.

There are many scholars who do not agree with Schumpeter's various formulations on imperialism and capitalism. That capitalism is benign, non-aggressive and benevolent; they are not willing to accept. They also reject Schumpeter's view that imperialism and capitalism are different and distinct. However, credit goes to him for putting the whole debate on capitalism and imperialism and their relationship on a much larger canvas. He tried to look for the causal factors for the emergence of imperialism on a larger canvas of human history. He also underlined the fact that there are vested interests in every society, which do influence political, economic and imperialist policies of the society. Thus he did not hold capitalism alone responsible for the emergence of imperialism. Rather, he holds various sections of the society responsible for such historical developments. In a word, he expanded the debate on imperialism and capitalism and their relationship in a very significant way. And that is not a small contribution for which he is being remembered even today.

4 Neo-colonialism

Colonialism has achieved a new guise. It has become neo-colonialism, the last stage of imperialism..... as monopoly-capitalism or imperialism is the last stage of capitalism.

KWAME NKRUMAH

We know that national liberation movements coupled with change in the balance of power in the international field was primarily responsible for initiating the process of decolonisation. On the road to decolonisation, independence of India in 1947 marked a milestone. In less than a decade after Indian independence, formal colonialism virtually came to an end, as most of the colonised world attained independence. But even when the process of decolonisation was on, a section of intellectuals and leaders came to the conclusion that the people of the erstwhile colonies would have to cover a long and arduous journey to totally free themselves from the indirect and subtle clutches of their ex-colonial masters. It was quite clear to them that ex-metropolitan countries continue to control and dominate their economic and political life through the operation of multinational companies and other international organisations. The elite sections of the newly freed countries were also in league with their erstwhile colonial masters. In other words, despite formal independence, there was not much material change in the situation as the people of ex-colonies continued to carry the yoke of dependency even during their post-independent era. It is the entire process of dependency and domination of the people of the ex-colonies at the hands of their erstwhile colonial master that has been described as a state of neo-colonialism or neo-imperialism. The quintessence of the concept of neo-colonialism/new-imperialism is that the so called sovereignty of these newly freed countries is a myth as they continue to be controlled and dominated by the Western capitalist countries – their erstwhile colonial masters.

Theorisation of Neo-colonialism

It was during 1950s and 1960s that the neo-colonialism as a concept was developed particularly in respect of the newly freed African continent. Kwame Nkrumah, the then president of Ghana is taken to be the main propounder of the theory of neo-colonialism/neo-imperialism. He enunciated his theory in his book, *Neo-colonialism: The Highest Stage of Imperialism*. His thesis on neo-colonialism is still popular among a section of progressive scholars. Nkrumah's major thesis is that neo-colonialism is the last stage of imperialism. Their forms and means may differ but their goal and destination, viz. control over the lives and resources of the people of ex-colonies continues to be the same. Nkrumah rebuts the popular notion that the import and investment of foreign capital would benefit the people of the erstwhile colonies. In fact, the basic purpose of foreign investment is to exploit and dominate the people and not to work towards their economic development and welfare. All this is being done to promote the vested interests of the Western capitalist countries. A number of scholars do believe that subsequent historical development have validated the basic thesis propounded by Nkrumah in his much celebrated book. For instance, Robert Young in his essay on 'neo-colonialism' asserts that "foreign capital is actually invested only in the areas wherein cheap labour and raw materials are available in abundance and political stability is also assured". Young makes the point by saying that Western countries do invest in China, Malaysia, Korea and not in the countries of African continent where there might be a genuine need for foreign investment.

Nkrumah also argues that foreign aid and cultural aids of various kinds on the part of the Western powers are meant actually for securing their domination over the countries of the Third World. He even goes to the extent of saying that such neo-colonial ventures of the metropolitan countries harm the real interest of the people of the Third World as well as the Western world. Actually, Western countries try to solve the internal problems of their own country, including inequality between the rich and the poor of their own society, through these neo-colonial stratagems. Robert Young moves a step forward and asserts that neo-colonialism is nothing more or nothing less than American colonialism. This is nothing but to build up an empire without formally owning any colony. Nkrumah goes even to the extent of saying that the cold war between two super powers was not going to serve any real interest of the people of the Third World. This is so because ultimately most of the aid comes in the form of military aid, which was hardly doing any good to the people of the poor countries. Nkrumah pleaded for the solidarity of the African countries to meet the challenges of neo-colonialism. Such a political and economic unity of the African people alone would ensure their freedom and welfare. For in such a situation, division of labour at international level would come to an end and the Western countries would be forced to come face-to-face with their own working class. That would lead to a new era of struggle, which would ultimately mark the end of the neo-colonial era. Samir Amin has further contributed towards a better understanding of the concept of neo-colonialism based on his study of the French colonies of the western Africa. He argues that the reason for the emergence of neo-colonialism in Africa lie in the balkanization of Africa and other institutional weaknesses. Robert Young is critical of formulations offered both by Nkrumah and Samir Amin. He believes that neither of them favour the rejection of the present model of economic development.

Some other scholars like Nuggi Wa Thiong find further fault with Nkrumah's basic formulation on neo-colonialism. According to him, Nkrumah attaches much more importance to the role of economic reasons and much less to political and cultural factors which play an equally important role in the entire process, if not more. Nuggi argues that the cultural dominance of the West, plays a dominant role in neo-colonialist ventures. According to him, major media for such cultural dominance are colonial language, cultural and political pattern and the presence of the descendents and progenies of the colonial masters. Nuggi has, in fact, extended the old thesis of Frantz Fanon that in the entire process the elite section of the ex-colonies have played a significant role. The elite of these areas attach themselves to their ex-colonial masters rather than with their own people. For instance, instead of opposing the multinational companies dominated by the Western countries, these elite actually support them. In the process, they are able to acquire a lifestyle and consumption pattern of the First World.

But scholars like Robert Young assert that the thinkers like Nuggi only promote the helplessness and haplessness of the African people. Besides, Robert Young further asserts that such generalisations are too general and flat to be acceptable. In fact, such generalisations avoid going into the roots of the problems and fail to confront the fundamental question as to why such things do happen? They also fail to distinguish between the cultural and political and economic dimensions of neo-colonialism. In fact, military-economic aspect of neo-colonialism is an integral part of the present day power-structure, whereas its cultural dimensions are the result of the historical development. Besides, neo-colonialism is not a universal and general principle– it could be applicable to certain areas and simultaneously not applicable to some other areas. For instance, Western intervention in Iraq, Afghanistan, Libya and similar other situations are certainly neo-colonialist ventures at domination. But similar type of intervention might not be possible in some other areas. Robert Young also finds another fault with Nuggi's analysis as the latter hardly underlines the fights and struggles of the victims against neo-colonial ventures.

Neo-colonialism and the Model of Economic Development

It is nobody's thesis that the Western capitalist countries have no policy and programme for the economic development of the Third World. Rather, in their scheme for the Third World, economic development has occupied a prominent place. It is a widely accepted view that the Western countries developed in the past at the cost of their colonies. But ignoring such glaring historical facts, the Western countries are now insisting that the Third World could develop through the Western model of economic development and modernisation. Initially, it was believed that two entirely different roads were open to the Third World countries; either they were to take to the capitalist road/model or the socialist road/model. Subsequently, Indian model underlined the model of mixed economy. However, here we are primarily concerned with examining the capitalist model of development under the new colonial phase. It was widely believed that in such a model, growth would be a constant and continuous process. It was also believed that through the process of industrialisation and urbanisation, the Third World countries would some day join the rank of the countries of the First World. But such a sanguine hope was subsequently belied. What is more, in this process, they have been irretrievably caught in the exploitative net of the Western countries. Naturally, a fundamental question was raised as to why the process and pace of development has been so slow and tardy in these countries? Many scholars started inquiring into such questions. Marxist scholars like Paul Baran made a major submission that multinational companies making huge profit from their neo-colonial investments do not invest the major part of their profit in these areas. Rather they ploughed it back to the metropolitan centres. And that is why their pace of development is slow and tardy. In fact, they are not interested in the development of these areas. Rather their primary focus is on maximising their profit.

Subsequently, some other scholars also put forward their own view on the subject. Their basic contention was that the western countries have been trying to impose their own model of economic development on the countries of the Third World. The trouble is that such a model of development is hardly in consonance with the experiences of the people of the Third World. These western countries also forget that they developed at the cost of the people of their colonies. They had also the advantage of having a captive market both for their own goods as well as for acquiring raw materials and labour at the cheapest possible rate. But these basic advantages are not available to the newly freed countries of the Third World. In fact, these countries are still dependent on their metropolitan countries. Moreover, the Western world is hardly interested in their development. Their primary purpose is the exploitation of these areas. Thus, old history of colonial exploitation and domination is being repeated once again, though in a much more subtle and indirect way.

However, of late the old rivalry between the Marxist and the liberal models has gone through a considerable change. With the collapse of the Soviet Union, it became abundantly clear that the traditional Marxist model was not in a position to compete with the Western model of development. Hence, there has been a change in their new model of development. Similarly, there have also been some changes in the old liberal model of economic development with greater emphasis on market forces rather than on the State. The new Western model of economic development is in the ascendant. It is also being asserted that new Western model could become universal and any country taking to this road could take major steps on the path to development. The other model of development has been argued by the Marxist leaders of the Latin America. They are firmly of the opinion that there could never be a universal model of economic development. This is so because historically the development of some countries has been at the cost of some other countries. Hence, according to them, the traditional Marxist thinking on capitalism and imperialism has to be reformulated and even replaced. These scholars formulated their thinking in the form of dependency theory and world model system. The quintessence of their thinking is that the countries at the centre of the circles develop at the cost of those which are at the periphery.

It is clear from the above that the present thinking on neo-colonialism has gone much beyond Nkrumah's basic formulations. Nkrumah believed that neo-colonialism could be understood by making in-depth study of cultural, political and economic lives of the people of ex-colonies and also the history of intervention of the Western world in these areas. Post colonial thinkers do accept some of the formulations of Nkrumah. But one major change is that now it is widely being believed that neo-colonialism could be understood more on regional basis rather than on universal one. For instance, the countries of Africa continue to lag behind on the scale of development, whereas some of the countries of South Asia, China and South East Asia are developing at a much faster pace.

Another major change in the understanding of neo-colonialism is that development is being taken in a much broader and integrated way. In its new avatar, development is being taken not only in terms of economic development but also in those of socio-political-cultural terms. In other words, the concept of economic growth as perceived by W.W. Rostow is no longer taken to be valid. At the same time, the traditional Marxist model of economic development has also failed. A new international economic order has emerged with the United States of America being the most dominant player. As a result, the Western countries intervention is increasingly becoming more visible and even the world organisations like IMF, World Bank and UNO are also playing a second fiddle to them. Besides, the role of the State in the entire process of development is being sidelined and market forces are gaining the upper hand. New international order is being run in the name of liberalization and globalization, though it is under considerable crisis after 2008. These post-colonial thinkers look at the whole process as being nothing more than the neo-colonial ventures. In the present system, the gap between the rich and the poor is widening. State is being sidelined and hence the poor are left to fend for themselves. Intervention in their favour is missing. The Western intervention in Iraq, Afghanistan and Libya, is taken as nothing short of neo-colonial ventures.

Thus, we find that the new international order has all the trappings of a neo-colonial world order. Some of the questions which Nkrumah raised in his book are still to be answered. Perhaps, his own answer might not stand the test of time. Neither the traditional Western model of economic development nor the present one is able to fully meet the challenge of the problems facing the people of the world. Similarly, the Marxist model has been rejected even by their own people. What is more, dependency theory and world model system have been found lacking to fully explain the present scenario and suggest a way out. They sound like too much of a general statement in the attempt to explain the problems of the developing countries. Some of these countries are developing at a faster pace while others are lagging behind. Thus, there is a gap even among the developing countries which could not be explained by dependency theory, as it places all blames at the doors of the foreign powers and fails to analyse the internal structure of some of these countries. And which is why some scholars are now talking in terms of popular development. It is also known as post-developmental theory. It has several positive characteristics. One, it is rooted in the grassroot movements. Secondly, it underlines the fact that the entire process of development should start from the bottom and not from the top, as it is being done today. In other words, there is the plea for 'bottom-up' approach rather than 'top-down' approach. In such a scheme, special care should be taken to protect the interests of the poor, the dispossessed and women. Besides, it should be based on the principle of self-reliance, use of local resources and basic needs of the people. In other words, such a concept of alternative development comes very near to the Gandhian concept of development. One would only surmise that the Gandhian path may offer a way out of exigencies of the neo-colonialist expansion. The future alone will fully answer the question. But hope persists in view of the new developments all over the world.

5 Post-colonialism/ Postcolonialism?

> *It is my argument that the central defining theme of post-colonialism or postcolonialist studies is the investigation of the mutually constitutive role played by the coloniser and the colonised, centre and periphery, the metropolitan and the native, in forming, in part, the identities of both the dominant power and the subalterns involved in the imperial and the colonial projects of the West.*
>
> ALI RATTANSI

Neo-colonialism and post-colonialism/postcolonialism overlap so much and so often that it becomes difficult to distinguish between the two terms. In fact, the basic roots of both these terms could be located in the history of colonialism and imperialism. But, on a closer examination, one could find subtle, yet significant differences between these two terms. As we have seen earlier, neo colonialism is the attempt of the developed countries of the West to control and dominate the socio-economic life of the countries of the Third World even during their post-independent era. But the post-colonialism/ postcolonialism is much more subtle, complex and a broad concept. One extreme of it marks the process of decolonisation which resulted in the emergence of the independent countries in the post-war period. Its other extreme underlines the fact that in the post-independent era, these countries were in the midst of multidimensional domination from which they found it difficult to extricate themselves. But postcolonial thinking does not end up by describing such a sad state of affairs; it also goes a long way to demand strong intervention to put an end to it. In other words, its strategy and tactics encompass the whole process from clearly describing the situation to planning strong measures to end such a plight. It is this entire process from description to intervention that covers the total ground of post-colonialism/postcolonialism.

But before we discuss the whole issue in a detailed manner, it would be relevant for us to distinguish and differentiate different terms used by the scholars to capture the quintessential nature of post-colonialism. Scholars have used three different terms to capture the entire process of post-colonialism. These are: post-colonialism, postcolonialism and postcoloniality. A scholar like Robert Young makes the distinction between these terms. According to him, post-colonialism could be viewed as a dialectical concept which denotes economic domination, at times even political domination along with the process of decolonisation which the newly freed countries faced in their post-colonial phase. On the other hand, postcoloniality underlines those economic material and cultural factors or the state of affairs, which are primarily shaped by international global capital and amidst which these newly freed countries have to operate. There has been also a debate on how the term 'post-colonialism' should be written – post-colonialism or simply postcolonialism, i.e., whether with or without a hyphen in between post and colonialism. Till the seventh decade of the last century, there was a general practice of it to be written with a hyphen. When written with a hyphen, it conveys the meaning of the period after the end of colonialism. Subsequently, scholars perhaps felt that when written with hyphen (post-colonialism), its meaning becomes too limited. Hence, there emerged a new practice of writing it without hyphen, viz. postcolonialism. In the process, its meaning and implications got widened. As a result, greater emphasis started being laid at its cultural aspects. It started being viewed as a two dimensional concept. According to a scholar like Vijay Mishra its two dimensions were (a) Oppositional, and (b) Complicit. Taken in its oppositional dimension, scholars prefer to write it in hyphenated form, i.e. post-colonialism. They also assert that in its oppositional dimension, it marks the historic turning point, when the newly emerged States come face-to-face with their metropolitan powers i.e. they face a situation of opposition and struggle. On the other hand, being written in non-hyphenated form (postcolonialism), it comes quite closer to the post-modernist tradition. Hence, postcolonialism sounds more pluralistic, bookish and complex. Hence, in this form it sounds more critical of the system and its emphasis on change is more emphatic. However, on this specific point, there is no general agreement among the scholars. For instance, a scholar like Loomba is of the opinion that colonialism, preceded by a predicate like post, assumes double meaning. One meaning of the term (post-colonialism) involves and marks the period after their independence for the newly freed countries. Its other meaning gets attached to post-modernist tradition. The trouble with the use of the term 'post-colonialism' is that it conveys a distinct feeling and meaning, as if colonialism as such has ended forever. But many scholars contend that might not be the correct description of the current situation in these countries. This is so because in these areas neo-colonialism is a working proposition. But a term like 'post-colonialism' creates the impression that it has disappeared for good. Similarly, the term 'postcolonialism' (used without hyphen) does not give due importance to the temporal aspect of the situation. Instead of placing emphasis on place, time and institutions, it more emphatically underlines feelings and thoughts of individuals in a much more significant way. Moreover, the concept of postcolonialism does not attach as much importance to the institution of the State and nationalism as it does to the problems of ethnic groups and minorities. For all these reasons, there is no unanimity among the scholars whether to use the term 'post-colonialism' or 'postcolonialism'.

Be as it might, let us move forward to discuss its basic formulations. The literature on this basic theme is so vast that it is difficult to even present its summarized version within the limited space available for our study. The essential point that needs to be grasped is that the use of the term like 'colonialism', 'imperialism', and 'neo-colonialism' underlines more prominently the unequal relationship between the newly emerged countries of the Third World and the more developed capitalist countries of the West, who have long records of exploitation and domination. On the other hand, the term like 'post colonialism' written with or without hyphen, carries with it deep concern for working towards the establishment of a just and equitable social order both at national and international levels. In the process, it gives a call for struggle against statusquoist forces within a country as well as against present international economic order marked by neo-imperialist drive. Like Marxism and feminism, it seeks a new path and means to face up the challenges posed by an unjust international order. However, it needs to be mentioned that the ideological foundation of post-colonialism could be traced back to Marxism of the non-European countries and feminism. In this way, the ideology of the post-colonialism does not end by offering trenchant criticisms of the Establishment at the various levels, but it also lays equal emphasis on philosophy and strategy for a sustained and determined struggle against all the forces of domination and exploitation. Besides, it also uses its penetrating interpretative skill to depict and delineate the material and cultural conditions which lead to the emergence of an unjust international order. At times it looks at the whole process from the viewpoints of the victims and not from the perspectives of exploiters and perpetrators of injustice.

Thus, ideologically it appears determined and committed for the creation of a just social order at every level. To that end, it pleads for the human intervention in various fields and at various levels. The ideologues of the school are fully conscious that concerted and collective efforts of the various creative and militant forces, presently scattered in different fields, alone could ensure such a transition. They are also aware that its success would primarily depend upon the close and objective analysis and correct assessment of unjust external system. More importantly, the real condition for such a radical change would be how the people of the erstwhile colonies do feel about the whole thing in the depth of their beings. In a word, it could be safely concluded that the primary concern of the post-colonial thinking is to create an alternative system marked by justice and equity. But it does not favour the replacement of the present unjust international order by another world order at one go, which has been the main attempt of traditional Marxism and feminism. In fact, it links up the various issues connected with gender, race, ethnic groups and other small groups. In the process, it virtually bypasses the institution of the

State and the feeling of nationalism which have been the mainstay of the present day order.

Historical Roots of Post-colonialism

There has been controversy about the historical aspects of the idea of post-colonialism. A number of scholars trace it to the fifties and sixties of the last century, i.e. its history could be linked up with the idea of decolonisation. During these periods, the basic question that was being raised was, as to what should these newly independent countries do with their colonial past? Should they get rid of it or should they reorientate it according to the needs of their future development or alternatively, should they follow their old pattern and path? Thus, they had three choices immediately after independence. In actual practice, choosing one of the alternatives was much more complex than it appeared on the face value. This was so because the elite classes who came to power were already well-entrenched in the old colonial culture. Besides, their lifestyle was greatly patterned on the Western culture and lifestyle. The struggles against the colonial rule which they had led earlier were basically inspired by their desire of replacing their own colonial master, rather than developing an alternative social and political culture. On the other hand, the Western metropolitan countries were more than keen to retain their hold on their ex-colonies. Thus, there was a good opportunity for an alliance between the elite classes of these countries and their ex-colonial masters. In fact, that became the main context for the emergence of neo-colonialism in the Third World countries.

Another factor that contributed to the emergence of neo-colonialism was the cold war phenomenon between the Western world led by USA and the communist countries led by the Soviet Union. To induce the newly freed countries to join the camp, the net of foreign aid, military aid, even trade was widely spread which the bulk of the Third World countries could hardly escape. Even the non-alignment movement led by Nehru, Tito, Nasser, Sukarno and others could not prove to be of much help in this respect.

But even during those days, there emerged a stream of thought in India which quite reverberated with the world view of postcolonialism. That was basically a Gandhian perspective, which was being carried forward by leaders like Rammanohar Lohia, Vinoba Bhave, Jayaprakash Narayan, J.B. Kripalani and others. They were for an alternative model of development with their primary focus on the lives of the common people. They were precursor to post-colonial thinking. Perhaps because they were not from the academic world or the world was too much enamoured of the Western model of development: their ideas were not taken seriously at least by the academicians and scholars. However, by 1960s the life and history of the communities who were on the periphery of the society came to constitute the syllabi of many universities in the Western world. Besides, the publication of Edward Said's book, *Orientalism* (1978) turned out to be a milestone in the history of post-colonial thinking. A lot of rethinking started on the various issues of the world. This process was further intensified after the collapse of the Soviet Union in 1991.

A major change that took place was that the market forces started taking over a lot of ground, which was earlier occupied by the institution of the State. This process even encompassed the Marxist countries including the People's Republic of China. Primarily based on the principle of free trade, a new international economic order emerged and then almost all the States fell in line. This is how the fortress of socialism virtually collapsed and neo-liberalism/capitalism emerged, trying to take over the entire world. Like the old capitalist system, it tried to cover and dominate the entire world. But it did evoke at least an ideological resistance from a section of scholars and social activists. In fact, it was in opposition to this neo-liberal/capitalist attempt at the world domination that post-colonialism emerged as a counter ideology. It makes an attempt to present a sober and serious critique of the new international order known as the system of globalization and liberalization. Post-colonial thinking is not so much enamoured of the Nation-State, its primary concern being the people living on the peripheries of the society. In this way, postcolonialism is equally concerned with the problem of internal colonialism.

In brief, we can say that the concern of postcolonialism goes much beyond the process of decolonisation. It tries to impress on the people the meaning of slavery and ways and means to get rid of it in the depth of their being. However, to that end, it does not go back to history through the path of any kind of revivalism even in its thought and imagination – whether ideological or institutional. In fact, its ultimate aim is to establish a just and equitable alternative by rooting out the old culture of colonialism. It aims at a system in which the people on the periphery of the society should get back their voice, their freedom, and ultimately they should have a clear picture of their identity. Thus, like post-modernism, the nature of postcolonialism is also pluralistic. Its primary aim is to enable the people on the periphery to raise their voice and give them a new inspiration and momentum and through them to establish a new system based on equity and justice.

Post-colonialism: An Appreciation

Admittedly, the decline of Marxism in the last two decades has primarily helped post-colonialism to emerge as an alternative ideology. Another point which needs to be underscored is that whereas Marxism concentrated on historical analysis of colonialism and imperialism, post-colonialism has mostly focused on the cultural aspects rather than on economic and political aspects. In the process, it has been able to attract the attention of quite a few prominent scholars and social activists. Hence, it has become a popular subject of study in the Western academic world. One reason for its popularity has been the dissatisfaction of scholars and academicians with the narrow groove in which classical Marxism has fallen. But post-colonialism has also attracted critical comments, particularly from some of the Marxist scholars. Some of the points that they mention could be summed up as follows:

(1) One of the major criticisms against postcolonial thinking is that its proponents do not speak in one voice: it does not have one major voice with which it could be identified. In fact, some of its proponents speak in different voices and that too with different emphasis. Not only that, it is also changing its colour and

complexion in the course of its historical evolution. Today post-colonialism is quite different from the one propounded by Cabral and Frantz Fanon. It was thinkers like Fanon who focused on its political and cultural aspect and in the process they promoted its deep understanding. That old understanding has been put up by Michael Hardt and Andrew Negri in a new formulation of their own. They are of the opinion that there have been deliberate attempts to divide the people between the White and the Black, and the people of Europe and those of the East. That has been primarily done to promote colonial interests. It is the post-colonial thinking which has opened a new path and perspective to go beyond the artificial division of the people of the Occident and the Orient. They further argue that the fact of the matter was that to establish the domain of the European self, there was a need to create an Oriental self. It was quite natural that such a divisive understanding was to be based on the foundation of violence. But an integrated understanding really opens the road for human liberation.

But the critics argue that such a deep and multidimensional understanding of the entire process of the past is missing from the present day post-colonial thinking. To be more specific, in the old understanding of post-colonialism, the struggles of the victims of colonialism constituted its integral part. But that is missing from the latest understanding as it is primarily focused on its cultured dimensions. Hence, it misses out on the other aspect of the situation, viz. political aspects and role of the human agency. In sum, the critics aver that the political aspect of human liberation is virtually missing from the present day discourse on postcolonialism. Arif Dirlik, one of the prominent scholars, has underscored such a critical view in a very effective manner. Scholars like him make two major critical points. One that the theory of knowledge of the present day post-colonialism takes out its cultural aspect from the entire political economy of capitalism and primarily concentrates on it. Such a limited and aspectual understanding of capitalism fails to realize the real strength of capitalism. Euro-centrism has been the central focus of the opposition and criticism of post colonial thinking. But they fail to understand that it is not a purely cultural construct, but it is the political dimension of the world capitalism. The second critical point which Dirlik underscores is that by overemphasing its cultural dimensions, the present day post-colonial thinking undermines the role of the revolutionary movements of the yesteryears. Hence, Dirlik would prefer to describe it as the past-revolutionary proposition rather than it being called as a post-colonial project.

Aijaz Ahmad is another prominent critic of the present day understanding of post-colonialism. He is also of the opinion that by overemphasizing cultural and undermining the political aspect of post-colonialism, they have belittled the real battle against world capitalism, which has got to be fought mostly on its political and economic fronts. Another critical point which Ahmad makes is that some of the present day post-colonial thinkers go the whole hog to reject the Western civilization *per se* and in fact they wrongly hold it as solely responsible for all the ills of the today's 'world'. Such an intellectual exercise, Ahmad asserts, leads to a state of senseless anarchism. Sumit Sarkar, one of the leading historians of India, is also of the same opinion. He further holds that in the latest post-colonial thinking the role of the institution of the State has been reduced to the very minimum and as such the role of the political action is virtually sidelined. According to him, history does not support such an understanding, Besides, Sarkar does not agree with their attempt to reject the entire tradition of European Enlightenment. Thus, Sarkar does not foresee any meaningful struggle and opposition based on the present day post-colonial thinking. He considers it as a big challenge to the entire Marxist thinking and tradition.

Some of the scholars have also attacked the post colonial thinking for its excessive emphasis on the pluralist identities and their politics. Kwame Anthony Appiah, an African intellectual, is of the opinion that the post-colonial thinkers have rejected the entire European tradition of modernity and enlightenment in the name of indigenous tradition and culture. He asserts that a totalistic rejection could not be taken as a sound intellectual proposition. What is more, some of the post-colonial thinkers of Africa are themselves well-entrenched in the European culture and way of life. Hence, they do not have the moral right to pose and act as the true representatives of the African culture and civilization. In this way, Appiah raises a question mark even against the intellectual honesty of some of these post-colonial thinkers from Africa.

Scholars have argued that by challenging the old understanding of colonialism, both of the Marxism and the liberal tradition, post-colonial thinkers moved much closer to post-modernism. In the process, it has created a serious intellectual problem. Sobhanlal Datta Gupta has raised a very valid point on this score, when he says that if the entire tradition of rationalism and progress is to be rejected in the name of their being a part of Euro-centrism, then that would certainly thwart and halt the further cultural journey of man. Amartya Sen also raises a pertinent point by saying that if human rationalism and communal identities are to be posited against each other, as some of the post-colonial thinkers appear to have held, that would lead to very serious problems. For instance, if we attach too much importance to identity politics, then every ethnic/communal group would take its own moral compass as being the last word on the score. In the process, a situation of conflict between rationalism and identity politics would be created. There would be the possibility of emergence of Talibani ideology negating the entire tradition of human culture.

In brief, one could safely conclude that postcolonialism has greatly extended the traditional thinking on colonialism and imperialism. Some of the aspects of their problem which have been ignored by Marxism and the liberal thinking has been enunciated by the post-colonial thinkers with greater coherence and clarity. Besides, it has also focused on the problems of the dispossessed, and those of internal colonialism. These ideas are its major contributions. But as it happens in the process of evolution of an ideological movement, some sort of change does take place in its nature and structure. As post-colonial thinking has moved closer to post-modernism it has become refined, nuanced and subtle but as a practical movement of thought and action, it is losing its verve and effectiveness. Besides, like any other ideological movement, it has failed to keep its various dimensions on an even keel. Gradually, its uni-dimensional character is coming to the fore. However, it goes without saying that post-colonial thinking has greatly enriched the intellectual discourse on colonialism and imperialism.

6 Nationalism

Nationlism is a state of mind which gives 'national' messages, memories and images a preferred status in social communication and a greater 'weight' in the making of the decisions.

KARL W. DEUTSCH

Nationalism is an emotionally surcharged political idea which has been playing a crucial role in the history of the world since the sixteenth century. The swift current of nationalism has changed the entire contours and complexion of the European continent during the nineteenth century. New nation-States emerged on the demise of the multinational imperialist States. This process was further intensified since the end of the First World War. In fact, even the causal factors leading to the First World War and the Second World War had also something to do with the forces of nationalism. In the post-war period, nationalism emerged as a powerful ideology and political movement. With the independence of India in 1947, the forces of nationalism got a further boost which ultimately led to the freedom of a large number of the countries of Asia and Africa. In fact, by the time the Soviet Union disintegrated in 1991, the process of decolonisation has been virtually completed. Subsequently, liberalization and globalization became popular ideologies all over the world. Thereafter, it started being said that the days of nationalism are gone and a new international economic order is taking over our world. In fact, during the last few decades, nationalism has been facing challenges from different quarters.

It is primarily being attacked as much as from internationalism from the outside as from ethnicity from within. Despite the concept of the Nation-State under attack, there are scholars who believe that nationalism is still a potent force. It would continue to play an important role even in the days to come. It is obvious that nationalism has been a controversial subject both as a concept and as an ideology. It has been full of contradictory and contrarian pulls. In some areas, it has played a progressive role leading to the independence of a large number of countries. But it has also played reactionary and retrogressive role in some other areas leading to the foundation of Nazi and Fascist regimes. Thus, the shadow of nationalism could be seen everywhere from national liberation movement to neo-colonialism and even on Nazism and fascism. Hence, it deserves a fuller examination. In the pages that follow, we would be examining its different aspects in a brief and concise way.

Emergence of the Idea of Nationalism

The concept of nationalism in its present form is a product of the European context. In some ways, it is also linked up with the coming of the Industrial Revolution. In the wake of the Industrial Revolution, the old identities and primordial loyalties got undermined. As a consequence, there emerged the need for new and larger identities. What strengthened the process was the fact of the social role of the religion going to the periphery. In the process, the feeling of unity and affiliation with one's own people and alienation and antagonism with other people gathered tremendous momentum. One can say that nationalism as an ideology emerged both out of geographical and political needs. Initially, the process started in the sixteenth/seventeenth century in Europe. The Treaty of Westphalia turned out to be a milestone on the road to nationalism. American and the French Revolutions gave it a further boost. The unification of Italy and Germany further intensified the process. Thus, the idea of a centralised and sovereign Nation-State got connected with the feeling of nationalism. It is not for nothing that Hans Kohn, a leading scholar of nationalism, looks at the institution of the State as a symbol of nationalism. The role of nationalism was very widely reflected in the emergence of independent Nation-States in the course of time.

Defining the Terms like Nation, Nationality and Nation-State

Though nationalism has been a dominant theme of political discourse, but it has not been an easy task to define it in a precise way. It has been differently defined at different stages of history by different groups of people. For instance, the feeling of nationalism has been used for enslaving people of the Third World by the European powers. On the other hand, it has played an equally important role in the National Liberation Movement of the Third World. It is clear that it carries within itself various contradictory forces and elements. It has also been intimately connected with other political concepts like nation, nationality and the Nation-State. All these concepts do share a lot of common ground among themselves. Hence, it has never been an easy task to define all these concepts separately and distinctively. But, without clearly understanding these terms, it is difficult to offer a precise definition of nationalism. Hence, we would try to understand some of these terms.

Let us first look at the institution of the State. Usually, the State is defined as a group of people inhabiting a well defined territory and who have a sovereign government at their disposal. Nationality is now being defined in terms of the membership of a sovereign State. In other words, it is being viewed in terms of citizenship. For example, every Indian who enjoys the status of the Indian nationality; he is accepted as the citizen of India. The term 'Nation-State' comes out of the Latin word, *Natio*, which when translated in English stands for an ethnic group. Thus, the nation is taken in terms of the feeling of emotional unity among the members of a particular group. In course of time, the terms like 'nation' and 'nationality' started getting defined more correctly. But at times, these two terms 'nation' and 'nationality' were also being used interchangeably. In the old books of political science, both these terms were used to symbolize emotional unity based on shared feelings of religion, culture historical, experience, etc. Thus, these two terms, 'nation' and 'nationality', are essentially informed by a deep sense of emotional unity. Subsequently, they acquired more political overtones as it came to be widely believed that when a nation/nationality was able to get a sovereign State of its own, it is turned into a Nation-State. While making distinction among terms like Nation-State, nation and nationality, J.H. Hayes, an eminent political scientist, asserts that the basis of Nation-State could be singular nation/nationality, but they in turn could exist even in the absence of it. That is so because their main basis is cultural and educational unity. And such a feeling of unity could emerge from regional, ethnic, religious, cultural and historical basis. However, it needs to be underlined that all these elements need not be present in each and every case. The real thing is the feeling of unity among the people.

However, of late, nationality is being primarily viewed in terms of the citizenship of a sovereign State. Similarly, nation is being viewed as a symbol of political independence, whether real or desired. We can take the example of our own country, India. Our national leaders even during the colonial rule strongly believed that India has been a nation since time immemorial, as there has been always a deep sense of unity among our people. But in 1940, Jinnah and his Muslim League started underlining the fact that the Musalmans of India constituted a separate nation. Hence, they must have their own State. In the same way, distinction between nation and Nation-State is also getting obliterated as today hardly any State is based on single nation and nationality. In fact, every State has become a conglomeration of more than one nation or nationality. Not only that, nation and State are also being used as interchangeable terms. For instance, India is being referred both as a nation as well as a State. What is more, even nationality as a political term is being used to symbolize the cultural unity of the people. Besides, they are also being used to represent an ethnic group. It is not universally true that every nation and nationality desire to establish their own Nation-State. Some of them would be quite happy to protect their ethnic and cultural identity. For example, what the people of Tibet under the leadership of Dalai Lama are asking for is to retain their ethnic and cultural identity. We find that there is great divergence of views in respect of terms like nation, nationality and Nation-State.

Defining Nationalism

Let us get back to our original question: What is nationalism? There is a lot of difference of opinion among the scholars about the nature and structure of the term, nationalism. Different scholars define it differently by underlining its different aspects. Giddons underlines its psychological aspect and defines it by saying that it symbolises the common denominator which is at the base among the people of a particular community or ethnic group. Another scholar, Hans Kohn looks at nationalism as a state of mind of a particular group/people which is constantly trying to adjust itself to political realities. Similarly, Karl W. Deutsch takes it as a mental state in which national memory, message, imagination, etc. play a crucial role in the collective decision-making.

But a scholar like Peter Alter finds all these definitions as being one sided. He is of the opinion that it should be defined in such a way that all its major aspects are equally illumined. To that end, he approvingly refers to the definition of nationalism offered by Eugen Lemberg. According to Lemberg, nationalism is that collective expression of ideas and norms which creates a distinct feeling among the members of a group that they have a separate and distinct identity and value system. In other words, in the process of the emergence of such identity, the outlines of such differentiation also gets well-defined. Thus, nationalism creates a sense of unity among the members of a particular group, at the same time it also generates a feeling of separateness from the others. In brief, the feeling of unity and separateness are the two sides of the same coin of nationalism. Another scholar, Theodor Schieder states that nationalism creates a distinct and specific emotional feeling which prompts a particular ethnic group/community to seek and become a political nation, rather than remaining just a social and religious group. On the basis of all these views, Peter Alter comes to the conclusion that we should look at nationalism as an ideological and political movement. In the process, it creates an undying hope of action propelling it towards its final goal and destination. Transcending all other identities, it gives the assurance to all members of a particular group that they belong to one nation and that is their supreme identity.

In brief, it could be said that nationalism prompts a group to look at itself as a political group and to demand and struggle for a Nation-State of its own in a collective way. As a result of such nationalistic feelings, an individual takes himself as a member of specific nation rather than of the entire humankind. In the process, he gets himself attached to the present political system. In fact, he puts his nation at the top of the ideal of his life. As such, he is prepared to make all the sacrifices and undergo all kinds of sufferings. The ruling group is clever enough to locate such intense feelings among the people and uses it for the promotion of its self-interests. C.J.H. Hayes is of the opinion that in our times, nationalism has taken the place of religion, creating the same kind of feeling of fervour and intensity. Hence, as in the case of religion, people are prepared to make supreme sacrifices for it. Thus, religion gets secularised and nationalism gets sanctified. But there are many scholars who opine that religion could not be linked up with the emergence of nationalism. They contend that there are many instances even from our own historical epoch when religion and nationalism have moved on parallel lines simultaneously.

Concept of Nation

Like in the case of nationalism, it is equally difficult to define the concept of nation, as it is subtle, equivocal and multidimensional. At its minimum, nation could be described as an awakened and dynamic group propelled by an intense feeling of unity. Karl Deutsch is of the opinion that a group living in far-flung areas could establish a common dialogue among its members on account of commonality of shared culture, racial memories, language, and religion. Bound by a strong sense of unity it allows itself, to be described as a distinct cultural group. But it has to try and attain the status of a sovereign State, if it is to be called a nation. But a scholar like Peter Alter believes that such definitions actually narrow down its meaning and dimension. One could cite many examples from modern history when a group considered itself being a nation even without getting the status of a sovereign State. He points out another limitation of such definitions of the concept of nation, as it might create the impression that there are as many sovereign States as there are nations in the world. But such a formulation would be far from the truth. History is a witness to the fact that a State could comprise many nations or a nation/nationality could be found scattered in different States.

Joseph Stalin, a Soviet leader, in his book, *Marxism and National State* considered the concept of nation in the Marxian perspective. According to him, any historically evolved stable community could be termed as a nation provided four basic elements permeate it. They are: linguistic, regional, economic and psychological and cultural unity. To him, these were the essential elements of a nation. However, Max Weber has his own view on the concept of nation. He asserts that a feeling of separateness from other groups as well as an intense feeling of unity is essential for a community to constitute a nation. But all the factors for unity like religion, linguistic, cultural and historical elements need not be present in every case. For example, Pakistan came into being on the basis of religion and Bangladesh on the basis of language.

Recent Thinking on Nationalism

In the last quarter of the twentieth century, there emerged some fresh thought on nation and nationalism. It needs to be mentioned that in the earlier period, historians and political scientists were forerunners in the realm of studies on nation and nationalism. Basically, political scientists were studying these concepts in the perspective of liberalism and Marxism. They were primarily concerned whether these concepts have affected the political systems in the world and the balance of power of the world politics? Historians' main focus of study was the working of different national liberation movements and the process through which different Nation-States had emerged. In such studies scholars like C.J.H. Hayes and Hans Kohn were the leading figures. They looked at the nation as a territory rather than a community. Hence, little attention was paid on the nature and structure of community, their cultural and social life. Max Weber also was a supporter of such studies. According to him, national consciousness had little to do with empirical realities like ethnic, linguistic and cultural unity. It has to do much more with the power-status of one's own State. The tradition of such studies is still popular in a section of academicians.

In recent years, a number of sociologists and anthropologists have been drawn to the issues relating to the concept of nation and nationality. Of late, the reason for such paradigm shift in the context of national liberation movement, is that these concepts are being looked upon as parts of an ideological movement. In recent times, the sovereignty of the State is facing challenge both at national and international levels.

The concept of the sovereign State is under pressure from different international organisations. At the same time it is also facing a challenge from various ethnic groups fired by primordial loyalties. As a result, the social scientists have started paying greater attention on these groups and the issues related to them. Thus, in new sociological perspective, nation and Nation-State are being viewed in a much more complex way. Nationalism could be viewed in different perspectives – at times as the ideology of an ambitious group or as a policy of a Nation-State or as devotion to one's own Nation-State. Besides, it could also be viewed as a social and political movement or could very well be viewed in the context of a nation-building endeavour. Similarly, the concept of a nation could be taken in multiple meanings. In one way, it could be taken as a part of Nation-State or the efforts made to establish such a State by a particular group. Similarly, the concept of a Nation-State is no longer taken to be that simple and concrete. In the entire scheme of the Nation-State, which of the two, nation or State, is more important, continues to be the most important question. Whether nation gets totally converted into a State, or State into a nation is a question which could not be easily and finally settled. Another question that continues to baffle us is whether the term the nation State could be used for all kinds of State or whether it could be taken as being relevant in respect of some specific States? Another question that has been often raised is whether a nation could encompass several States or whether a State could encompass several nations? Similarly, another question being asked is whether nationality could be viewed simply as a legal membership of a

State or could it be taken in the sense of ethnic group? All these questions have brought about a new perspective on these concepts. A number of scholars are engaged in studying these concepts in a new perspective. However, on account of the limitations of space, we would confine our study in respect of three prominent scholars who have made pioneering studies in this area. They are: Ernest Gellner, Benedict Anderson and Anthony Smith. We would be making a very brief and quintessential presentation of their views.

Ernest Gellner

Gellner looks at the institution of State in secular terms and which is why he opines that the primary purpose of the State is to establish and look after the problems of law and order. He finds the symbol of its authority in the institution like police and judicial system. It is because of these institutions that the State differentiates itself from other organizations and institutions. He also believes that the modern State is the product of industrial society. He is also of the opinion that industrial society totally destroyed the value system and norms of the old society. Hence, the modern State tries to create a uniform national feeling through propagation and dissemination of national culture. Thus, Gellner asserts that the State is prior to the emergence of Nation-State. In other words, nation is created through the efforts of the State and its work. Hence, he concludes that a nation is nothing more than a consciousness. He furthers opines that on account of the shared culture, the member of a particular community develops a feeling of rights and duties among themselves. In the process, that community assumes the form of a nation. Similarly, while defining nationalism, Gellner asserts that as a special form of patriotism, it has come up only in recent times. Thus, Gellner believes that it is the elite culture, when it is taken to the masses, gives birth to the feeling of nationalism and nation-building. As such, the State plays a crucial role in the entire process.

But there are scholars like Liah Greenfield and J. Eastwood who violently disagree with Gellner's views. They point out the most glaring flaw in Gellner's definition as it fails to identify the special features of nationalism. Some other scholars have pinpointed another weakness of Gellner's views as being totally inapplicable to the Indian situation. This is so because in the case of India, nation came first and it was followed by the emergence of the Indian State. Thus, Gellner's entire definition falls flat in the case of India.

Anthony Smith on Nation and Nationalism

Anthony Smith is another thinker who has his own views on the concepts like nation and nationalism. He defines nation as a group inhabiting a specific area and bound by economic unity and whose every member has an equal feeling of rights and duties. Besides, the group is also embedded in historical myth, racial memories and popular culture. With all these characteristics as prerequisites, the group could claim to be a nation. Thus, according to Smith the roots of nation and nationalism could be located in the nature and structure of ethnicity. Smith believes that the fundamental constituents of ethnic identity are myths, memories, symbols, and values which could be taken as being 'permanent cultural attributes'. For Smith, these permanent features are quite in contrast with ephemeral dimensions of collective will, attitude, even sentiment which make up the day-to-day fabric of ethnic consciousness. What works as further cementing force for the ethnic group is the strong attachment among the members of the group to a specific area and also a sense of unity among the elite section of that ethnic group. In brief, Anthony Smith is known as a proponent of ethnic nationalism.

Scholars have pointed out a number of flaws in Smith thinking about nationalism. As Thomas J. Scheff points out that Smith's distinction between 'permanent cultural attributes' and 'ephemeral dimensions' could not be always taken to be valid as it is nothing more than 'a priori judgements' that sentiments are ephemeral. Secondly, Smith ignores the fact that ethnic nationalism might arise because of a sense of alienation, even on account of resentment against unfair exclusion, whether political, economic or social. Similarly, inclusion in these areas could undercut the feeling of nationalism. Thirdly, in Smith's scheme of things it is difficult to distinguish between nation and an ethnic group. But the fact of the matter is that every ethnic group does not end up as constituting a nation with a strong sense of nationalism.

Benedict Anderson on Nationalism

Anderson is an influential thinker on the theme of nationalism. In his book, *Imagined Communities* he argues that a nation is nothing more than a product of human imagination, for the members of a nation do not know each other, nor could they ever assemble at one place. Hence, they could not be taken to be constituting a real society. In fact, they could at best be an imagined community. As even their sense of unity is also the result of their imagination. Anderson finds the cultural roots of nationalism in the decline and erosion of religions and religious certainty. He believes that nationalism gives similar meaning to the lives of the people which was earlier provided by religion.

Anderson's critics do assert that his definition of nation is neither realistic, nor does it cover the concept of nation in its totality. As Thomas Scheff points out that Anderson's formulation fails to explain why an imagined community is chosen over an actual one. In other words, why does one feel closer to the people one does not know than with the people one knows? Anderson's explanation fails to explain this puzzle.

It is in the above perspective that scholars like Liah Greenfield and J. Eastwood believe that full light on the theme of nationalism is yet to be thrown. These two scholars also try to define nationalism in their own way. They assert that nationalism is a way of thinking in which the concept of the nation stands at the centre. They further opine that the nation stands for an ethnic group which is marked by a feeling of equality and sovereignty which also lies with them. Every member is competent to provide the leadership and as such he could become the part of the elite group. It is because of the fact that every one enjoys equal respect; hence they are prepared to sacrifice everything for it. In this way, they believe that nationalism is a cultural event and feeling. It is a kind of consciousness and as such it provides the basis for political action. In the absence of the nation, neither nationalism nor the project of nation building can take place.

Political and Cultural Nationalism

There are two strands of nation and nationalism which have drawn the attention of scholars in recent times. They are described as political and cultural nationalism.

Political Nationalism

Political nationalism is primarily based on the basic principle of unity and equality among all people of the nation. Here national commitment comes from the freedom of the people. An eminent scholar like Ernest Renan believes that in the whole scheme of things, the free will of the people is so important that it would not be an exaggeration to say that a nation is virtually backed by the daily referendum of the popular will. Hence, even if all other factors in making of the nation are present, but if the feeling of equality and unity are missing, then, it would be difficult to sustain its existence in the long-term. In fact, at some stage of their national existence, the people of a particular territory start taking themself as a nation. At such a stage, nationality and citizenship become one and the same, i.e. they become identical. The history of USA, France and Great Britain are illustrative examples of political nationalism. In all these countries, it was through citizenship that the feeling of intense nationalism grew up in the course of historical developments. In the process, the provision for equality before the law played a crucial role. Despite people having religious, linguistic and ethnic differences, dignity and integrity of individuals, his liberty, equality and rights have become the real component of nationalism. The life of such a nation is marked by intellectual liberalism and strong faith in the existence of people with diverse background.

Cultural Nationalism

A tradition of cultural nationalism has also been in existence side by side with political nationalism. In such a conception of nationalism, there has been an emphasis on ethnic and religious aspect of nationalism. In such a scheme of cultural nationalism,

nationalism comes to stay much before the State comes into being. This is so because in such a situation, it is religion and ethnicity that play a crucial role and not the fact of the State being organised as a political entity. Thus, the primary basis of cultural nationalism is the commonality of religious and ethnic experiences, which ultimately lead to the process of nation-making. Here, unlike in the case of political nationalism, free will of the people does not play a very important role, for an individual is already a member of a cultural nation. The decision for his membership of the State is already made through history and culture of the group. Very often cultural nationalism as compared to political nationalism is considered to be much less democratic. It could even be anti-democratic. There is not much scope for encompassing other religious and ethnic groups. But it would not be correct to say that popular will is totally absent from the realm of cultural nationalism. In the process of acquiring a State or while confronting an adversary State, popular will plays an important role. In fact, in such a situation, there is a great scope for manipulating the popular will for promoting the interest of the powers that be. Besides, minorities may suffer from the feeling of insecurity. The possibility of conflict is much greater in a nation governed under the system of cultural nationalism.

7 *Historiography of Colonialism and Nationalism in India*

The historiography of Indian nationalism has for a long time been dominated by elitism – colonial elitism and bourgeois-nationnalist elitism.

RANAJIT GUHA

The term 'historiography' stands for historical writings of historical events of a particular period, both for the purposes of recording as well as for their varying interpretations. Today, there is virtually a general agreement among historians that history writing is much more than a mere collection of historical data or facts and other evidences. It is being widely believed that interpretative aspects of history writing is far more significant than mere collection of historical data and evidences. It is a well established opinion that the same historical event and even evidence could be viewed differently by different historians. This is so because in the entire process of history writing, historian's worldviews and his ideological moorings are bound to impact his historical perception. That is the reason why the same historical events are interpreted and evaluated differently by different scholars.

In this chapter, we propose to give a bird's-eye view of the historiography of colonialism and nationalism in India. There are five prominent schools which deal with the historiography of colonialism and nationalism in India. They are: the imperialist, the nationalist, the Marxist, the Quasi-Marxist-Nationalist, and the subaltern. We propose to make a brief but critical presentation on all these schools.

To start with, it would be relevant to underline the basic issues underlying all these schools. Basically, there have been four major questions which impinge on the entire process. First, what is the relationship between colonialism and Indian nationalism? To be more specific, is it true that the leaders of the Indian national movement by making an independent judgment decided to work out and pursue their policy and programmes in the interest of the people of India? Or is it a fact that all these policies and programmes of our national movement were formulated in response to the initiatives taken by the colonial rulers? In other words, could it be said that it was while responding to the British initiatives that our leaders set up the national goal, tried to find the appropriate means to traverse the journey or were they working independently of the British initiatives taking into account the real interests of the people of India? A second set of questions are: which section of the people of India was the worst victims of the colonial rule? And which section/class did initiate and remain steadfastly in the forefront of the national struggle? Did the national movement mostly benefit the elite classes? Or did it bring benefit to all sections of the Indian people? What did ultimately happen to the poor and the dispossessed of India both in the process of the journey as well as at the end of it? The third set of relevant questions are: was the entire national movement initiated and run by the Indian elite and that too in its own interest? Or was the movement actually run by the common masses in different parts of the country in different periods and on different issues and it is they who paid a heavy price for their bold ventures? Could these scattered movements of the people be characterised as the national movement? Or is it a fact that putting aside the people's initiative, ultimately the elite grabbed the movement and used it for their own self-promotion? The fourth set of questions are: what was the real role of the British colonialism in India? Was it just an alien rule whose only purpose was to promote the colonial interest? Or was it also committed to bring about a progressive civilization and to train the Indian people in the art of self-government? In the following pages, we will find that different scholars look at all these questions in their own perspective and accordingly find their own answers.

The Imperialist School

The imperialist school is as old as the British rule itself. Its proponents comprised viceroys, colonial administrators, political elite and other protagonists of the British rule. The basic contention of this school has been that the British rule was Providential for the people of India. Hence, its primary purpose was to promote the interests of the people of India. Thus, all talks about the exploitation of the people of India is meaningless and without any foundation whatsoever.

Romila Thapar, the noted historian, has rightly pointed out that in the beginning of their rule, the British had a great need to acquire a deep understanding of the Indian people, their history, culture and religion. This process went through several phases. First of all, the Orientalists tried to understand the Indian culture, language, civilization and society. Those were the days of William Jones and his Asiatic Society of Calcutta. The attempt was to explore and explain the various aspects of Indian life. One of the primary objectives of such initial endeavour was to make the task of the colonial administrators easier through a clear understanding of the working of the ancient Indian institutions. These scholars also underlined the fact of Aryan immigration to both India and Europe. They also talked of Indo-European languages. Max Muller, a German scholar, took forward their work in an energetic manner.

Apart from the Orientalists, there was another class of British scholars during the nineteenth century, who took a lot of interest in Indian studies. They also challenged some of the basic formulations of the Orientalist school. They were inspired by the Utilitarian school led by Bentham. They contended that the ancient culture of India suffered from many infirmities and flaws. If the people of India were to be put on the path of progress and prosperity, then, one has to promote individualism and rationalism in their lives. This could be achieved through a series of progressive laws energetically intervening in the social and religious life of the Indian people. James Mill's book, *History of India* underscored the same line of thought. The Christian missionaries were of the same opinion. We must keep in our mind that during the nineteenth century, the process of industrial revolution in England had gathered momentum. Hence, the need for acquiring raw materials and assured market for them were the primary concerns of the British rulers. Hence, it was necessary to intervene in the social, economic and religious life of our people, making them more conducive for the promotion of British industries. Therefore, pinpointing some of the major weaknesses (real or imagined) of the Indian society became the major plank of the British colonial policy.

Subsequently, such an imperialist viewpoint was further extended by scholars like Reginald Coupland and Percival Spear. Their basic contention was that the British rule has provided a training ground for self government for the people of India. Not only that, ultimately they also transferred power to the people of India. This was a kind of the liberal perspective on the part of the imperialist school. The more conservative view was yet to come. This was provided by scholars like Anil Seal, Galldan, Broomfield and Judith Brown – all of them belonged to the Cambridge School of History. They went much further than the earlier scholars in defence of the British imperialist position. They argued that India was not even a nation-in-making, what to talk of its being a nation. In their view, India was nothing more than a conglomeration of the communities-religious, linguistic and caste interests. It is this conglomeration of different groups which provided the social base for all political actions. In their opinion, India could never develop a strong national identity as the people of India could never transcend and overcome their varying primordial loyalties. Hence, there has never been any possibility of emergence of genuine nationalism in India. In fact, the so called national movement was nothing more than a galaxy of local movements. Moreover, it simply represented the class, individual and communal interests of the Indian elite. These scholars also believed that a number of leaders were seeking favours from the British and in the process, they even competed with each other. Not only that, in the opinion of these scholars, even popular mobilization was done to promote their own interests. These national leaders were in position to assure the local leaders and their communities that they too would be able to avail the fringe benefits. And that was the primary reason why local leaders got attached to the national leaders. These scholars even put the national leaders like Gandhi, Nehru and Patel in the same category of self-seekers. They also contend that it was certain initiatives taken by the British in the field of education and legislature which offered new opportunities through which the people got attracted to the national movement. Some of these scholars engaged themselves in regional studies to support and substantiate their basic contentions. On the basis of their regional studies, they concluded that the local movements promoted the local community interests and not so much the national interest. This is, in brief, the major intellectual contention of the imperialist school. They do not find a genuine conflict between the colonial ruler and those who led the Indian national movement. In fact, they look at the whole process as being a part of competition and co-operation between the Indian elite and the colonial administration.

It is nct all surprising that the Indian scholars have strongly reacted and refuted the basic formulations of the imperialist school. S.Gopal, one of the leading historians of India, was of the opinion that the imperialist school rejects the entire tradition of selfless service, idealism and self-suffering which dominated the national movement throughout its existence. Another Indian scholar, Tapan Roy Choudhary, while ridiculing the entire thesis of the imperialist school, characterised it as nothing but animal politics. One could only add that such a low view of man and his working even goes beyond the Machiavellian politics. In fact, such a low view of man is nothing but a direct assault on his dignity, integrity and all the idealism he has upheld throughout human history. Such a low view of human nature is also falsified by human history, which is full of instances of sacrifice and self-suffering for the larger cause of the people.

The Nationalist School

Diametrically opposite to the imperialist school, there has been an Indian nationalist school. This school is not a mere by-product of the national movement, but has also played a crucial role in its emergence and growth. In fact, it has strengthened the national movement in every possible way. There is a long list of its initial proponents comprising Dadabhai Naoroji, R.C. Dutt, S.N. Banerjee, Lokmanya Tilak, Bipin Chandra Pal, Lala Lajpat Rai, Swami Dayanand, Swami Vivekananda, Aurobindo Ghosh and Mahatma Gandhi to name just a few of the nationalist leaders. The subsequent academic protagonists comprised such stalwart historians like R.C. Majumdar, Tarachand, Bisheshber Prasad, B.R. Nanda, B.N. Pandey and a host of other academicians and scholars. All these leaders and scholars greatly contributed to the emergence and growth of this school. The basic postulates of this school could be summed up as follows:

(i) It goes to the credit of this school that it has greatly exposed the exploitative and domineering nature of the British colonial rule. Not only that, these scholars have further asserted that it was through use of force, fraud and political manipulation that British occupation in India was made possible. In the process, East India Company looted and took away an enormous amount of wealth from India, which in turn played a crucial role in the coming of the industrial revolution in England. In subsequent years, India was made a captive market for the British industrial goods and for the acquiring of cheap raw materials. This process of exploitation was further expanded by the investment of the British capital in India. All these resulted in the destruction of different aspects of the Indian life, including economic, political and social life, which in turn led to mass pauperization of the Indian people. In brief, they reject all the major contentions of the imperialist school in respect of the benevolent nature of the British Rule.

(ii) The second major thesis of the nationalist school is that basically the Indian national movement was based on the Indian situation, its history, culture and the experiences of the Indian people. In other words, they contend that the racial memory of our illustrious cultural and religious heritage had played a crucial role in the emergence of the Indian national movement. They refute the imperialist school's contention that the Indian national movement did arise in response to the British initiatives. The proponents of this school further contend that India has a great tradition of cultural nationalism and the British had hardly any big role in the emergence of the Indian nationhood. They further argued that the ancient Indian culture with its high social norms and values has been the precursor of some of the ideas like liberty, equality, universalism, dignity and integrity of man which today are considered to be the symbol of Western modernity. In any case, our ancient heritage does not contradict and run counter to these modern values. In other words, our cultural and religious values have greatly contributed to the emergence of Indian nationalism.

(iii) The nationalist school also contends that the Indian national movement represented the sum total of the interests of the Indian people and was never fired by sectional interest of any class. It took a popular form under the leadership of Mahatma Gandhi. In other words, it could be said that the British colonialism destroyed the social fabric of India and even tried to undermine its culture. The real roots of Indian nationalism lay in the collective memory of our old cultural and patriotic history and the shared opposition of our people to the British rule.

The major attack on the basic formulations of the nationalist school has come from the imperialist school as well as the Marxist school of the various persuasions. Basically, the critics contend that the nationalist concept of the ever existing Indian nationhood, is nothing but a product of their imagination. Their notion of the Indian nationhood is devoid of all empirical realities. According to the critics, the entire movement was under the firm grip of the elite which successfully manipulated it for their self promotion. The people did participate in the movement but at critical junctures their interests were ignored for the sake of those of the elite. Some of the interests and concerns of the common people did become a part of the national programmes, but that was done more to seek their support and participation, rather than out of genuine concern for them. Hence, once the struggle was over, their interests were kept in cold storage and the elite took away its lion's share.

The Marxist School

The Marxist School has primarily displayed its intellectual dependence on the writings of Karl Marx, particularly on a series of essays which he wrote, analysing the British occupation in India, in formulating its perspective on the nature and structure of the British colonialism and the Indian national movement. In these essays, Marx makes it clear that the nature of the British occupation in India was entirely different from its earlier occupation. The earlier invaders had settled down in India and integrated themselves in the mainstream of the Indian society and culture. Some of them even lost their war on the cultural front with India, even though they had been the winners on the battlefield. But the British occupation has been of different nature and importance. In fact, the British society has crossed the stage of feudalism and entered into a capitalist phase by the time they came to India. Hence, the British colonial rule had twin impacts – both destructive and constructive. In other words, while its destructive role could be seen in ending the autarkic system of the village life in India, its constructive role was displayed in ushering India into a capitalist system of production. In the process, it caused untold sufferings to the people of India, but there is no denying the fact that it played a progressive role in laying the capitalist foundation in India.

Indian Marxist scholars like R.P. Dutt, A.R. Desai and others have been repeating these Marxian formulation ad nauseam. However, some other Marxist scholars like Sumit Sarkar have disfavoured such wholesale adoption of Marxian formulations. Sarkar has been of the opinion that while concept like class and class consciousness are good tools of social analysis, but their machanical application might create many problems. Hence, a more nuanced, flexible and intellectually ingenious approach is needed for using these Marxist tools of social analysis. Some of the Marxists do concede that all classes contributed their share in the national movement. Hence, contributions of none of the classes could be ignored while analysing the Indian national movement, and a multi-class approach would be more appropriate. However, here our purpose is not to go into the different strands of the Marxist formulations. Rather, a summarised version of their formulations would serve our purpose. They are being summarised as follows:

(i) R.P. Dutt, who is taken as the most prominent ideologue of the Marxist School in his book, *India Today* follows the Lenin's line of thinking on imperialism. He divides the British colonialism in three phases – mercantile, industrial, and financial. This is nothing but the Indian version of Lenin's theory of imperialism. Though, tactics, strategies, policies, and programmes did differ from phase to phase, but the basic purpose remained the same: the loot of the Indian wealth and making India subservient to the British capitalist interest.

(ii) Following Karl Marx, the Marxist scholars do concede that the large-scale destruction of the Indian social and economic fabric did take place on account of the British colonial rule, which in turn led to the mass pauperization of the Indian people. But like Karl Marx they argue that was a part of the destructive and constructive role of the British rule in India. It led to the destruction of the feudal order but also played a constructive role in laying the foundation for the capitalist system in India. In Marxist parlance, capitalism being the higher stage of social development, they do look at it as a positive step. Under the British rule, big changes took place both in the productive system as well as in the nature of Indian social structure. For example, it led to the emergence of a modern State system and of different and new classes in the Indian society. It also led to distinct improvement in the transport and communication system. But these Marxist scholars do agree with the nationalist school that all these developments were taking place in the interest of the British rule. But they do not forget to add that these measures virtually changed the social structure of India, giving it a positive and progressive character.

(iii) These scholars do accept that these changes brought about a primary contradiction between the interest of the Indian people and the British colonial rulers. And that might have provided both distant and precipitating causes for the emergence of the Indian national movement. They lay greater emphasis on the class character of the Indian national movement.

(iv) Marxist Scholars have always been in a state of dilemma in respect of their understanding and characterization of the Indian national movement and its class character. Similarly, they also failed to accurately and adequately characterize the leadership of Mahatma Gandhi. There were many reasons for such failures. One, they had the mechanical faith in the theory of class analysis and class struggle. Hence, they could never clearly see the empirical nature of the Indian situation. Similarly, they could not once for all decide the class character of the Indian national movement. This was so because they had to take into account both the basic Marxian theoretical proposition and also the empirical realities of the Indian situation. On top of it, they were also to follow the guidelines given by the international communist movement led by the Soviet leadership. All these created a lot of confusion and they could not go into the empirical realities of the Indian situation in their own independent way. Hence, they continued to remain confused and could not take a clear stand and final decision on all these counts. For example, they could not decide who is their primary enemy, the international bourgeoisie in the form of the British imperialism or the Indian bourgeoisie which was leading the national movement.

It is such indecisiveness on the basic issues, both in terms of theory and praxis which made them change their position quite frequently. And which is why at times they tended to support the Non-cooperation Movement, but at other times they fiercely opposed the Quit India Movement. Not only that, at times, they tended to drive their own lonely ideological furrow and at other times they were quite keen to pursue the policy of the United Front at the behest of the Soviet leadership. These contracdictory policies were their primary weakness. They could never free themselves from the clutches of the international communist movement. According to Bipan Chandra, their primary weakness lay in their failure to make a distinction between the 'primary contradiction' and the 'secondary contradiction'. They could not reconcile between these two types of contradictions. While underlying the bourgeois character of the Indian national movement, they failed to take into account its multi-class character. Besides, by linking the strategic move of the national movement in its forward and backward movements to its class character, they could easily go into long slumber under their own ideological cloak.

The Quasi-Marxist-Nationalist School

Bipan Chandra and his associate scholars have tried their best to work out a genuine reconciliation between the Marxist and the nationalist school formulations. Hence, I have called their approach to the historiography of colonialism and nationalism in India as being Quasi-Marxist-Nationalist School. Their basic formulations could be summed up as follows:

(i) These scholars contend that there was a primary contradiction between the interest of the British imperialism and those of the Indian people. There was hardly any scope for any genuine reconciliation between the two. It was on such a solid foundation that the Indian national movement emerged and grew.

(ii) These scholars do accept that there might have been some secondary contradictions between different classes of people in India. But what is not to be forgotten is the fact that they never superseded the primary contradiction that existed between the British colonial rule and the people of India.

(iii) The Indian national movement was not a movement of any single class of India. It always had a multi-class foundation. Therefore, it could be legitimately described as having a multi-class foundation. Hence, all said and done, it was a people based movement – a popular movement in which people drawn from all classes participated. This became more obvious once Mahatma Gandhi took over its leadership.

(iv) It is true that the Indian national movement did intensify the nationalist feelings of the Indian people. In the process, it strengthened the foundation of the Indian nationhood. But in the process, it did not completely overtake their primordial loyalties to their own groups based on language, religion, caste and region. There was not much contradiction between their national identity and their social and cultural identities. It was a kind of attempt at multi-culturalism – much before this term came into the political discourse of the Western academia.

(v) Indian intelligentsia played a crucial role in the course of the national movement – contributing significantly to its nature and structure, both in terms of its ideology and organisation. It also tried to bring about reconciliation between different classes. It also played a crucial role in the transfer of power which took place in 1947. These scholars also contend that the transfer of power in 1947, which took place between the Indian bourgeoisie and the British imperialists was in the words of Antonio Gramsci, 'position of war' in which the Indian people were involved.

Thus, we find that Bipan Chandra and his associate scholars have made a bold attempt to reconcile the major formulations of the Marxist and the nationalist schools. But in the process they had to take the help of Mao Ze Dung's ideological formulations of primary and secondary contradictions. They have used this basic ideological tool to explain the relationship between the people of India and the British imperialism in terms of 'primary contradiction'. On the other hand, according to them, contradiction among the different classes of the Indian society was in the nature of 'secondary contradiction'. It goes without saying that by its very nature the primary contradictions existing between the two adversaries were irreconcilable, whereas there were good chances of reconciliation in case of secondary contradictions.

However, the basic question remains whether by such nuanced ideological understanding the poor could forget their suffering and deprivation. This question has been raised by Ranajit Guha and his associate scholars in a big way. They belong to the subaltern school which has challenged all other schools.

The Subaltern School

The Subaltern School is latest to join the rank of historiographers on colonialism and nationalism in India. Ranajit Guha is the chief propounder of this school of thought in India. A brief statement about its main theoretical perspective is given in the introduction part of Ranajit Guha's book, *Subaltern Studies* Volume I. In that introduction for the clarification of this main theme, he offers definitions of elite as well as of subaltern classes. According to Guha, the elite class, comprising both indigenous and foreign origins, constitutes the most dominant class. But the indigenous section of the elite class also comprises two types of people. One section of this class has nationwide spread, whereas another section of this class is confined to certain areas. In other words, the latter is dominant only at the regional level, but the other section enjoyed all-India dominance. According to Guha, the subaltern class comprises all these remaining sections of the Indian people, after the elite classes have been deducted from the total population of the country. These subaltern classes comprise impoverished zamindars, poorer section of the rural elite, upper middle class peasants and a host of similar other classes. The upper middle class peasants ordinarily identify themselves with the elite and at other times also with subaltern classes. Guha's purpose in defining these classes in such detailed way is to show the behaviour and character of the national movement and also to expose the contradictory character of some of these classes. Guha's main formulations could be summed up as follows:

(i) The elite classes have dominated the field of history writing for a long time. In such a scheme of things, both the indigenous elite class and also those of foreign origins have always joined hands. Their dominance has continued even in the post-independent era.

(ii) The elite classes have always laid the claim that they have played a crucial role in arousing and consolidating the mainstream of Indian nationalism. But Guha contends that the indigenous elite class was never inspired by high ideals. Rather, it was always fired by both individual as well as its class interests. Hence, it adopted a twin policy of cooperation and competition with the colonial administration. Not only that, even inside the country it again carried the same policy of cooperation and competition with other indigenous classes.

(iii) According to Guha, the history of the national movement penned by the indigenous elite class is nothing but the glorification of its role in the national movement. In the process, it only underlines the acts of sacrifices made and sufferings undergone by its own class. In fact, it totally ignores the cooperation and compromises it has made with the colonial administration for its own selfish interest. Ridiculing such history writing, Guha wryly comments that it is nothing less than the spiritual life story of the elite classes. However, he concedes that this kind of history writing has its own advantage. Through such history writing, one gets a close view of the nature and structure of the colonial State, its action and also about the ideology of the elite classes. Not only that, one could also see the real ideology behind various strands of historiography.

(iv) Guha makes it clear that from the tradition of such history writing one could hardly get a real understanding of contributions of the subaltern classes in the cause of the national movement. In fact, it presents a faulty and distorted view of participation and the role of common man in the Indian freedom struggle. Such a distorted picture of history looks at such participation of the common people only in terms of the charismatic personality of some national leaders or in the form of some selfish groupism or in terms of deteriorating law and order situation. Guha is firmly of the opinion that with such a distorted perspective, one could hardly explain the massive participation of the people, in some of the national movements like the Non-Cooperation Movement, Civil Disobedience Movement and Quit India Movement. According to Guha, in all these movements, the participation of the people did not move in vertical direction, rather it moved in a horizontal order. Peasant participation in particular was massive in all these movements, though other sections of subaltern classes also participated in them. Such massive participation was also based on the understanding of the subaltern classes about their exploitation and domination by the elite classes. The elite classes could never represent the voice of the people of India. Peasants and the working classes, while facing exploitation and domination at the hands of the upper classes, could still claim their own identity and their own voice in the entire process. However, Guha concedes that the politics of subaltern classes was not that powerful, so as to constitute a full fledged national liberation movement on their own. Guha would also like to make it a point of study, as to why people failed in such endeavour. But one thing is certain that historiography of the elite classes would have to be rejected in any case as its study of the Indian national movement is inadequate, unauthentic and one sided. Hence, there is a need for establishing a new school of historiography which will amply study the cross-currents of the politics of both the elite classes and subaltern classes including the process of their co-existence. According to Guha, historians of the subaltern school are trying their best to establish such a new tradition of historiography.

In brief, the subaltern school has tried to understand and study people's struggle, their trials and tribulations and it is only in such perspective that it attempts to look at the history of colonialism and nationalism in India. The main formulation of this school is that the subaltern sections of the Indian population comprising peasants, industrial workers, the rural poor, handicraft workers and others have enough of sociological, anthropological and other kinds of ample literature on their life and culture. They also have daring and romantic stories of struggle against the colonial administration, as they were the worst victims of colonial rule.

However, a number of scholars have taken critical views on many of the basic formulations of the subaltern school. They view these basic formulations as being exaggerated and one sided. It is also interesting to note that such critical views are coming from a host of Marxist scholars. For example, Sumit Sarkar is of the opinion that in the latest tradition of this school, the real hero, the subaltern class, is missing from the main focus of the study. Its intellectual concerns, Sarkar asserts, are gradually shifting towards the politics of the educated classes of the colonial era. Thus, its attention is getting divided and blurred. Bipan Chandra has expressed his surprise that the subaltern school is echoing the opinions and perceptions of the imperialist school as far as the nature and character of the national movement is concerned.

Romila Thapar has also taken a critical view of the basic contentions of this school. She is of the opinion that these scholars refuse to make broad generalization based on their historical writings and studies. They take every study on its own which has hardly anything to do much with their other studies. Hence, in the process of counting trees, they totally ignored the overview of the woods. Besides, they have also failed to provide an alternative vision of nationalism. Moreover, there is no central point in their studies. Hence, their different studies could not be assessed based on any central point of their own.

In the view of the above, we find that several schools of historiography on colonialism and nationalism have come up in recent times. Perhaps the basic reason for such divergent views is the pluralistic nature of our society. We have different classes, castes, religious groups, regional variations and there are different visions of our nationhood. In the process, the colonial rule also played a crucial role in promoting these divergent visions based on their policy of divide and rule. However, it has to be accepted that nationalism has played some role in bringing some coherence and consonance among these divergent voices and visions. It is true that it did not succeed totally, as its message of unity could not ensure rightful participation and shared lives among all these divergent groups. It was on that account that India was divided. The challenge of establishing unity amidst diversity is still there. These different schools of historiography of colonialism and nationalism also symbolise in some way the same problems of diversity and even divergence. Each school tries to take a group and grab a segment of the whole reality. Hence, each one of them is bound to be partial and inadequate on its own for the fuller understanding of the total reality. One cannot depend on any one of these schools for the fuller understanding of the Indian situation. Nor could we choose any one of them as a sole tool of social analysis. We have to adopt multi-pronged strategy to that end.

PART II

Different Aspects of the British Challenge

Let us only make common cause with her (Indian) people; let them feel that we are there to give more than we receive; that their interest are not traversed and frustrated by selfish aims of ours; that, if we are defending ourselves upon the line of the Hindu Kush, it is them and their interest that we are defending even more and far more than our own. Unless we can produce conviction in the mind of India, in vain shall we lavish our thought and our resources upon a merely material defence.

WILLIAM E. GLADSTONE

India was never conquered by the English sword – not by military valour, but by a subtle and cunning diplomacy. To have used force . . . would have roused the warring chiefs to a sense of mutual danger, and united them against the common enemy. Lulled by professions of a purely commercial interest, the native chieftains vied with one another in extending opportunities of trade to the British in return for military service rendered by these armed merchants in subduing local rivals. Too late they found that the mailed fist which encompassed the ruin of their enemies was turned with equal effectiveness against themselves.

LALA LAJPAT RAI

8 British Occupation of India: An Overview

The trader's scale turned overnight into the ruler's sceptre.

RABINDRANATH TAGORE

The gradual occupation of India by the British in the course of the eighteenth and nineteenth centuries was more than a mere amazing and even bizarre act in the arena of world history. That England, a tiny country both in terms of population and territorial size, could occupy and master a big country like India, with such an ancient culture, is a fact which cannot be taken as just an unexpected accident in human history. Obviously, it raises questions of a fundamental nature regarding the actual strengths and weaknesses of both the parties involved in the process. Thus, our study will have to delve into the deeper processes and recesses of history, and as such it has to go beyond a merely descriptive and chronological account of how India was gradually enslaved by the British. Primarily, one has to tackle two fundamental questions. One, why could not India either at the central level or even at the level of regional powers – all of which were much bigger than England – successfully resist the British aggressive attempts? In other words, what was wrong with our polity or economy which prevented us from successfully thwarting all British attempts at the occupation of India? On the side of England we have also to confront a fundamental question: how could a company (the East India Company) of profit-seeking merchants equipped with a weighing scale in its hands, turn itself into a power-weighing and power-wielding sceptre? With a view to go into the nitty-gritty of these questions, we propose to delineate and analyse the actual conditions as well as the motive force of their history that led to the British occupation of India. To do that, we have to go back to the middle of the eighteenth century when the initial steps towards British occupation of India were being taken. We could begin our study with a peep into the decline of the Mughal Empire, resulting in the emergence of regional powers in India, which virtually took over the bulk of the Indian territory leaving the Mughals only with a symbolic presence.

There is virtually a near unanimity among the scholars of Indian history about the sharp decline in the glory, inner vitality and visible might of the Mughals after the death of Aurangzeb in 1707. A number of historical facts are cited in support of such a formulation. One, the Marathas who had earlier resisted and fought against Aurangzeb's aggressive moves, succeeded in plundering the area around Delhi in 1738. But what really exposed the soft underbelly of the Mughal Empire was Nadir Shah's sack of Delhi during 1738-39, which gave a mortal blow to the glory and prestige of the Mughal Empire. It soon emboldened and encouraged the Afghan ruler Ahmad Shah Abdali (also known as Durrani), who not only took over Punjab but also sacked Delhi during 1756-57. He even defeated the Marathas at the battlefield of Panipat in 1761, which gave a big blow to their ambition of inheriting and wearing the imperial mantle of the Mughals. In brief, it was clear by the middle of the eighteenth century that something had already eaten into the vitals of the Mughals and their empire. However, there is no unanimity among the historians about the nature of the debilitating disease afflicting the Mughal body politic. Three groups of scholars have differently accounted for the decline of the Mughal Empire. Historians like Jadunath Sarkar have underscored the faulty policies of Aurangzeb, including his prolonged fight for supremacy in the Deccan region. That war virtually drained the Mughal imperial army – the mainstay of the empire. This, coupled with his anti-Hindu policy and the personal failings of his successors and the nobles of the court, led to the decline and the final demise of the Mughal Empire. The second group, comprising Marxist scholars led by Satish Chandra and Irfan Habib, have laid their hands on the weaknesses and infirmities of the institutional and economic set up of the Mughal imperial system. In their view, the Mughal's system of jagirdari and iniquitous agrarian system were the chief villains of the piece. A third group of scholars underline the fact that it was not the economic crisis but the loosening of the Mughal central authority that encouraged overambitious zamindars, often backed by the peasants of their own caste, to assert their local authority, which finally resulted in the emergence of a number of regional powers. A detailed examination of all these formulations is beyond the scope of this book. Perhaps it was the cumulative impact of all these causes, which might account for the decline of the Mughal Empire. It is sufficient here to say that by the middle of the eighteenth century the central striking power of the Mughals had considerably weakened, leading to the emergence of a number of regional powers. An understanding of the dynamics of these regional powers is also needed, as it was from them that the British gradually took over the entire country. Besides, the British also faced, fought and eliminated three rival European powers, namely, Portugal, Holland and France from the field of Indian trade. It was by gradually subduing both regional Indian states as well as her European rivals that England took over the entire Indian territory and became its ruling power. We would now briefly describe the landmarks of the process through which the British occupied the Indian territory and became its ruling power. But let us first have a look at the major regional Indian states that the British had to face subsequently.

Major Regional States of the Eighteenth Century

In the wake of the decline of the Mughal central authority, a number of Indian regional states emerged. It is relevant to note here that states like Hyderabad, Bengal and Awadh were earlier an integral part of the Mughal Empire. But subsequently they emerged as autonomous states acting mostly on their own, though they also kept a semblance of allegiance with the Mughal central authority. Hyderabad was reorganised as a state by Nizam-ul-Mulk who had earlier been a wazir at the Mughal court at Delhi. He was made a subedar of the Deccan in 1724, and by the time he died, in 1748, he had succeeded in establishing Hyderabad as an independent state, though he never formally severed its umbilical ties with the Delhi throne.

Bengal was another regional power that emerged on the ruins of the Mughal Empire. Murshid Quli Khan was appointed as the Governor of Bengal by the Mughal emperor in 1717. Soon he, for all practical purposes, became his own master, though he continued to send a tribute to the Mughal court. He died in 1727 and was succeeded by Suja-ud-din who, in turn, was succeeded by Alivardi Khan, an army commander, in 1739. Alivardi Khan made Bengal virtually an independent power, as he stopped paying tribute to Delhi and made all official appointments on his own. After his death in 1756, he was succeeded by his grandson Siraj-ud-daula who fought and lost the Battle of Plassey with the British, which virtually laid the foundation of the British Empire in India.

Awadh also belongs to the same category of successor states of the Mughals, along with Hyderabad and Bengal. Saadat Khan became the Mughal Governor of Awadh in 1722. He successfully subdued the local zamindars who had earlier refused to pay land revenue. He made Safdar Jung as the deputy governor and even appointed him as diwan and made this office totally free from Delhi's control. Safdar Jung succeeded him during 1740 and took Awadh further on the road to autonomy. After his death in 1754, his son Shuja-ud-daula became the Governor of Awadh. Shuja aligned himself with Ahmad Shah Abdali at the Battle of Panipat, against the Marathas, and maintained his autonomous status. This was challenged only in 1764 when he, along with the Mughal Emperor and the Bengal Nawab, lost the Battle of Buxar.

The Marathas, Sikhs, Jats and Afghans primarily constituted the rebel groups who subsequently succeeded in emerging as powerful regional powers. The Maratha Kingdom was initially set up by Shivaji in 1674, who had started his political career as a rebel against the Mughals. But it was Balaji Vishwanath who, as the all-powerful Peshwa, built up the basic structure of the Maratha state power. On his death in 1720, he was succeeded by Baji Rao who further strengthened and expanded the Maratha territory by taking over Malwa and Gujarat. In 1737, the Maratha army invaded Delhi and even held the Emperor captive for some time. When

Baji Rao died in 1740, he had vastly expanded the Maratha Empire. In 1740, his son Balaji Baji Rao succeeded him, who is also known as Nana Saheb. When Shahuji, the Maratha king died in 1749, Nana Saheb consolidated his position further and virtually became the supreme authority in Maratha affairs. In fact, in the course of its historical development, the Maratha state-structure underwent a political and administrative metamorphosis which, though apparently leading to its physical – spatial expansion, came to contain within itself the seeds of its destruction. The centralised state-structure solely headed by Shivaji was gradually turned into a multi-polar military confederacy with its in-built system of mutual jealousies and rivalries. Besides, it ultimately turned into a system of nominal monarchy with the Maratha king at Satara, while real power came to be exercised by the Peshwas with their *gaddi* at Pune. This metamorphosis of the Maratha state contributed a great deal to its decline and ultimate demise.

Maratha glory reached its peak when they even forced Alivardi Khan of Bengal to cede Orissa to them. The Marathas also remained in constant struggle with the Nizam of Hyderabad. In the Mughal durbar also, the Marathas started playing a big role and during 1752-53 the Mughal Emperor came under their protection. One fundamental weakness of Maratha rule, however, was that they were more interested in exacting *chaudh* and *sardeshmukhi* from the area they overran rather than in establishing a permanent administrative set up. But it was the Maratha defeat at the Third Battle of Panipat in January 1761 at the hands of the Afghan ruler, Ahmad Shah Abdali, which gave a big blow to the Maratha ambition of wearing the imperial mantle of the Mughal Empire. Nana Saheb died soon. Subsequently, a succession war broke out, which provided an opportunity to the British in 1772 to intervene, and then onwards Maratha power declined leading finally to its eclipse.

The Sikhs were another group of people who built up a powerful state in Punjab in the eighteenth century. Earlier, Guru Nanak Dev had founded the Sikh Panth as a part of the Bhakti Movement. But soon the Sikhs acquired the reputation of a fighting servant of God rather than a suffering servant. Guru Arjun Dev was executed by the Mughal Emperor, Jahangir. The situation became worse when the ninth guru of the Sikhs, Guru Teg Bahadur, was executed by Aurangzeb in 1675 in Delhi. As a sequel, his son, Guru Govind Singh, who established the Khalsa Panth in 1699, turned the Sikhs into a warlike militant group. He soon tried to build up an autonomous state located at Anandpur, but was ousted from there by the combined forces of the Mughals and chieftains of Himachal. The death of Aurangzeb (in 1707) changed the situation, but the Guru was murdered in October 1708. However, his chief follower, Banda Bahadur, continued the rebellion till his execution in March 1716. The Sikh rebellion did not wane and by 1761 they came to control a vast territory in Punjab. But there was no well-organised central Sikh authority till the gap was filled by Ranjit Singh who built up a powerful state by the first decade of the nineteenth century. He died in 1839. Soon Punjab was caught in royal family feuds, as well as the power struggle among Sikh chiefs, which helped the British to takeover the Sikh state by 1849 after the second Anglo-Sikh War.

In the east of Punjab, a small kingdom of Rohilkhand was founded by Ali Muhammad Khan, an Afghan chief. And yet another kingdom, established by another Afghan chief, Ahmad Khan Bangash, emerged around Farukhabad. These kingdoms were small in size and the only thing notable about them was that at the time of the Third Battle of Panipat they aligned themselves with Ahmad Shah Abdali. In the south-west of Delhi a number of Rajput principalities had also come up. Generally, they did not face much of a problem with the Mughals except in the case of the Mewar Kingdom. But when the Mughal Empire weakened, the Rajput chiefs gradually asserted their independence.

The Jats, who were primarily located in and around the Delhi-Mathura region, also succeeded in establishing a Jat kingdom at Bharatpur in Rajasthan. The Jats had a long history of rebellion against the Mughals since the days of Jahangir, but it was the Jat chieftain Suraj Mal, who consolidated the Jat kingdom at Bharatpur during the middle of the eighteenth century. At one stage, his kingdom spread from Ganga in the east to Agra in the west and from Delhi in the north to the Chambal in the south. However, after the death of Suraj Mal in 1763, the Jat kingdom lost much of its sheen.

That leaves us with south India wherein Mysore emerged as a powerful state during the eighteenth century, under the Wodeyar dynasty. But a radical change took place in 1761 when Haider Ali, an officer of the Mysore army, took over the political power. He soon launched a programme of modernisation of his army with French assistance. Haider Ali expanded his kingdom by taking over Malabar and Calicut in 1766. Soon Mysore emerged as a powerful regional power in south India under the dynamic leadership of Haider Ali and his son Tipu Sultan. Travancore was also another state which had an independent status even during the heyday of the Mughal Empire. It reached its full glory in 1729 under the headship of King Martanda Varma. He modernised his army and introduced a state monopoly in trade that led to a considerable increase in state resources. Travancore survived the Mysorean invasion of 1766 and was known for its progress, displayed in the field of irrigation, transport and communication. It had an equally good reputation in the field of art and culture. However, in 1800, Travancore, ultimately, succumbed to the British pressure as it agreed to the presence of the British Resident.

We have briefly delineated the state of affairs in India during the eighteenth century, along with the condition of major Indian regional political players. For a better understanding of the process of the British occupation of India, we have to go through a brief history of the East India Company's encounter both with European rival powers as well as with the Indian regional powers. The whole process is so chronologically intertwined that it becomes a difficult task to untangle them and make a neat presentation. To unravel this, a brief history of the Company's encounter and its ultimate victory over both its European rival powers and with the regional Indian states would be presented here separately. This would provide a clear picture of the entire process of the British occupation of India. But let us first look at its encounter with the European powers.

The East India Company and its European Rivals

As we know, the East India Company was set up by a Charter with a privilege to carry on trade in the area east of the Cape of Good

Hope. It was a shareholders company to be governed by 20 elected members who constituted its Court. In the initial years, it concentrated on its trade with the Spice Islands. But very soon it came to discover that some of the Indian products, primarily textiles, could be used as barter for the South-East Asian spices – making its entire business exceptionally profitable. But it also realised that in this venture it faced a major challenge from three European powers, namely, Portugal, Holland and France, as they were also competing with the British for the control of the Indian trade.

It is also relevant to note that the Portuguese were the first European power to enter into the arena of Indian trade after the opening of the Atlantic route. Vasco da Gama of Portugal had reached Calicut, on the Malabar Coast, in 1498, after discovering a new sea route through the Atlantic to India. Prior to that, Indian trade in the west was dominated by the Arabs on account of their control over the land route as well as the Mediterranean sea route. The Portuguese were the first to open their factories in India and dominated the Indian trade throughout the sixteenth century.

But the Portuguese suffered their first defeat at the hands of the British in 1611 near Surat. The British inflicted another defeat on the Portuguese in 1620 and they were finally expelled by the Mughals from Hugli in Bengal in 1633. The Portuguese hold on India further declined when, in 1634, they entered into an agreement with the British for a good commercial relationship. This was followed by two other treaties between these two powers in 1654 and 1661 respectively, which not only guaranteed the British right to the eastern trade but also bound both powers to act jointly against the Dutch in India. Consequently, except Goa and Diu, the Portuguese virtually lost their interest in the Indian trade. The Dutch were another power who had opened a number of factories in India in the middle of the seventeenth century. The Dutch East India Company was set up in 1602. What was more, a warlike situation developed when a large fleet of Dutch ships reached Swally, near Surat, forcing the British to suspend their trade at Surat. However, by 1667 they reached an agreement by which the Dutch agreed not to interfere with the English settlement in India as a *quid pro quo* of the British surrender of all claims of trade in Indonesia. Gradually, the Dutch lost more ground when their naval expedition to Hugli failed in 1675. Their position further weakened, and by 1695 the Dutch were finally expelled from India by the British.

The third power that competed with the British was France. Though it was a latecomer to India, it did put up a stiff competition and even fought with the British for the control of the Indian trade. In 1668, the first French factory was opened at Surat. Subsequently, Chandernagore near Calcutta was built up by them during 1690–92. The French position in this part of the world was further strengthened when they occupied Mauritius in 1721, and soon they also acquired some foothold on the Malabar coast. By the 1740s the British and the French emerged as the main rival powers in India. The British conflict with the French is known as the Carnatic Wars which covered a period of twenty years from 1744 to 1764. The First Carnatic War had its genesis in the Austrian succession-war in Europe, with its overspill in India as the British and French were on opposite sides in that war. The British took the initiative and seized some French ships on the east coast of India, which prompted the French to attack and capture Madras with support from their naval force located in Mauritius. In a clever move, the British sought the help of the Nawab of Arcot who sent troops to Madras but his forces were badly defeated by the French forces. This provided a new sense of confidence to the French officials led by Dupleix. When the hostilities ceased in Europe by 1748, there was an agreement between the two powers by which the French got back all their possessions in North America and they, in turn, returned all British possessions in India. The Second Carnatic War started on the issues of succession both at Hyderabad and Arcot in which the French and the British were supporting the opposite groups. In 1750, the French obtained several concessions from the new subedar of the Deccan at Hyderabad, including Dupleix being appointed Governor of all Deccan dominions to the south of the Krishna river. In return, he stationed a strong French military contingent at the Deccan court under the French General Bussy. But Robert Clive sent a strong contingent to Arcot and in the process the French General got captured and was beheaded. Subsequently, Chanda Sahib, the Nawab of Arcot, was also murdered. Thus, the

Second Carnatic War was ultimately lost by the French and the prestige of the British soon skyrocketed. This led to the recall of Dupleix – the main architect of French policy in India. He was replaced by a pliant French Governor, Godeheu, who suspended the French action and chose to negotiate with the British.

The French and the British forces had their final round of armed engagement, which came to be known as the Third Carnatic War. In the backdrop of the war was the outbreak of the Seven-Year War (1756–63) among European powers and their colonies in Europe. In 1756, the British captured Chandernagore, a French town near Calcutta and Siraj-ud-daula had a tiff with the British as he gave shelter to the French. That led to a Nawab–British confrontation during 1756-57. In south India, a confrontation between these two powers could not take place as the British forces had been committed to Bengal and the French reinforcement could not arrive there before 1758. On their arrival, French forces launched an offensive which resulted in the capture of a large chunk of territory under the British, including the port at Vishakhapatnam. Meanwhile, the British reinforcement from Bengal also reached Madras. But due to internal problems of the French Army, including lack of coordination between the land and naval forces, the French could not take full advantage of their initial gains. And finally on 16 January 1761, the French surrendered Pondicherry, followed by the surrender of their possessions on the Malabar Coast. Earlier, French forces had been defeated at Wandiwash on 22 January 1760. At the end of the Seven-year's war in Europe the treaty of the Peace of Paris restored the French possessions in India to them. However, the French East India Company was formally wound up in 1769. In a way that marked the end of the French attempt to take over the Indian trade from the British hand. Thus the British succeeded in eliminating all three major European rivals from India which left a free field for them alone.

The British Occupation of India: Its Encounter and Victory Over the Regional States

We have already delineated the state of Indian affairs, including the decline of the Mughal Empire and the emergence of a number of regional states. Now, let us turn to the British face-off with the Indian states. Our story covers a period of one hundred years starting with the British victory at the Battle of Plassey (1757) and ends with the final annexation of Awadh by the British Empire in 1856, followed by the 1857 rebellion and the Crown's takeover (1858) of the Indian Empire. In the process, the British encountered and subdued the Marathas, Tipu Sultan of Mysore and the Sikhs – all major political players of the period.

The British Occupation of Bengal and Awadh

It would be relevant here to highlight how the British acquired a foothold in India which ultimately enabled them to enter and subdue all its rivals, both Europeans and Indians in due course. After coming to India, towards the beginning of the seventeenth century, the East India Company concentrated on business for many years by continuously trying to be on the right side of the Mughal authorities. Sir Thomas Roe was the first resident English envoy to be received at Jahangir's Court in 1617. However, after opening a factory at Surat in 1613 they sought its fortification in 1625, but the Mughal authorities refused to give permission. A golden opportunity came to the Company in 1639 when it succeeded in obtaining Madras on lease from a local king who was promised 50 per cent of the customs revenue. It was a very good bargain for the Company as they got an opportunity to fortify the area as well as a right to mint their own coins. Soon they built up the Fort St. George at Madras. This was followed by the fortification of Bombay Port which was transferred to the Company by the British king in 1661. The British king had received it as a dowry from the Portuguese king. British factories had also been opened in eastern India, including Hugli in Bengal. In a clever move to build up a centralised authority, the Company officials put all its other establishments under the control of Fort St. George at Madras. Another milestone was reached by the Company when it got permission from the Mughals to do customs-free business. However, during the 1680s Aurangzeb seized British factories at a number of places but soon the Company got them back after making a lump sum payment. Thereafter, there was no looking back for the Company.

In 1698, it obtained the zamindari right to collect revenue from three villages of Sutanuti, Govindapur and Kolikata in Bengal. In 1700, all Bengal factories were put under the control of Fort William at Calcutta. Another major development occurred in 1717 when the new Mughal Emperor Farrukhsiyar gave the company permission to use its coins throughout the Mughal territory along with the freedom to do customs-free business. Thus by the middle of the eighteenth century, the East India Company was more than a mere trading company. With factories at the important corners of the country and control over the ports of Bombay, Madras and Calcutta, and with an army at its disposal, it had become a dominant power. With the introduction of a large number of army personnel during the Anglo–French conflict in India, the Company was confident regarding its own strength.

Bengal was the first state where the Company's newly acquired strength was tested vis-à-vis the Indian states. The period from 1757 to 1764 virtually brought about a radical change in the fate of Bengal as well as that of the Company. Here the Company enjoyed customs-free business which became the real bone of contention between the Company and the local Nawab. In 1756, Siraj-ud-daula succeeded Alivardi Khan who had virtually made Bengal independent. Siraj had developed serious grievances against the Company which was acting a little too independently. The Company's officials were not only misusing their right to customs-free business but they were also indulging in the fortification of its factories without the Nawab's permission. Siraj attacked Fort William, which precipitated the crisis as it brought into the open the conflict between the Company and the Nawab. This led to the Battle of Plassey where the Company's forces defeated the Nawab's army.

The Battle of Plassey marked a turning point in the fate of India as well as that of the Company: the British occupation of India had started with a big bang. What actually led to the defeat of the Nawab's forces had been debated since the day it occurred. Perhaps two things proved decisive. Robert Clive's strong contingent from Madras and the betrayal of the Nawab's officials including Mir Jafar. Siraj was killed and Mir Jafar succeeded him on Bengal's throne. The Company wanted its pound of flesh and made undue financial demands on him which he was unable to meet. Ultimately, he succumbed to the pressure and was forced to step down. Mir Kasim, his own son-in-law, succeeded him in September 1760. He began to act in an independent manner and shifted his capital from Murshidabad to Monghyr and also reorganised his army and the bureaucracy. Soon he fell from the grace of the Company as he protested against the misuse of the Dastak (customs-free business) by the Company's officials, which was resulting in a huge revenue loss for the Nawab. When the Company tried to pressurise him, he refused. In the process he was replaced by Mir Jafar with the open support of the Company and some courtiers and financial magnates of Bengal. He sought the support of the Mughal Emperor, Shah Alam, as well as the Nawab Shuja-ud-daula of Awadh. This led to the battle royal at Buxar where the Company's forces again became victorious. This virtually sealed the fate of India and was a real turning point on the road to the British occupation of India. Mir Jafar was made the Nawab with the open support of the Company. But the real power remained vested in the hands of Robert Clive, the Governor of Bengal. And the Nawab for all practical purposes became the titular head. In 1765, Robert Clive entered into an agreement with the Mughal emperor and got the *diwani* right of Bengal, Bihar and Orissa for the Company in lieu of a lump sum payment to the Mughal Emperor. Thus the Company came to have the real control of the financial administration of Sube-Bengal. The real significance of the Company's victory at Plassey and Buxar followed by its *diwani* right was that it became the real ruler of the Sube-Bengal reducing the status of the Nawab to a mere puppet in its hand.

With Bengal under its thumb, the Company set its eyes on the Sube-Awadh. By the treaty of August 1765, a war indemnity of Rs 50,00,000 was imposed on Awadh and the Mughal Emperor Shah Alam got some area around Allahabad as a part of the bargain. Shuja-ud-daula, the Nawab of Awadh, tried to regain his position by reorganising his army, but the Company tightened its noose around his neck by forcing him, in 1773, to make a monthly payment of Rs 2,10,000 to each brigade of the Company stationed in Awadh or Allahabad areas. The Awadh Nawab fell in the debt-trap of the

Company. That enabled the Company to directly interfere in the affairs of Awadh. Soon the Company got hold of a sizeable part of Awadh's territory around Banaras, earlier held by Chait Singh. Subsequently, the Company forced the Awadh Nawab into an agreement excluding the Mughal Emperor from all future Anglo–Awadh transactions and posting a British Resident at the Nawab's court. The Awadh Nawab did get some respite when his debt to the Company was reduced by Rs 50 lakh in view of his strong protest. But with the death of Asaf-ud-daula in 1797, the new Nawab, Saadat Ali agreed to pay an enhanced sum of Rs 76 lakh. But when, in subsequent years he expressed his inability to pay such huge sum, he was forced in 1801 to cede a large chunk of his territory, comprising Rohilkhand, Gorakhpur and Doab to the Company. This gave a mortal blow to Awadh's glory and might. This state of affairs continued till Awadh was finally annexed by the East India Company in 1856.

Annexation of Punjab

After the defeat of the Marathas at the hand of Ahmad Shah Abdali the Sikhs took advantage and established their own states, known as 12 misls. Subsequently, Ranjit Singh subdued them and built-up a big and powerful empire which extended not only from the Sutlej to the Indus but also to trans-Indus regions like Dera Ismail Khan and Dera Ghazi Khan. However, the British were keeping a watch over Punjab's affairs and in 1809 they entered into a treaty with Ranjit Singh – known as the Amritsar Treaty. Accordingly, Ranjit Singh had to forgo his claim over the trans-Sutlej areas. However, not much of the problem existed between the Sikhs and the British till 1839. But after the death of Ranjit Singh in 1839, there was a succession feud which provided an opportunity for the British to interfere in Sikh affairs. This resulted in the first Anglo–Sikh War in 1845 which resulted in the Lahore Treaty, which reduced the status of Punjab to a British dependency. This was followed by the Second Anglo–Sikh War in 1849 which finally ended in the annexation of Punjab to the British colonial empire. Thus from 1757 (Battle of Plassey) to 1856 (final annexation of Awadh) the entire eastern and northern India came to be occupied by the British.

The British Occupation of the South and Western India

In southern and western India, the main challenge to the British trade and territorial ambition came from two major state systems – Mysore, and the Marathas. In subsequent sections, we would have a bird's eye view of the processes through which the British subdued these regions and finally occupied them.

After the disintegration of the Vijayanagar Empire the state of Mysore was built up as an autonomous state by the Wodeyar dynasty. Soon, Haider Ali, one of the military officers of the Mysore army, captured power after overthrowing the Wodeyar dynasty of Mysore and the boundary of Mysore state extended from the Krishna River in the north to the Malabar Coast in the west. As we have seen earlier, Haider Ali and his son Tipu Sultan tried to build up a very powerful, militarised and centralised state with an ambition to control entire south India. Thus the East India Company perceived a threat from Mysore State and decided to tackle and subdue it.

There were four wars that took place between the British and Mysore State between 1767 and 1799, when Mysore was finally taken over by the British. It has to be remembered that three major powers existed in the region, viz., Hyderabad, Mysore and the Marathas; all of which were struggling to establish their political and territorial supremacy. The British had their own political game and, more often than not, they took advantage of the rivalries of the regional states among themselves. The First Anglo-Mysore War took place during 1767–69, when Haider Ali, with the support of the Marathas and the Nizam of Hyderabad attacked the British near Madras and forced them to sign an alliance treaty with Mysore. The treaty provided that they would support each other in case of a third party attack. The Second Anglo–Mysore War broke out in 1781 when the British succeeded in subduing Haider Ali by neutralising the Marathas and the Nizam. Haider Ali died in 1782 and was succeeded by his son Tipu Sultan. Tipu Sultan continued the war and forced the British to sign the Treaty of Mangalore which gave him a temporary respite. When Lord Cornwallis became the Governor-General he managed to bring the Marathas and the Nizam on his side. Meanwhile the Third Anglo–Mysore War started when Tipu Sultan attacked Travancore State which was allied to the British. The war continued from 1790 to 1792 in which Tipu ultimately surrendered half of his territory to the British. But he remained defiant and the British forces had a final showdown with him in 1799, which resulted in his defeat and his death. Tipu's dominions were divided between the Nizam and the British. The British restored the Wodeyar dynasty, but Mysore lost its independence and became a British dependency.

Anglo–Maratha War

The Marathas had suffered a great setback when they were decisively beaten by Ahmad Shah Abdali at the Battle of Panipat in 1761. But the British, after consolidating their position in Bengal and Awadh, were looking for an opportunity to settle a score with them. The opportunity came when Raghunath Rao sought British help for becoming the Peshwa, as he was facing opposition from the Council of Regency headed by Nana Phadnavis. That led to the First Anglo–Maratha War (1775–82), which resulted in the Treaty of Salbai in 1782, by which Madhav Rao Narayan was recognised as the real Peshwa. The other consequences of the Treaty of Salbai were that the British acquired control of Salsette and Bassein and also established a foothold in the internal conflicts of Indian states. This peace treaty with the Marathas helped the British to concentrate on Mysore and other states, as the lull continued for 20 years on the Marathas' front. Meanwhile the Marathas were gripped by internal dissension and local Maratha chiefs tried to expand their areas as much as possible, which obviously weakened the central Maratha authority. However, they refused the British offer of subsidiary alliance with them. This was followed by Holkar's victory over the Peshwa's forces in the year 1800 which prompted the Peshwa Baji Rao II to accept the British offer of subsidiary alliance in 1802 by signing the Treaty of Bassein. According to this treaty, the Peshwa had to pay a huge sum as subsidy. Besides, he agreed not to enter into any alliance with any other power without

British consent. However, the Treaty of Bassein was rejected by the Maratha chiefs which led to the second Anglo-Maratha War (1803-05). Consequently, the treaties of subordination were imposed on a number of tributaries of the Marathas. Besides, most of the territories controlled by Sindhia, including Delhi and Agra, were taken over by the British. Moreover, the British acquired the right to be the final arbiter in any disputes among the Maratha houses. The third Anglo–Maratha War erupted when Peshwa Baji Rao tried to unite all Maratha chiefs against the British during 1718-19. The Marathas were badly beaten, which resulted in abolition of the office of the Peshwa and his dominions were taken over by the British. Thus, the Maratha dream of inheriting the Mughal imperial mantle was finally dashed to the ground.

The defeat of the Marathas opened the road for establishing the Company's paramountcy over the Rajputana region. Some of these Rajput states like Ajmer, Udaipur and Jodhpur, were under the Maratha's sway earlier. In the wake of the Maratha's defeat, bigger states like Udaipur, Jodhpur, Ajmer and Jaipur, were forced to accept British paramountcy through individual treaties with them in 1918. Subsequently, similar treaties were imposed on smaller Rajputana states like Kota, Bundi, Bikaner, Jaisalmer, Banswara, Dungarpur Pratapgarh, Karauli and others.

Soon, the British turned their attention to the Himalayan region. They were engaged in several battles with Nepal, which had emerged as a powerful state. That ultimately led to the Treaty of Sugauli by which the British got control of the Terai region as well as areas of Kumaon and Garhwal. Besides, the Gorkhas had to withdraw from Sikkim. And they also agreed to keep a British resident at Kathmandu. All this led to further consolidation of the British power in India.

British Policy towards Frontier Regions

No study of the British occupation of India would be complete without referring to the frontier policy of the British. Basically, there were two major frontier regions – the north-west and the north-east. In the north-west, Sikhs were the major power and the annexation of Punjab in 1849 had cleared the road for pursuing a forward frontier policy in the region. In fact, the British had always been concerned over the developments in the north-western region as they were apprehensive about the Russian desire to advance in Central Asia. When Russia and France signed a treaty in 1819, the British concern reached an alarming stage. They responded by occupying Kutch in 1819 and subsequently forced a number of unequal treaties on the Amirs of Sindh. They, also played their clever policy of 'divide and rule' between the Sikh rulers and the Amirs of Sindh and Afganistan. All this led to the First Anglo–Afghan War (1839–41), which went against the British. Partly to compensate for their loss of face and partly to build up an inner rampart against Russia, the English were prompted to make unabashed use of fraud and force and succeeded in occupying Sindh in 1843. The annexation of Sindh brought universal condemnation for the British but it hardly deterred them: they continued to take an acute interest in the region. Their Russo-phobia reached a feverish pitch after the Crimean War (1854–56). Consequently, in 1876, the British occupied Quetta and Baluchistan. Soon they went in for the Second Anglo–Afghan War and got Abdur Rahman installed on the Afghan throne. However, the region continued to remain turbulent in view of the tribal raids and uprisings and the British continued to pursue a forward policy. Ultimately it was in 1893 that an agreement was signed resulting in the demarcation of the northern-western frontier of India, which came to be known as the Durand Line, named after the chief negotiator, Sir Henry Durand. However, the region continued to be volatile and subsequently Chitral (1895) and Tirah (1897) were taken over after military expeditions. Subsequently Lord Curzon constituted the entire region as a new province called North-Western Frontier Province (NWFP) in 1901.

The situation in the northern-eastern region was equally turbulent. Burma had emerged there as a powerful state during the eighteenth century. The British fought three wars with Burma: the first one during 1824–26, the second in 1852 and the third one in 1885. As a result of the first Burmese–British War, the King of Burma was forced to cede Assam and Nagaland as well as Arakan and Tenasserim, followed by annexation of Cachar in 1830. In the second Indo–Burmese War, Rangoon was captured and Pegu was annexed. In the third war, upper Burma was added to the British Empire. It was only after the Act of 1935 that Burma was separated from the British Indian Empire.

All these successes emboldened the British officials to seek further expansion and annexations. Subsequently, using the 'Doctrine of Lapse' a number of Indian states like Satara (1848), Sambalpur and Baghat (1850), Udaipur (1852), Nagpur (1853), Jhansi (1854) and Berar (1853) were annexed. Thus by 1857, a large part of India, both in terms of population and territory had come under the direct control of the British. The rest of Indian territory and population were left under the control of the Indian princes who themselves were under the indirect control of the British under the policy of Paramountcy.

This is the brief history of the British occupation of India. We have seen that the eighteenth century in India was marked by the decline of the central authority of the Mughals. But fortunately it did not lead to a total power vacuum in the country as the political space vacated by the Mughals was gradually occupied by a number of regional powers. One of these regional powers, the Marathas, even made a serious bid to inherit and wear the imperial mantle of the Mughals. The Sikhs in the north and Tipu Sultan in the south at some stage became equally powerful. Besides, historians have also dug up enough data to support the thesis that the regionalisation of Indian political power did not destroy the economic and social fabric of the country. In fact, before the British occupation, India was doing pretty well on the economic front. Why all this could not help our people to successfully resist the British takeover is an issue, which has been a subject of debate among our historians for a long time.

A number of practical explanations have also been advanced by our scholars for the inability of our people to face up to the British challenge. One, the regional powers in India were constantly at loggerheads with each other, always trying to occupy as much territory as possible by overstepping on each-other's toes. It resulted in frittering away of their energy and resources. More than that, such a cut-throat competition among the regional powers provided the British with an opportunity to play one region against the other, and subdue them one by one, instead of facing the collective might of all Indian states. Mysore–Maratha rivalry is an illustrative case. Besides, these regional powers were also weakened by court rivalries and intrigues. Mir Jafar's treacherous role in the Battle of Plassey is a case in point. The second reason for the failure of the Indian states was their incapacity to mobilise enough resources to match and surpass the Company. The financial magnates of India found the British Company more creditworthy and trustworthy than the Indian princes. Besides, the Company used ruthless methods to force the local states and nawabs to extend larger and larger amount of subsidies, which greatly facilitated British operations in India. The resource crunch on the part of the Indian princes resulted in irregular payments to their army which often created demoralisation and dissensions among them. Perhaps, the technological superiority of the British also played a role, as it succeeded in neutralising the numerical superiority of the Indian army. A large number of British troops in India were inducted during the Anglo–French War, which also helped the British in consolidating their position in India.

However, in respect of the British occupation of India, one of the central theoretical questions is: what was the primary strength, which enabled the British to occupy India so easily? Scholars have tried to find its direct correlation with the unprecedented ascendance of the Western World in the course of the last few centuries, prior to the British occupation of India. One theoretical explanation is that in the wake of the Renaissance followed by the Reformation and the Enlightenment, the European mind was freed from the shackles of superstitious belief. That made human 'reason' as the powerful and final arbiter in all human affairs, pushing claims of 'revelation' in the background. That led to the secularisation of society which, in turn, promoted a deep spirit of enquiry, innovation and inquisitiveness. As a result, the old ideas and instrumentalities, viz., compass, gunpowder, printing press, charcoal, saltpetre, navigational aids, borrowed from the older civilisations, were put to better and more effective use for long sea voyages as well as in forging new weapons. Their innovative use helped their mariners to reach places as distant as South and North America in the West, and China and India in the East. In sharp contrast to that, the East, for various reasons, including those being old civilisations, lacked such an adventurous, innovative and outgoing spirit. Perhaps that settled the scale in the favour of the British.

A related question is, why of all the rival powers who were struggling for colonial possessions, England alone could forge ahead. The explanation is not far to seek. In the European subcontinent, Germany and the Italian States were still divided, and France suffered from the excesses of revolutionary ferment. Holland did not possess much natural resources and Spain and Portugal were still being dominated by priests and soldiers. And they also lacked a sufficient number of innovative middle classes. England had a sufficient store of coal and iron ore and a surging, innovative middle class and also superior naval force. All that was lacking was an adequate supply of capital which came from the plunder of India. That worked as a launching pad both for the initiation of the industrial revolution as well as for colonial possessions. Thus it is not all surprising that England surged ahead of all its European rivals and occupied India in a period of less than a hundred years.

To sum up, the seed of decline of the Mughal Empire could be traced to Aurangzeb's religious bigotry and his overambitious expansionist venture into the Deccan – a policy which not only alienated a large chunk of the Indian populace but also led to the overstretching of the imperial resources. However, what hastened the process of its decline and ultimate demise, was the fact that his successors, one after another, turned out to be political weaklings. It is true that in the wake of the decline of the Mughal Empire, a number of regional powers did emerge with a fair chance to occupy the political space vacated by the Mughals. Unfortunately that hope was soon belied as they crumbled under the weight of British political machination as well as their superior military might. What added to their failure were their mutual recriminations and rivalries. The elimination of the rival European powers had been made possible partly due to the British superiority in naval power and partly due to its capacity to influence and manipulate the contours of the European power politics. Admittedly, the new intellectual revolution which had galvanised Western Europe during those days also facilitated the British game in the foreign land. It had unshackled the human mind and helped to build up a string of new secular institutions. Besides, it had widened the arena of individual's freedom and even initiated a new discourse on religious affairs. All this created a new mindset which prompted the British to set out for a foreign 'kill'. All this helped the British in occupying the bulk of the Indian territory in a remarkably short span of time and at the minimum cost in terms of men and materials.

With this brief story of the British occupation of India, we would take up a study of its impact on Indian society in the subsequent chapters.

INDIA
in 1561
English Miles
0 300 600
Akbar's Dominions
K. = Kingdom
PERSIA
KABUL
Kabul
Peshawar
KASHMIR
Srinagar
Ghazni
PROV.
Kandahar
PANJAB
Sialkot
Lahore
HIMALAYAN STATES
Multan
TRIBES
Panipat
Delhi
RAJASTHAN
Sihwan
SIND
Agra
Ajmer
Gwalior
Benares
RAJAS
HIMALAYAN STATES
AFGHAN
BENGAL
Patna
BIH
Chitor
Patan
MALWA
Prayag
Dacca
KACHH
GUJARAT
Ahmadabad
Ujjain
Cambay
GONDWANA
Chittagong
Diu
ORISSA
Surat
KHANDESH
BERAR
Daman
AHMAD-
NAGAR
Bassein
Bombay
Chaul
Puri
VARIOUS RAJAS
GOLKONDA K.
Bidar
BIDAR
ARABIAN
SEA
Bijapur
BIJAPUR K.
BAY OF
BENGAL
Goa
Masulipatam
Honawar
Nellore
VIJAYANAGAR EMPIRE
Mangalore
Pulicat
Andaman Is
Lacadive Is.
Calicut
Tanjore
Negapatam
Cochin
Quilon
CEYLON
Maldive Is.

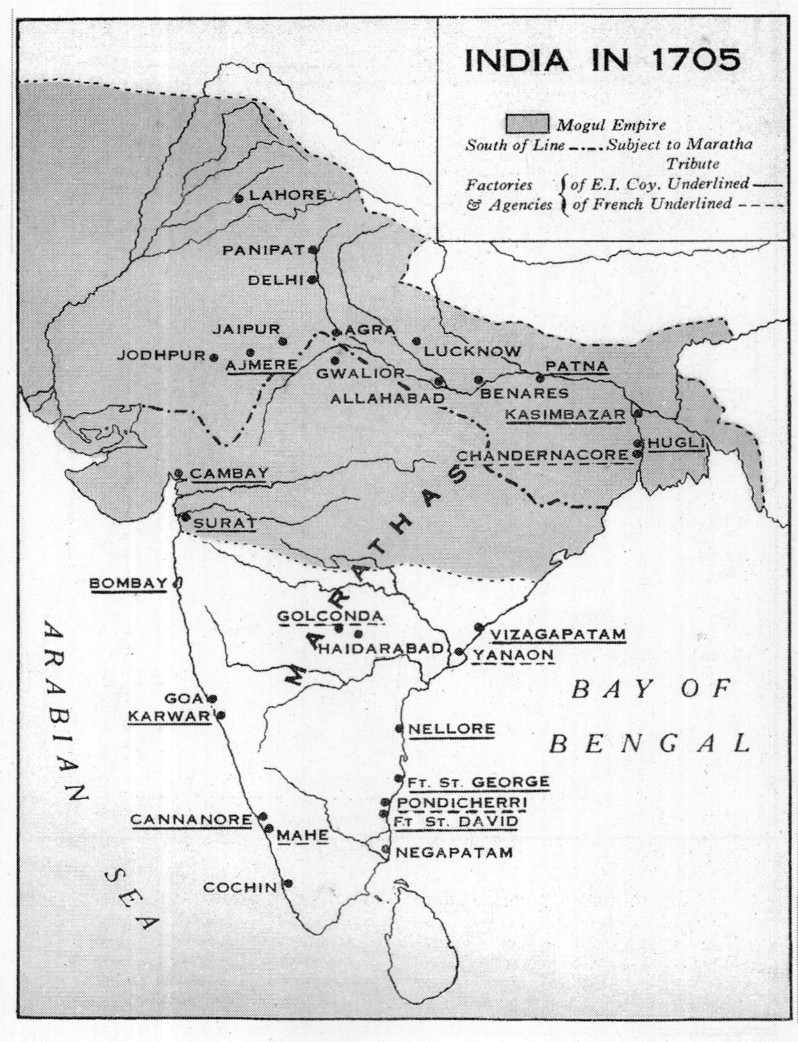
INDIA IN 1705
Mogul Empire
South of Line Subject to Maratha Tribute
Factories & Agencies of E.I. Coy. Underlined
of French Underlined
LAHORE
PANIPAT
DELHI
JAIPUR
AGRA
JODHPUR
AJMERE
GWALIOR
LUCKNOW
PATNA
ALLAHABAD
BENARES
KASIMBAZAR
HUGLI
CHANDERNACORE
CAMBAY
SURAT
MARATHAS
BOMBAY
GOLCONDA
HAIDARABAD
VIZAGAPATAM
YANAON
GOA
KARWAR
NELLORE
BAY OF BENGAL
ARABIAN SEA
FT. ST. GEORGE
PONDICHERRI
FT ST. DAVID
CANNANORE
MAHE
NEGAPATAM
COCHIN

Kabul
Peshawar
Kandahar
AFGHANS
Jihlam R.
Chenab R.
Ravi R.
Lahore
Multan
Sutlaj R.
Indus R.
Panipat
Ramnagar
ROHILKAND
NEPAL
Delhi
Bareilly
Ganges R.
RAJPUTS
Agra
Jumna R.
OUDH
Lucknow
Cawnpore
Jodhpur
Gwalior
Salbai
Kara
Hyderabad
Chambal R.
Allahabad
Luni R.
Benares
Baxar
Patna
Monghyr
Murshidabad
Cooch Behar
MAHRATTA
BEHAR
Plassy
Chinsura
Chandarnagar
Ahmadabad
Indore
Bhopal
Calcutta
BENGAL
Baroda
Narbada R.
Junagarh
Balasore
Mahanadi R.
Broach
Asirgarh
Nagpur
Somnath
Diu
Surat
Tapti R.
CONFEDERACY
Cuttack
Bassein
Salsette I.
Bombay
Aurangabad
Godavari R.
Wargaon
Poona
Kardla
Bankot
Purandhar
NIZAM'S
Hyderabad
Ellore
Bijapur
DOMINIONS
CIRCARS
Masulipatam
BAY OF BENGAL
Karnul
Goa
Cuddapah
ARABIAN SEA
MYSORE
Mangalore
Bangalore
Madras
Seringapatam
Cannanore
Mysore
Mahe
Pondicherry
CARNATIC
Calicut
Tanjore
INDIA in 1795
Cochin
Madura
British Territory
British Protected States
Mahrattas
Scale of Miles
0 50 100 200 300 400
WAXTYPE
GEORGE PHILIP & SON, LTD.

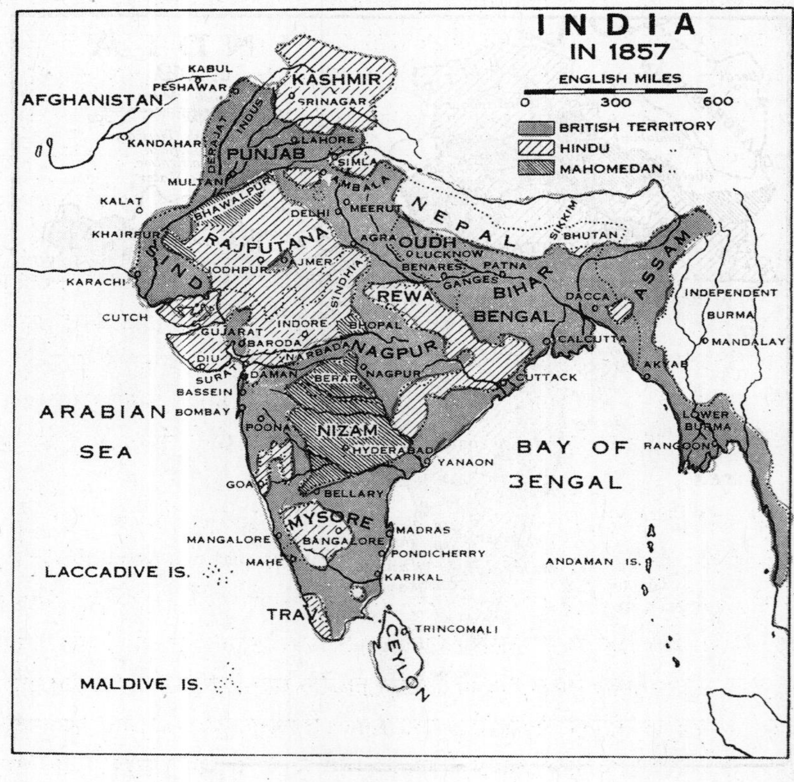
INDIA
IN 1857
ENGLISH MILES
0 300 600
BRITISH TERRITORY
HINDU ..
MAHOMEDAN ..
AFGHANISTAN
KABUL
PESHAWAR
KANDAHAR
KASHMIR
SRINAGAR
LAHORE
PUNJAB
INDUS
DERAJAT
SIMLA
MULTAN
AMBALA
KALAT
BHAWALPUR
DELHI
MEERUT
NEPAL
SIKKIM
BHUTAN
KHAIRPUR
RAJPUTANA
AGRA
OUDH
LUCKNOW
SIND
JODHPUR
AJMER
BENARES
PATNA
GANGES
BIHAR
ASSAM
KARACHI
SINDHIA
REWA
DACCA
INDEPENDENT
BURMA
CUTCH
INDORE
BHOPAL
BENGAL
MANDALAY
GUJARAT
BARODA
CALCUTTA
DIU
NARBADA
NAGPUR
AKYAB
SURAT
DAMAN
BERAR
CUTTACK
BASSEIN
ARABIAN
SEA
BOMBAY
POONA
NIZAM
LOWER
BURMA
HYDERABAD
BAY OF
BENGAL
RANGOON
YANAON
GOA
BELLARY
MYSORE
MADRAS
MANGALORE
BANGALORE
PONDICHERRY
MAHE
ANDAMAN IS.
LACCADIVE IS.
KARIKAL
TRA
TRINCOMALI
CEYLON
MALDIVE IS.

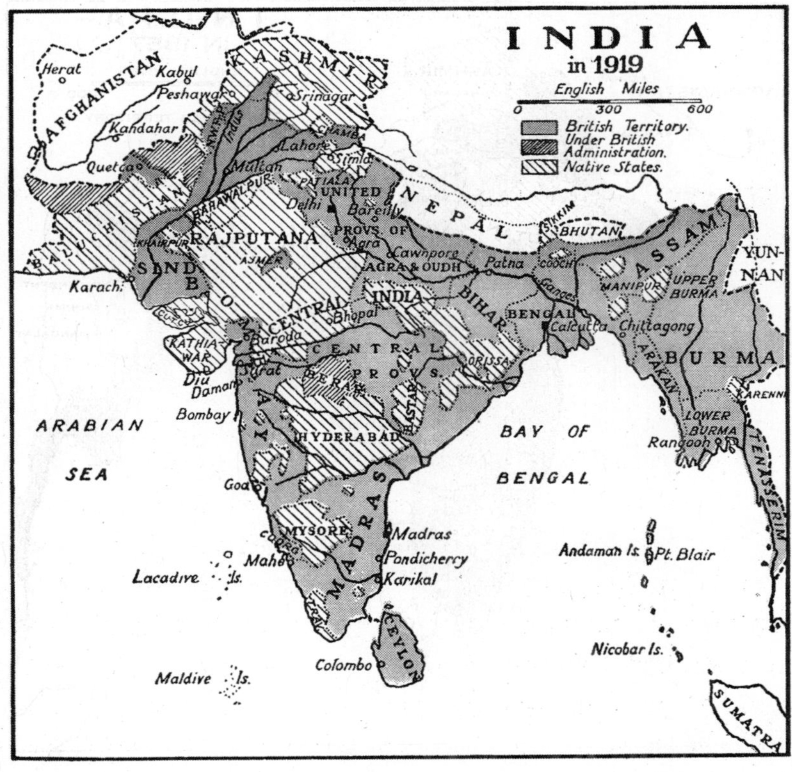
INDIA
in 1919
English Miles
0
300
600
British Territory.
Under British Administration.
Native States.
AFGHANISTAN
Herat
Kabul
Peshawar
Kandahar
Quetta
KASHMIR
Srinagar
Lahore
Multan
Simla
PATIALA
BAHAWALPUR
BALUCHISTAN
KHAIRPUR
RAJPUTANA
Delhi
UNITED
Bareilly
PROVS. OF
Agra
AJMER
Cawnpore
AGRA & OUDH
NEPAL
SIKKIM
BHUTAN
ASSAM
YUN-NAN
Patna
COOCH
Ganges
MANIPUR
UPPER BURMA
Karachi
SIND
CUTCH
KATHIA-WAR
Diu
Daman
CENTRAL
INDIA
Bhopal
Baroda
BIHAR
BENGAL
Calcutta
Chittagong
ARAKAN
BURMA
Surat
CENTRAL
PROVS.
BERAR
ORISSA
KARENNI
Bombay
ARABIAN
SEA
HYDERABAD
BAY OF
BENGAL
LOWER BURMA
Rangoon
TENASSERIM
Goa
MYSORE
Coorg
Madras
Mahe
Pondicherry
Karikal
MADRAS
Lacadive Is.
Andaman Is.
Pt. Blair
Nicobar Is.
CEYLON
Colombo
Maldive Is.
SUMATRA

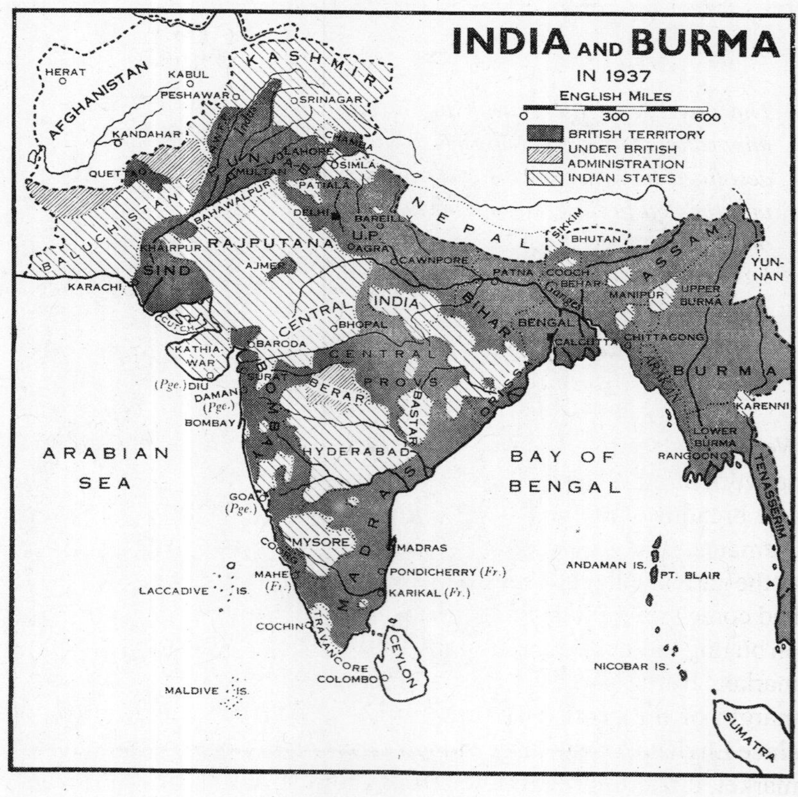
INDIA AND BURMA
IN 1937
ENGLISH MILES
0
300
600
BRITISH TERRITORY
UNDER BRITISH ADMINISTRATION
INDIAN STATES
HERAT
KABUL
AFGHANISTAN
PESHAWAR
KASHMIR
SRINAGAR
KANDAHAR
CHAMBA
QUETTA
LAHORE
SIMLA
MULTAN
PATIALA
BALUCHISTAN
BAHAWALPUR
DELHI
BAREILLY
NEPAL
SIKKIM
BHUTAN
RAJPUTANA
U.P.
AGRA
KHAIRPUR
CAWNPORE
AJMER
SIND
PATNA
COOCH BEHAR
ASSAM
YUN-NAN
KARACHI
MANIPUR
UPPER BURMA
CENTRAL INDIA
BIHAR
CUTCH
BHOPAL
BENGAL
BARODA
CALCUTTA
CHITTAGONG
KATHIA-WAR
CENTRAL PROVS.
BURMA
ARAKAN
(Pge.) DIU
SURAT
BERAR
DAMAN (Pge.)
BOMBAY
BASTAR
KARENNI
ORISSA
LOWER BURMA
ARABIAN SEA
HYDERABAD
BAY OF BENGAL
RANGOON
GOA (Pge.)
TENASSERIM
MYSORE
MADRAS
COORG
ANDAMAN IS.
PT. BLAIR
MAHE (Fr.)
PONDICHERRY (Fr.)
LACCADIVE IS.
KARIKAL (Fr.)
COCHIN
TRAVANCORE
CEYLON
NICOBAR IS.
COLOMBO
MALDIVE IS.
SUMATRA

9 British Rule and Indian Agriculture

The poverty of the Indian population at the present day is unparalleled in any civilized country; the famines which have desolated India within the last quarter of nineteenth century are unexampled in their extent and intensity in the history of ancient or modern times. ...A population equal to half of that of England has been perished in India within a period which men and women, still in middle ages, can remember.

RAMESH C. DUTT

We have already seen how the British colonial rule spread its network of political and economic tentacles throughout the length and breadth of India. To that end, it had adopted a strategy of outmaneuvering and outforcing its major European rivals as well as the native regional powers. As we know, the East India Company had come as a trading company and hence it initially concentrated on buying Indian goods cheap and selling them dear in the European market. In the process, the Company made good money as the margin of the profit was pretty high. But there was a problem: since England did not have enough exportable goods for the Indian market, it had to bring bullion to pay for the Indian goods. In this process, a large amount of British gold and silver had to be brought to India.

The Company got a golden opportunity when it managed to get the *diwani* rights of Bengal, Orissa and Bihar in 1765 in the wake of its victories at the battlefields of both Plassey (1757) and Buxar (1764). One major positive result for the Company from its newly acquired *diwani* rights was that it could buy Indian goods by paying from the accumulated fund from its land revenue exactions. In other words, the Company easily received sufficient funds for buying Indian goods without bringing the bullion from England. What was more, the earnings from Indian goods sold in the European market went straightway to the treasury of the Company located at London and was never ploughed back to India. Thus the quantum of land revenue collection became very crucial and critical to the trading capacity of the Company. Therefore, it became imperative for the Company officials to exact the maximum amount of land revenue from the Indian tenants, even by resorting to force and fraud. Such a callous and inhuman policy had its disastrous impact on Indian agriculture.

In this section we would concentrate on examining the various land revenue systems introduced by the British and their implications for the Indian peasantry. Commercialisation of agriculture in India, which led to the change of its cropping pattern, is another issue which we would take up for our study. But before going into the details of these issues, let us present a brief and succinct account of the state of rural life and the agrarian system prevalent in pre-British India.

Indian Rural Society in the Pre-British Days

There is a near unanimity among scholars about the salient features of rural India in the pre-British days. Briefly stated, they are:

1. First, self-sufficiency and interdependence were the hallmarks of rural life in India. Such a system ensured every one's contributions as well as shares in the economic life of the village, putting it permanently on an even keel. It further proved to be a real bulwark against any major change or disruption of rural life on account of any political change. Thus it not only marginalised the role of the State but also ensured stability and continuity of its socio-economic-cultural life.
2. A unique land ownership pattern was the second feature of our village life. Generally, the land ownership was vested either in king or in community or in the peasant

proprietors. But the traditional Indian system did not fall within any of these categories. Here the peasant families did enjoy hereditary rights to cultivate the land from generation to generation but they were mostly using their own family labour for cultivation. Besides they did not have the right to buy and sell land and hence they could not be categorised as the peasant proprietors.

3. Third, according to the traditional land revenue system, Hindu kings could only collect one-sixth of the produce from the peasant cultivators. But the kings could not dispossess or change the hereditary rights of the cultivators. The Mughals made some changes in the land revenue collection system, including payment in cash and collection through intermediaries. But even they did not have the right to dispossess the actual cultivators, so long as they were willing to pay the rent. And that is why kings, over the ages, tried to have control over the village and not inside it.
4. Fourth, on account of the caste system there was a real interdependence among the various groups of the village. Apart from the cultivating families, there were other groups, viz., carpenters, blacksmiths, potters, barbers, oilmen, cobblers, scavengers, washermen and weavers, who mostly worked as service-providers. Brahmins took care of the ritual and religious ceremonies of the village. Thus an army of village artisans took care of every need of the village population. In lieu of their services, they were either allotted a piece of village land for cultivation or were given a fixed measure of grains at the time of harvest. By and large, these artisans got raw materials for their produce in and around their village. The rest of their needs were met at the weekly local markets. Thus a kind of village-autarchy did prevail in traditional India which is why major political changes at the national level hardly created any ripples in the village life.

There is an extensive debate among scholars about the overall pattern of the village life in the pre-British era. On the one hand, B R Ambedkar and a number of Marxist scholars believe that the entire traditional life was based on a subtle and shrewd system of exploitation of the depressed classes by the dominant upper castes. On the other hand, Mahatma Gandhi and a number of other scholars are of the opinion that the entire village system was marked by complimentarity and harmony, and not by exploitations and exactions. In our view, it is difficult to say at this stage with so much historical distortions and accretions in between, whether the village life was so idyllic or exploitative, as pointed out by some of the scholars. In our times, all that one can say is that the system would not have survived for millenniums had it been that unjust and exploitative. Despite differences of opinion among scholars, there is almost a general agreement on the quintessential characteristics of the Indian agrarian system: that there was no landed aristocracy in India with the kind of proprietary right which the European manors enjoyed. Nor was slavery and serfdom an integral part of our agrarian system, as was prevalent in Europe. Besides, there was no system of private ownership of land, not even peasant proprietorship, as it was the village which virtually remained a unit of revenue assessment.

Indian Agriculture under the British Rule

The introduction of a new land revenue system and the subsequent commercialisation of Indian agriculture brought about far-reaching changes in the nature and structure of Indian agriculture. Let us discuss how these changes came into effect.

New Land Revenue System

The British introduced three different systems of land revenue fixation and collection, which came to be known as: (a) Zamindari, (b) Ryotwari and (c) Mahalwari. Before going into their details, let us get an overview of the expectations they had from the new land revenue system. We have already seen that soon after the Company got the *diwani* right (in 1765) its primary aim had been to collect as much land revenue as was humanly possible. With its newly acquired authority, the Company unscrupulously extracted the maximum land revenue from peasants, so much so that Bengal suffered an unprecedented famine during 1769-70, which virtually wiped out one-third of its population. Alarmed by this, they experimented with a new system of revenue which was called, 'farming'. The quintessence of the new system was that the job of the revenue collection was given to the highest bidders. The new system only accelerated the pace and process of the ruination of the peasantry. What perhaps prompted the Company officials to look for another system of revenue collection was the fact that ruination of agriculture had also adversely affected Company's trade as some of the export items, like silk and cotton were intimately linked with agriculture. This search led to the introduction of yet another new system of land revenue collection which came to be known as zamindari or Bengal Permanent Settlement under Lord Cornwallis. There were two major components of the new system: (a) the quantum of land revenue would be fixed once and for all; and that (b) the job and responsibility for its collection would be given to zamindars. The major rationale behind permanent fixation of the quantum of land revenue was that it would rid the system of its corruption and would also eliminate its uncertain and fluid character. It was further argued that the permanent settlement would encourage zamindars to make investment for the improvement of land, as the increased income would entirely remain with them on account of the fixed nature of the land revenue to be paid to the Company. But the Company was the net gainer in the entire process, as the revenue was to be fixed on the point of absolute maximum. How the new system helped the Company could be illustrated by a simple fact: the quantum of land revenue doubled between 1765 and 1793 – a period less than thirty years. The other question as to who should be given the job of revenue collection was decided by Lord Cornwallis in favour of the zamindars. The rationale behind the zamindari system was that it would be much easier to get the revenue collected through a small number of zamindars, rather than collecting it directly from thousands of cultivators. Perhaps, the real calculation was that zamindars would also provide a strong social support base for the Company–Government. The quintessence of the zamindari system was that the zamindars were given private property right in land: they could own, sell, purchase and mortgage it and their successors could also inherit it. The only limitation was that in case of non-payment of the fixed rent, a zamindar was bound to lose his zamindari. Thus for the first time private property right in land had been introduced in India.

It did not take long for the pernicious consequences of the zamindari system to come to light. Peasants, of course, were its worst victims. They were soon reduced to the status of tenants and subtenants as they could be dispossessed of their lands at a zamindar's whim or fancy. The high quantum of rent virtually broke their back, reducing them to a state of penury and poverty. What was more, they had hardly any avenue even to ventilate their grievances, what to talk of their being redressed. It was only during the later part of the nineteenth century that peasant occupancy rights were recognised by new tenancy legislations. Though the zamindars enjoyed their newly acquired prosperity, a number of them did lose their zamindari as and when they failed to pay their rent in time. Interestingly, the Company officials also had their own grouse against the permanent settlement system: they found in it a stumbling block to increase the revenue at their sweet will. It is for this reason, perhaps, that the permanent settlement system could cover not more than 20 per cent area of British India – prevailing only in Bengal, Bihar, Orissa and north Madras areas. It was this desire to enhance the quantum of revenue collection, which prompted the Company to look for another system which came to be known as Ryotwari.

Ryotwari System

Ryotwari system of land revenue collection was first introduced in Madras by its Governor Thomas Munro. In this system the land revenue was to be collected directly from the cultivators instead of being collected through intermediaries as under the zamindari system. But the new system did not establish peasant proprietorship as they were to pay the rent directly to the government, which was supposed to be the owner of the land. The apparent rationale behind the introduction of Ryotwari system was that it was better suited to the Indian tradition where the cultivators had enjoyed certain rights since time immemorial. Perhaps the real reason behind the introduction of the new system was the Company–Government's need for enhanced revenue on account of its continuous engagement in war with its rivals. It was also argued that though the Company would be getting more revenue, the peasants would be paying less, as intermediaries would be eliminated from the system. Ideally the Ryotwari system was supposed to be based on fixation of the rent for each Ryot and each field. A Ryot was to be given a choice to accept or reject the offer made by the government for a particular piece of land. However, in actual practice it did not happen as the quantum of rent was fixed arbitrarily by the Company officials and both force and fraud were used to extract maximum rent from the cultivators. The system had become obnoxious and repressive, which was brought out by the Report of the Madras Torture Commission in 1855. Subsequently, the Ryotwari system was also introduced in the Bombay Province, where too it encountered similar problems.

Mahalwari System

Mahalwari system was another system of land revenue collection, which was primarily introduced in north-west provinces and subsequently in Punjab and some parts of the central provinces. In these areas, initially an attempt was made to collect the land revenue through the Talukdars of these areas, but it failed primarily on account of excessive rent demand from the Company–Government. This prompted the British to shift their attention to local zamindars (landowners) who were actual cultivators and the village community. In Mahalwari system, the entire village or Mahal was taken as a unit, and thus rent was fixed for the entire Mahal, though every cultivator had a joint responsibility for payment of the rent. Generally, the rent was collected through the village pradhan or any other cultivator of high standing in the village. Mahalwari system was also supposed to be based on detailed field survey to assess the potential of the produce as a basis for the fixation of the rent. But in actual practice, such detailed field surveys were never conducted and the rent so fixed remained too high. Soon the entire system virtually broke down under the weight of high rent. Subsequently, an attempt was made to retrieve the system by the Regulation of 1833 which did bring some relief to these cultivators. But on the whole, Mahalwari system also ruined the cultivators giving a field day for moneylenders.

It can be fairly concluded that all the three new land revenue systems, ultimately, resulted in fixation of high rent and harsh ways of its collection. Besides, what further aggravated the miserable conditions of the Indian peasantry was a system of cash payment of rent and that too during the harvest time when the prices of the agricultural produce were always low.

Commercialisation of Indian Agriculture and its Consequences

Commercialisation of agriculture was another major change brought about by the British rule. New crops and other agro-based products were being produced for the market and not only for local consumption. It is true that some kind of commercialisation of agriculture was already prevalent even in the pre-British days, particularly after the Mughals had introduced the system of cash-payment for land revenue. But the British brought about a major change both in quantitative as well as qualitative terms. In other words, the new system differed from the old one in that now the Company–Government started forcing Indian peasants to produce agro-based exportable goods. Initially, it attempted to force the Indian peasants to produce those agro-based goods, that were in great demand in the European markets. The process was further intensified once the industrial revolution began to gather momentum in England. This led to a new strategy on the part of the British to concentrate on the export of those Indian agricultural goods, which would work as the raw materials for the British industries. Such a strategy also solved their problem of the adverse balance of payments in respect of China. There was a good market in China for Indian agro-products like cotton, ivory and opium, and their export to China would mitigate the problem of balance of payment arising out of the import of Chinese tea by the Company. Thus in view of the demand for Indian agro-products, both in China and in the European market, the British concentrated on the acquisition of products such as indigo, cotton, raw-silk, opium, pepper, etc. Different strategies were adopted to induce production of these exportable goods by Indian peasantry, which ranged from binding the producers by advancing a paltry sum to open use of force and fraud. In the process, the Company did not hesitate to treat the workers in tea-gardens of Assam as virtual slaves.

The question that is often asked is why the commercialisation of Indian agriculture did not help peasants as it did elsewhere in a similar situation. The reasons are not far to seek. First, small peasant families who were predominantly engaged in the production of these goods were not doing it by choice but under compulsion. Second, they were not free to market their goods on competitive prices. They had to supply these goods to the Company under the threat of force. Hence by producing these goods, they did not get enriched, instead they were impoverished. What was more, the earnings of these exports went to the Company's account in London, and they were never ploughed back to India. Nor could India import British goods on those accounts. Hence the export of these goods led to the impoverishment of India and not to its enrichment.

It is true that in subsequent years a number of steps were taken by the British to improve the state of affairs in the field of Indian agriculture. This included new irrigational facilities by new canal systems particularly in Punjab, western UP and some parts of Madras. Besides, the new tenancy laws of 1859 and 1885 did give some relief and protection to the impoverished tenants. But all these measures proved too inadequate to tackle the problem actually faced by the Indian cultivators. Even where some positive results came out of these measures; they were confined to some areas like Punjab, western UP and parts of Madras. And there too, it was only a small group of privileged few who actually benefited from it.

Taking a synoptic view, certain other consequences of the British intrusion in the Indian agrarian system could also be traced out. Some of these long-term consequences were: rural indebtedness, fragmentation of landholdings and emergence of certain new classes in respect of rural India, viz., moneylenders, landless labour and absentee landlords in the form of zamindars. In sum, it was the British intrusion in the field of Indian agriculture which led to the total disruption of the millennium-old village systems, destroying its social as well as its economic fabric.

Finally, so far as the overall balance sheet of the impact of the British rule on Indian agriculture is concerned, there are two diametrically opposite views on it. Some of the Marxist historians like A R Desai and R P Dutt are of the opinion that with all its limitations, the British rule played a positive and progressive role in respect of the rural life of India, as it elevated it to the status of national agriculture and linked it up with the national and even world market. On the other hand, a number of nationalist leaders, including Mahatma Gandhi, held the British rule squarely responsible for total ruination of the rural life of India, leading to the mass pauperisation of the peasantry.

In our view, if foreign slavery would have been that liberating force in human history, it would not have been such a hated system inviting fierce human anger and defiance. It is not for nothing that in the social history of man thousands have laid down their lives in the process of resisting it. Slavery is nothing but a direct and frontal attack on the dignity of man. Hence, it is a total travesty of truth to say that slavery could ever become a tool of human liberation and social progress.

10 British Rule and Indian Industries

The bones of the cotton weavers are bleaching the plains of India.

LORD BENTINCK

We have already seen how Indian agriculture was ruined under the British rule on account of excessive exactions of land revenue and by its forced commercialisation. Equally pernicious and destructive was the impact of the colonial rule on Indian handicraft industries, which were the mainstay of the Indian economy during the pre-British days. In the subsequent sections we propose to analyse the basic strategy adopted by the colonial administration for the destruction of Indian handicraft industries and the consequences thereof on the Indian economy. Before delving into details, it would be expedient to make a synoptic presentation on the nature and structure of the Indian handicraft system prevalent in pre-British days.

The Nature of Indian Handicraft Industries in the Pre-colonial Era

We have seen earlier that one of the chief characteristics of Indian village economic life was its self-sufficient and autarchic nature. An average Indian village not only produced enough food and clothes but also took care of its other material needs, primarily through village artisans, viz., cobbler, potter, oilman, blacksmith, carpenter and silver-smith. The socio-religious ceremonial needs were taken care of by the village brahmin and barber. Drawn primarily from environment-friendly local resources, these goods were produced and consumed locally. These artisans were supported by the village on the basis of a *Jajmani* system and not on a commercial basis. In brief, self-sufficiency and interdependence were the hallmarks of a traditional Indian village.

In the urban areas, the nature and structure of handicraft industries were slightly different. Here goods were being produced on a commercial basis, both for local as well as the world markets. For instance, the Indian textile industry had no rivals in the world. Besides, India enjoyed a high reputation in metal work, stone-work, dyeing, pottery and leather work. What was more, some of these high-quality items were being produced for the elite section of the society: kings, nawabs, and high officials both civilian and non-civilian. These urban handicrafts had their market all over the world. Thus, these urban industries were taking care of the needs of every section of the society, from the commoner to the king. And these urban artisans ranged from bangle-markers to weapon-forgers. However, Indian villages were generally not within the orbit of these urban industries, as their needs were being met by the village-artisans. Besides, a part of urban goods was being produced only for the elite section of the society and for export to other countries. All these factors contributed to a limited market being made available to artisans. Consequently, they faced problems both in the process of capital formation as well as in the field of technological innovations.

British Rule and Indian Handicrafts

We have earlier noted that the East India Company was set up around A.D. 1600 with an exclusive trading right in the East. Initially, textile was one of the major items which the British East India Company traded with India. The Company had to compete with other European companies particularly the Portuguese, Dutch and French for the control of Indian trade market. Besides, it had to struggle to keep itself on the right side of the Indian rulers, including the Mughal Emperor. Despite these challenges, even in the initial stages, the Company did a flourishing business in India, as Indian goods were in great demand in European markets and the profit margin was quite high. For India too, it was not a bad bargain as its textile industries got a boost on account of expanding demands. Moreover, since England did not have many goods to be exported to India, the Company had to bring British bullion (gold and silver) to pay for the goods bought from the Indian market. At that stage, a mutually beneficial commercial relationship existed between India and the Company.

However, in subsequent years, two major developments occurred, which changed the entire relationship. The gradual elimination of other European companies from the Indian region by the British East India Company indeed facilitated its monopolistic control over the Indian market. By the middle of the eighteenth century, the East India Company had successfully accomplished this task. A second and more decisive event, which virtually changed the fates of both India and the Company, was the latter's victory at Plassey (1757) followed by its victory at Buxar (1764) and the grant of *diwani* right to it in 1765. These momentous events entirely changed the relationship between India and the Company. Rabindranath Tagore captured the entire scenario in his poetic words when he said that the 'weighing scales in the merchant's hands changed into the imperial sceptre'. One can add that the Company continued to hold the weighing scale in one hand but had got a sword in the other, to back up its freedom to turn and twist it the way it liked to do. In other words, a fundamental change was brought about even in respect of the Company's commercial dealings in India – as they did not have to be governed by the market forces alone on account of newly acquired political power.

The period between 1757 and 1947 had been divided by the Marxist scholars like R P Dutt and others into three phases (based on the Leninist `s theorisation pattern): the phase of commercial capitalism 1600–1800); the phase of industrial capitalism (1800–60); and the phase of finance capitalism (1860 onwards). During all these phases different strategies were adopted by the British which impacted the Indian industries. It would be expedient for us to dissect and analyse the British colonial policy during these three stages and see how they impacted the Indian industries.

Commercial Capitalist Phase: The First Phase (1600-1800)

The hallmark of this phase of the East India Company's trade with India was that it wanted to maximise its margins of profit by buying goods in the Indian market at the cheapest possible rates and selling them at the highest possible rates in the European market. Before the victory at Plassey, it had to compete with other European companies in the Indian market and also had to deal with Indian rulers. On the whole, its trading patterns were being governed by the market forces. Besides, it had to bring British bullion to India to pay for the Indian goods. In the post-1765 period it, however, managed to overcome all these restrictions. Through the *diwani* rights (the collection of the land revenue) of Bengal, Bihar and Orissa, it evolved and perfected a system of land revenue collection by maximum exactions and extortions from the hapless Indian peasants. A second major revenue source for the Company–Government came from taxes on internal trade items like shops, looms, sheep, cattle, and sundry professions. The third source of income for the Company was seizure of wealth from native rulers, merchants and bankers. The cumulative impact of all these mobilised resources was that the Company was able to solve one of its fundamental problems: how to pay for the purchase of Indian goods without bringing bullion from England. Now, it started paying for them from the surplus of land revenue collections. Not only that, its surplus revenue was subsequently used to wage war and acquire more territory, leading to the further enhancement of its financial strength. The Company–Government experimented and perfected ruthless and rapacious methods for maximum exactions and extortions from the Indian people. These measures can be listed as follows:

(i) Maximum exactions from the Indian peasantry in the form of land revenue collection either directly or through intermediaries.

(ii) Blatant use of force and fraud to force the Indian producers to sell their goods at the minimum price. At times, the forcibly fixed price was less than 35 per cent of the market price. To make the system more ruthless, the Company soon got rid of Indian merchants who used to work as middlemen between the Company and the producers. And it replaced them by a system of *gomastas* who followed a no-holds barred policy to force the producers to sell their goods to the Company at unremunerative prices. One of the techniques used was to 'bulldoze' the producers to take some advances on behalf of the Company. And once they fell in the advance-trap they could never get out of it. For instance, according to a regulation of 1789, any producer failing to deliver goods in time to the Company would have to pay a penalty of 35 per cent on his advances.

(iii) The Company officials engaged in private business using their position to engage in private extortions.

(iv) Loot and extortions from the Indian princes, bankers and merchants.

(v) The profits derived from the exports of goods.

All these measures started telling upon the health of Indian handicrafts. Forcible imposition and compulsory fixation of prices on the handicrafts producers started making the whole business unremunerative and many of them started closing their shops. Thus the process of de-industrialisation had set in. In fact, at this stage, the Company–Government was hardly concerned with the problems of the Indian people as its primary concern remained maximum revenue generation from trading. Another point, which deserves special mention here, is that the proceeds from the Company trading in Indian goods were directly deposited in the Company's account in London and were never brought back to India, either in monetary or material terms. They were treated as a kind of tribute from India, which became a major constituent of primary capital accumulation in England. This, in turn, contributed significantly to the emergence of industrial revolution in England. Thus a direct linkage was established between Indian impoverishment and British enrichment.

Industrial Capitalism: The Second Phase (1800-1860)

Around the close of the eighteenth century, England started

emerging as an industrial country having crossed the threshold of the industrial revolution. What really brought about the industrial revolution in England is beyond the scope of this book. However, there is no denying the fact that the plunder of India certainly was a contributory cause to it. Be as it may, the important point is that once the industrial revolution gathered momentum in England, it had big implications for the Indian handicraft industries. Indian handicrafts, including textiles, were still popular in England and other European markets, and export from India was still a profitable business. But England had a greater need for a captive market for its industrial goods. India, in view of its vast size, population and the Company–Government's control over it, made a tantalising proposition. But the destruction of the Indian handicraft industry was a pre-condition for turning her into a captive market for British industrial goods. Hence, a more concerted and concentrated strategy was evolved to achieve that objective. The ending of the monopolistic trading right of the Company was another pre-condition to open up the Indian market for the British goods. This created a lobby of 'free traders' in England who demanded an immediate end of the monopoly of the East India Company over Indian trade. This resulted in the Charter Act 1813, which abolished the Company's monopoly over Indian trade. The Indian market was further opened by the Charter Act of 1833. Thus India was turned into a free zone for the flow of the British industrial goods. However, the real challenge was to destroy the Indian handicraft industries, which alone could turn her into a captive market for British industrial goods and a supplier of raw materials for the British industries. A sixfold strategy was adopted to achieve these twin objectives.

(i) Manipulation of export and import duty with a view to making Indian goods more expensive in the British markets and the British industrial goods less expensive in the Indian markets.

(ii) Maximisation of land revenue collection by adopting various methods and stratagems so that enough funds could be generated for buying goods from the Indian markets.

(iii) Commercialisation of Indian agriculture so as to turn India into a supplier of raw materials for British Industries.
(iv) Opening of the Indian hinterland by developing means of transportation, making it possible for the British goods to reach out to the remotest corner of the country.
(v) Spread the network of the British administrative machinery even to the remotest area and new legal and judicial system, so as to ensure the safety of trade routes as well as to make secure the British financial-commercial interests. The entire structure of the legal system, including Indian Penal Code (IPC) and Criminal Procedure Code (CrPC), was raised during this phase.
(vi) Promote the English medium-based western education so as to generate enough low-paid manpower to lower rungs of the administrative machinery at the minimum cost. It was not accidental that the Macaulay system of education was introduced during the phase.

All these measures soon yielded their desired results. The cumulative impact of the new strategy was the total destruction of the entire structure of Indian handicrafts, making it possible for the British goods to reach each and every corner of the country. As a result, India soon became a supplier of raw materials for the British industries. India went through a process of what historians have called 'de-industrialisation', which was primarily responsible for mass pauperisation and impoverishment of our people. Even one illustration could prove the point: from 1814 to 1835 the export of the British cotton clothes to India increased by 51 times, whereas that of India to England decreased by 13 times. Cotton Mills of Lancashire were built up on the ruins of Dacca, Murshidabad and Surat and some of these cities went through the process of de-urbanisation as well.

Finance Capitalism: The Third Phase (1860-1947)

In the later part of the nineteenth century, capitalism matured in England and also in some other European countries like Germany, France, Belgium and Holland. This led to a cut-throat competition among European powers, which ultimately resulted in the First World War. Meanwhile, capital accumulation had taken place in England and they were looking for new investment opportunities. With India under their thumb, there was no better place where the British capital could be invested. Besides, India was also endowed with abundant raw materials along with the availability of cheap labour. Moreover, the system of rapid transportation including railway had opened up the Indian hinterland. Hence around 1860, British capital started getting invested in India. The main areas of British investments were railways, irrigation projects, banking and insurance. British investment grew rapidly and by 1914, the total investment came to the tune of 500 million British pounds.

However, there were a number of problems in this phase of finance capitalism in India. In the first place, there was no genuine desire to lay down a sound base with strong infrastructure for rapid industrialisation of India. The idea behind the British investment was to strengthen its stranglehold on Indian people and also to maximise their profits. It was not driven by a genuine desire to put India on the right track of industrialisation. For instance, financial institutions like banks never supported genuine Indian entrepreneurs in a big way. Second, no attempt was made to encourage Indian entrepreneurs to work for the rapid industrialisation of India. For example, till 1924, no attempt was made to give protection to the Indian industries. Besides, there was no attempt to develop heavy industries, which alone could have worked as the motive force of industrialisation. Other factors responsible for the limited, retarded and lopsided growth of Indian industries were lack of well-trained technical hands and lack of purchasing power of our peasantry, which constituted the bulk of our population. Third, the bulk of the British capital invested in India was essentially raised from Indian plunder, which was shown as 'public debt'. Besides, India had to pay for so many expenses from which it derived no benefits. Perhaps the drain of wealth from India to England was much more than the British investment in India.

Indeed, the early nationalist leaders were genuinely aghast at the excessive exploitative nature of the British rule in India, resulting in the mass pauperisation of our people. It was on that account that one of the early nationalist leaders, Dadabhai Naoroji, propounded his oft-quoted 'Drain Theory' which underlined the process of the British enrichment at the cost of the Indian people. The quintessence of his 'Drain Theory' was that Indian wealth was being drained out to England on account of 'home-charges', high salaries and allowances of the British employees in India, and a huge amount of profit on the British capital investment being taken away to England.

Thus, the British colonial rule, adopting different strategies at different stages of its rule, consistently destroyed the traditional base of Indian handicrafts both in urban and rural areas. In the process India went through a phase of rapid de-industrialisation which broke the economic back of the Indian people – reducing them to a state of penury and poverty. Even when an attempt was made to start certain industries in India, it was more out of a profit-motive rather a genuine desire for creating a sound industrial base in India. This could be proved by the simple fact that no attempts were made to develop heavy industry by the British entrepreneurs. Nor were the Indian entrepreneurs encouraged in these directions. Therefore, it was not surprising that on the eve of its independence, India continued to be an industrially backward country despite century-old British rule.

A corollary issue, emerging out of the discussion about the impact of the British on the industrial structure of India, relates to the Marxist theory of growth of capitalist production and its progeny, imperialism. For a long time, the Marxists have been offering their own explanations for the decline of the Indian handicrafts industries, rise of capitalist production and imperialism. Karl Marx put forward a basic formulation that in its initial stages, capitalist system had played a progressive role. He wrote: 'The cheapness of articles produced by machines and the improved means of transport and communications furnish the weapons for conquering foreign markets.' Similarly, Lenin also said that imperialism was the highest stage of capitalism. He further tried to establish a direct correlation of monopoly capitalism with imperialism and militarism. He also called it a stage of finance capitalism. Indian Marxists have been repeating these Marxian formulations ad nauseam without subjecting them to critical evaluation in the context of India. They have also been asserting that with all its limitations, the British rule played a progressive role as it introduced a higher system of production in India. In brief, this has been the position of Marxist scholars like A R Desai, R P Dutt and others.

However, a section of Indian scholars have always rejected the Marxist thesis of capitalism and imperialism. Even the early nationalists who never outrightly rejected the British rule, were of the opinion that plunder of India played a crucial role in the coming of the industrial revolution in England. Dadabhai Naoroji was perhaps the first to propound the 'Drain theory' through which he conclusively proved that it was the transfer of the plundered wealth of India which triggered the industrial revolution in England. But, he was not the only one to propound this theory. A number of other scholars like Cunningham, William Digby and Brooks Adams have been equally enthusiastic supporters of this line of thinking. Adams, in fact, tried to establish a chronological correlation between the British occupation of India and the coming of the industrial revolution in England. He wrote:

'Plassey was fought in 1757 and perhaps nothing has ever equaled the rapidity of change which followed. In 1770 the fighting-shuttle appeared, and coal began to replace wood in smelting. In 1764 Hargreaves invented the spinning-jenny, in 1779 Crompton contrived the mule, in 1768 Watt matured a steam engine, the most perfect of all vents of centralising energy. . . . In themselves, inventions are passive, waiting for the sufficient store of force to have accumulated to set them working. That force must always take the shape of money, and not hoarded, but in motion'. Arguing further in the same vein Adams concluded: 'Before the influx of the Indian treasure and the expansion of the credit which followed; no force sufficient for the purpose existed, and had Watt lived fifty years earlier, he and his inventions must have perished together'.

Back home in India, the socialist leader Rammanohar Lohia has also faulted the Marxist–Leninist theory of capitalism and imperialism on several counts. He particularly challenged their validity in the Indian context. Lohia in his paper on 'Economics after Marx' took up the Marxist theory of capitalism for a critical evaluation. Lohia asserts that Marxist–Leninist theory on capitalist production and its overspill, imperialism, does not have intellectual legs to stand on. According to Lohia, if we take the Indian context, the emergence and growth of industrial revolution and capitalist production occurred in the following manner:

(i) The British came for trading purposes.
(ii) On account of certain weaknesses of the Indian political set up they succeeded in occupying India through political intrigues and superior military force.
(iii) They unabashedly indulged in the plunder of India and transferred the wealth of India to England, including gold and silver.
(iv) It was this plundered wealth of India which provided the basic capital which spurred the industrial revolution and capitalist production in England.

On the basis of this historical sequence, Lohia concluded that capitalism and imperialism grew together and reinforced each other. Thus, he challenged Marx's assertion that capitalism ever played any progressive role in respect of colonial labour. He writes: 'There is no greater collapse of human intelligence than when an Indian or any other colonial repeats parrot-like the Marxist formula that capitalism had at one time been progressive, but has now ceased to be so. Capitalism has at no time been progressive to the colonial masses, it has increasingly wasted their economic and spiritual welfare' (Lohia: Economics after Marx).

In brief, the British rule had a disastrous impact on the entire industrial structure of India. During the entire period of the British rule, there was a total dichotomy between the economic interests of the British and those of the Indian people. Initially, the British interest lay in buying Indian goods at the minimum price and selling them with the maximum margins of profit in the European markets. In the process, the British had hardly any compunction in using both force and fraud to achieve their basic objective. Subsequently, with the coming of the industrial revolution in England, they doggedly pursued their policy of turning India into a captive market for their finished goods and also as a supplier of raw materials needed for their factories. At a still later stage of their rule, the British found it more profitable to make capital investment in India so that it could be wedded to cheap labour and raw materials, which were easily available in India. Thus the maximisation of their margin of profit and pocketing the bulk of the economic surplus extracted from the Indian people remained a common and constant refrain of the British colonial policy. If in the process, some stray industrialisation took place in India that was an unintended fringe benefit for the Indian people. In any case, that was hardly an adequate compensation for the process of de-industrialisation which India went through under the British rule. As one of the early nationalist leaders, G Subramaniya Aiyer put it: 'Millions of workmen who pursued hereditary occupations, who called into exercise their intelligence and imagination, and who therefore, led a life of decent means and self-respect, have been reduced to a condition of abject poverty having become agriculture labourers or day-labourers in towns.'

11 Evolution of Educational Policy in Colonial India

We must at present do our best to form a class who may be interpreter between us and the millions whom we govern – a class of persons Indian in blood and colour, but English in taste, in opinions, in morals and in intellect.

LORD MACAULAY

The British colonial rule made tremendous impact on our educational system, on the nature and structure of syllabi of our academia, the institutional structure and even on our educational policy. But this momentous task was attempted and achieved in various instalments covering different periods. In the process, the British educational policy in India went through several significant changes. In this chapter, an attempt would be made to trace out the changing pattern of the colonial education policy in historical terms. As a background, we would be looking at the basic nature and structure as our pre-colonial educational system. Now it is a widely accepted view that there was a widespread extension of education in the pre-British days. Dharampal in his book, *The Beautiful Tree* based on his in-depth study of Madras Presidency, successfully demonstrated that school education was quite widely spread there. Regional language used to be the medium of instruction in schools. Not only that, even the institutions of higher learning existed in the different parts of the country.

In these institutions of higher learning, the medium of instruction was either Arabic, Persian or Sanskrit. It is a matter of controversy whether caste system played any significant role in the institutions of learning. Some scholars do assert that education was widespread among the upper castes, particularly among the Brahmins. However, Dharampal's study controverts such assertion. Based on the finding of his study, he is of the opinion that school education covered virtually all the castes. Dharampal's findings are also supported by several educational surveys on the regional levels, carried out in Bombay, Madras and Bengal at the behest of the East India Company. These surveys also support Dharampal's view and contention that school education was quite widespread in different parts of the country. In fact some of the officers of the East India Company were so much impressed by the educational pattern prevailing in India at the school level that they even went to the extent of using this system of education for the poor in England. It started being called as the Madras System of School Education in England. Strangely enough, the foundation of the school education was weakened with the coming of the Company Raj in India. It so happened that the village people became so poor under the weight of the various policies of the Company that the old educational system could no longer be sustained. Thus, in the course of time, the people of India came under the grip of the illiteracy with all its concomitant consequences.

The Orientalist and the Education System

Before the East India Company took over the Diwani rights in 1765, it hardly took any interest in the educational problems of India. However, it was supportive of Christian Missionaries work who were trying to spread Christianity through institutions of primary health care and education. But the grant of Diwani rights in 1765 brought about a radical change in the whole situation including its thinking on education. The Company became quite keen to seek the support of the elite classes of India.

Warren Hastings, the Governor of Bengal, took keen interest in the entire process. On his initiative, a code of Gentoo (1776) and Mohammedan code (1781) was put in black and white. This was followed by the study of Sanskrit grammar by Charles Willkins in 1779. Soon a Madarsa was set up in Calcutta (1781), followed by a Sanskrit College in Benaras in 1792. But in the field of education, the most significant work was carried out by William Jones who set up the Asiatic Society in Calcutta in 1784. Under the auspices of the Asiatic Society, old Sanskrit manuscripts were collected and put in a systematic way in the Asiatic Society library. Some of them were even edited and translated. Not only that, an academic journal was also brought out by the Asiatic Society known as *The Asiatic Researches*. Subsequently, Fort William College was founded to impart training to the employees of the Company. It needs to be mentioned that the average employee of the Company was hardly involved in these educational endeavours. Only a handful of big officials were associated with all these major educational initiatives. It is also to be remembered that in the initial stage of its rule, the Company was not clear about its exact role in the various walks of Indian life, including in the field of education. However, all these educational initiatives taken by a few of the top Company officials could be taken as the foundation for the company's subsequent work in the field of education.

Charles Grant's Educational Project

Charles Grant was an official of the Company. He is known for his keen interest and initiative for introducing English education in India, much before Macaulay successfully introduced it in 1835. Grant was firmly of the opinion that the Indian society has got corrupted and it has missed the straight path. He wanted Christianity to be widely introduced in India in a big way as a remedial measure. But he could not push through his project in a big way as the king George III disfavoured such initiative, as it might antagonise and alienate different sections of the Indian society. Hence, nothing much came out of Grant's proposal in any concrete form. In the course of the parliamentary debates, it became quite clear that the real purpose of Grant's proposal was to facilitate Christian missionaries entry into India. Thus, during 1798, Grant's proposal was rejected. But Grant and his associates did not lose hope and continued to work on their proposal. Some of the Christian missionaries did come to India and started working for the spread of Christianity especially in some areas of Bengal. The persistent effort of Grant and his associates did yield the desired result in 1813. At the occasion of the renewal of the Company's Charter, Grant's proposal was accepted. Under the new dispensation, the missionary work was to be allowed in India. Besides, simultaneously it was also decided that a grant of rupees one lakh was to be provided for being spent in the educational field, particularly for the spread of scientific study in India. Perhaps this initiative was taken as a counter balancing measure against the entry of Christan missionaries in India, or to appease the Orientalist lobby which was making such demands for a long time.

Towards the Introduction of English Education in India

By 1821, the Company was well-established and stabilized in India. It had acquired greater self-confidence and self-assurance. It was during that year that the question of spending the grant of rupees one lakh for the educational purposes, which had been provided earlier, came up for actual implementation. There was some surplus revenue during the same year. It was around the period that Sanskrit College had been founded in Calcutta. Thus, a congenial ground was emerging for a major new initiative in the educational field. Hence, in 1823 a Central Committee for public instruction was set up to consider and chalk out a new educational policy. There was prolonged debate among the members of the committee and sharp differences of opinion developed on the ideological lines. One half of the committee members were in favour of introduction of English education in India, whereas the other half favoured the oriental system of education. Due to sharp differences among the members of the committee, the final decision was left to the Governor General. The Governor General, in turn, left it to be decided by Lord Macaulay, who was the legal member of the Executive Council of the Governor General. Macaulay belonged to the group of administrators, who were in the favour of the introduction of English education in India. He conveniently drew the minutes on the subject and got it approved on 2 February 1935. It was a historic decision to introduce English education in India, ignoring the Orientalist plea for the continuation of the old system. It was a historic and momentous decision, which not only affected the nature and structure of the Indian education during the colonial era, but continues to rule the roost even today. It also led to the emergence of the new English educated elite, whose one section raised the banner of revolt though another section of the group continued to lend support to the colonial rule.

Let us try to understand the historical background to this historic decision. Let us recall that with the renewal of the Company's charter in 1813, the gate of India was opened for the Christian missionaries work. These missionaries in the course of pursuing their missionary work, had also opened a number of schools. Alexander Duff was one of the most prominent among these missionary groups. He was firmly of the opinion that the religious conversion of the Hindus, was a pre-requisite for the betterment of the Indian society. He had an institution which ultimately turned into the Scottish Church College of Calcutta. Another thing which needs to be underlined is that was the time when the Indian society was going through a great intellectual churning. A large number of people particularly in Bengal, were trying to acquire English education, so that they could get jobs in the Company's offices. Besides, there were also a number of modernist and enlightened people who were going all out to imbibe the new scientific spirit. Most prominent among them was Raja Rammohun Roy. Another historical background has also to be mentioned. It was the same period during which the Utilitarian thinkers were getting popular in England. Bentham, James Mill and Malthus were most prominent among them. They were critical of the Indian cultural ethics and social system and favoured multi-pronged intervention to ameliorate the Indian condition. Inspired by the Utilitarianism, many young people started working in India. James Mill, who wrote, *History of India* was one of them. He was also a staunch critic of the Orientalist school. This book got him good name and he was appointed in the Company's office in India. Subsequently, his son, John Stuart Mill, also joined the rank. Thus, a new school of thought emerged, which was deadly opposed to the Orientalist way of thinking. So, when in 1823 a proposal for opening a Sanskrit College in Calcutta came, even Raja Rammohun Roy was opposed to it. He was of the opinion that the Company should work for the introduction of scientific ideas in India. But Roy failed to persuade the Company at that stage. Not only that the Sanskrit College was opened in Calcutta in 1823, it was soon followed by the foundation of the college for the study of the classical languages in Delhi in 1824. But the coming of the William Bentinck as the Governor General in 1828 led to radical changes in the situation. He was inspired by the Utilitarian ideas. With the support of Raja Rammohun Roy, he succeeded in abolishing the nefarious system of 'sati' in 1829. Not only that, by 1930 English was introduced as a subject in the old institutions of Benaras, Delhi and Calcutta. By that time in 1833, the Company's Charter was due for renewal, Macaulay came as a law member of the Executive Council in 1834. Under the new Charter Act, the amount of the grant was raised from rupees one lakh to ten lakhs. But in the preceding years, a fierce debate was on, between the Orientalists and the modernists, who favoured the introduction of English education in India. The modernists had argued that the regional languages of India were not developed enough to work as the medium of instruction for the modern education. Hence, the only choice was Arabic/Persian or Sanskrit. But they were not considered good enough to work as a vehicle for modern education because of their old moorings. Hence, a number of people favoured the introduction of English education in India. Macaulay was one of them. He favoured it by saying that a single shelf of European library might outweigh in terms of knowledge all that is contained in all the books of the traditional languages. He also argued that English was even ahead of other European languages. It was also popular among the elite classes of India and was quickly acquiring the status of the language of the trade and commerce in India. But the most telling argument which he offered was that it would lead to the creation of a new class in India, which would provide the social support base for the colonial administration. Besides, this new group would be Indian, only in terms of 'colour and blood', but in respect of morals, ethics and in the way of thinking, it would be like the Englishmen. It was with this background that Macaulay got his education minute passed in February 1935, which was approved by the Governor General in March 1935. Macaulay would be ever remembered not only for the introduction of English education in India, but also for his remark about the English educated elites which have turned out to be true in the literal sense. After 1935 things started moving fast. Soon a medical college was opened in Calcutta. Another landmark was the setting up of a committee under William Adam, a Baptist Missionary, to prepare a detailed report on the vernacular education in India. Thus, two roads were opened after 1935 in respect of education in India, one leading to the introduction of English education in India and the other in respect of vernacular/regional language education.

Charles Wood's Dispatch of 1854

Charles Wood's Dispatch turned out to be another milestone on the educational road of India. Wood was the Chairman of the Board of Control of the Company. He had been asked to put forward an integrated note on the educational policy for India. In his dispatch he pleaded for a double pronged educational policy – the English medium classes for the elite and vernacular education for the common masses. Wood also suggested some changes in the Macaulay's policy. Thus, whereas Macaulay had favoured the English medium education for all, Wood stood for the education through vernacular languages for the common man. He was of the opinion that the common man could easily acquire and internalize new knowledge through the medium of vernacular language. He went to the extent of suggesting that even in the English medium institutions, there was a need for the introduction of the vernacular languages. Similarly, in vernacular medium institutions, English as a subject needed to be introduced. He laid greater emphasis on primary and secondary education. So far as the contents of the syllabi were concerned, he laid great emphasis on humanities and languages. Subsequently, at the provincial level, the Department of Public Instruction was set up. Besides, provision was to be made for the grant-in-aid for different institutions. Subsequently, universities were set up in the presidencies of Bengal, Madras and Bombay. Wood's dispatch wanted trained teachers and good textbooks to be provided for the school level education. The Dispatch also raised the question of provision for medical and engineering education. Even the question of woman's education was not left untouched by the Dispatch.

Despite all these positive aspects, scholars have found many loopholes in the Dispatch. It had failed to tackle the problem of general literacy. Besides, it did not touch upon the basic issues of an education policy for a self governing State. However, it needs to be emphasised that in the wake of the Dispatch, a new era of English education, as well as vernacular teachings began. It encompassed all institutions from primary to the institutions of higher learning. Along with the opening of universities in three presidencies, a number of colleges were also opened in different parts of the country. Similarly, the number of schools also went up in a big way. At all these institutions, English came to occupy a distinct place including primary level education. However, the problem of general literacy remained appalling as it did not exceed more than one per cent of the total population.

The Hunter Commission

The period between the year of Dispatch (1854) and the year (1882), when the Hunter Commission was set up, saw marked improvement in the field of education from primary to the higher level institutions. But there was a problem with the Christian missionaries. They were protesting that the government was interfering too much in the educational affairs through the instrumentality of the grants-in-aid. Hence, they were pleading for education to be left in the private hands. Besides, considerable time had lapsed after the Wood's Dispatch of 1854. In view of all these problems, the Hunter Commission was set up in 1882 to consider and report back to the government on these issues. One of the major recommendations of the Hunter Commission was to relieve the government from the responsibility of general literacy. It favoured education to be left in private hands. This led to the opening of many schools and colleges. But such mushrooming growth of educational institutions created problems of the absence of good provision for teaching and other infrastructural facilities. As a result, Lord Curzon set up the Indian University Commission in 1902. Based on its report, he got passed the Indian University Act in 1904. The new Act made several changes in respect of university education as well as in the administrative field.

It greatly enhanced the chances of the State interventions in the life of the educational institutions, which is why it faced stiff opposition from the Indian leadership. Subsequently, the partition of Bengal further alienated the Indian leadership from Curzon's administration. In the course of the Swadeshi Movement, which had risen against the partition of Bengal, the issue of national education occupied a dominant position. A number of national institutions for education were set up. Leaders like Aurobindo were in the forefront of such initiatives. He also became the Principal of Calcutta National College. However, with the decline of the Swadeshi Movement in the subsequent years, these national institutions also lost their sheen. In the process, they made their own contributions to the cause of Indian nationalism. Many of those, including teachers and students, who were earlier associated with these national institutions joined the national movement and valiantly fought for the freedom of our country.

The next major step in the field of education was reflected in the government's resolution on education which was passed on 21 February 1913. It was conceded in the Resolution that till 1912 the pace and direction of development in the education field had been tardy. Thus, till date only five universities and 185 colleges had come up which were too meager in the view of the vast size of the land and population of our country. Admittedly, there was need for vast expansion in the field of education at various levels. Besides, it was also felt that the government must play a much bigger role in the field of education, particularly at the secondary level. The need for the massive expansion of primary education was also underlined. All this led to the increased role of the government in the field of education.

The Act of 1919 also marked another milestone in the field of education. Dyarchy was set up at the provincial levels and education formed a part of the concurrent list on which both provincial government and central government could legislate and act. However, in the process, educational growth became uneven in different provinces. In 1921, the Government set up the Central Board of Education. However, it was disbanded within a few years. But let us recall that was the time of non-cooperation movement led by Mahatma Gandhi. Once again like at the time of the Swadeshi Movement, a number of institutions of national education like the Gujarat Vidyapeeth, Kashi Vidyapeeth, Bihar Vidyapeeth and several institutions of similar kinds came up. The primary emphasis on these institutions was the nationalist education system through the medium of regional languages. These institutions played a major role in arousing and sustaining the deep sense of nationalism in the country.

Subsequently, the government set up Hartong Commission in 1927 to consider the issues relating to education and give recommendations. The Commission submitted its report in 1929. The Commission recorded the fact that there had been a great increase in the educational field both in terms of the number of institutions as well as in terms of enrollment. But the Commission did express its dissatisfaction with the state of affairs in the primary education. It also made some recommendations in respect of secondary education, particularly relating to the service conditions of the teachers and even expressed its concern about them. It also gave its views on higher education and stressed the need for greater initiatives in the field of research and tutorials. The Commission was of the opinion that there was a need for laying emphasis on the female education. The government did take some steps in the light of those recommendations which led to some improvement in the field of education.

The Act of 1935 gave great role to the provincial government in the field of education. The Act did away the system of dyarchy under the Act of 1919 and granted full provincial autonomy. Thus, barring a few institutions which still remained under the control of the central government, education as a subject came under the purview of the provincial government. In 1935, on the basis of the Hartong Committee Report an Advisory Board for education policy was revived. Subsequently, Abbot and Wood Committee was entrusted with the task of making recommendations in the field of education and training programmes for teachers. After the formation of the Congress in the provinces, Mahatma Gandhi presented his basic education programme, also known as the Waradha Scheme of Education. B.G. Kher Committee looked into the issues connected with the basic education. The Committee recommended that in the rural areas, children till the age of fourteen should receive basic education. But in September 1939, the Second World War broke out. Failing to get any concrete assurances on the issue of Indian independence, the Congress resigned from the office. Hence, a great opportunity for doing something concrete in the field of education was lost. In 1943, the central government set up the Sargent Committee to make fresh recommendations in the field of education. The Sargent Committee did make some recommendations for the education of children between the age of 3 and 6. It also recommended free and compulsory education for the children between the age of 5 and 11. It also felt the need for a provision in respect of adult education. It favoured education till secondary stage through the medium of mother tongue.

Scholars have taken a very critical view of the Sargent Committee's recommendations. They have argued quite convincingly that even if these recommendations would have been implemented fully, they could have taken India to a stage at which England was already in 1939. Secondly, the committee had kept the education system of England as an ideal for making its own recommendations. But Indian conditions and problems in the field of education were quite different from England. Hence, the intellectual foundation of the report was wrong and faulty. However, after receiving the Report of the Committee, the government of India asked the provincial government to take measures towards its implementation. In 1945, a new department of education was founded at the central level followed by the establishment of the University Grants Committee in 1946. Meanwhile, political scenes changed and India became independent in 1947.

In the above survey, an attempt has been made to take an account of the British educational policy in the colonial era. It would be expedient for the study to look at some of the statistical data in respect of the Indian education, just on the eve of independence in 1947, when the British left the country. Let us remember that around 1947, the population of India was around 400 million. The number of primary institutions during 1946-47 was 1,72,000 and the number of the students on rolls were 13 million approximately. There were 17,258 middle schools and the number of students in those schools were around 3.6 million. So far as higher education was concerned during the same period, there were 17 universities and 297 colleges and the total number of students in these institutions were around 96,800. On paper, these figures might look quite impressive, but if one looks at the vast population of India, these figures look inadequate and meagre. A second weakness of the colonial educational policy was that it was mostly confined among the upper castes of Hindus and the elite section of the Muslim population. The bulk of the downtrodden like dalits, adivasies women and Muslims virtually remained outside the system. Thirdly, no serious attempt was made to impart technical education to the Indian people. Fourthly, bulk of the people had remained illiterate and no serious attempts were made to spread general literacy among our people.

Finally, it needs to be mentioned that the Macaulay system of education had led to the emergence of a new elite group, which had developed a highly colonised mentality. It is true that it was this section of elite which had raised the banner of revolt against the colonial rule. But that was a minuscule section of the Indian elite. The bulk of them remained victims of the slavish mentality. Only when Mahatma Gandhi became the leader of the national movement and the people responded to his call, that some of the elites joined the ranks of the freedom fighters. What was more, the Indian elite had little respect for the common man, their language, culture, their way of life and what they had. Thus, Macaulay's system of education has created a barrier between the elite and the common masses, which has turned out to be unbridgeable, even in the post-independent era. It is this elite class which continues to dominate every walk of our national life. However, scholars also point out that it is through the English education that India had achieved the status of world power in the field of knowledge industry. It has opened the door for modern scientific knowledge. It is also said that it was one section of the elite which revolted against the British rule and led India to independence in 1947. The fact of the matter is that the debate about the positive and negative aspects of the Macaulay's system of education is still on and might not be settled for a long time, as the stakes are too high at least for the elite.

12 Constitutional Development in India During British Colonial Rule

After all, we framed the constitution ... of 1935 because we thought it was the best way ... to hold India to the Empire.

LORD LINLITHGOW

The British Raj gradually provided a constitutional framework for India which was primarily raised to meet the challenge of the national movement. But it did provide a broad constitutional framework which greatly impacted the constitution of free India. In this chapter, an attempt would be made to trace the evolution of constitutional development during the colonial period.

Let us recall that it was the British victory at Plassey (1757) and Buxar (1764) that virtually laid the foundation of the Company Raj in India. But it soon became clear in the minds of the British political leaders that the Company could not be left free to rule India according to its whims and fancies. Some kind of an overall supervision and control over the Company rule would have to be made by the British Parliament and the British political elite. It was this line of thinking which led to the making of the Regulating Act of 1773 which was framed on the basis of a report of the Parliamentary Committee. Accordingly, it became incumbent on the part of the Company to keep the British government informed of its moves both in civil and military affairs. Besides, through this Act, the governor of Bengal was raised to the status of the Governor General of India and as such governors of Madras and Bombay presidencies were made subservient to him. Moreover, a four member Executive Council was also set up to aid and advise the Governor General. Besides, a Federal Court was also set up in Calcutta. Subsequently, such political control over the Company Raj was further tightened by the Pitt's India Act of 1784. Under the new dispensation, the Board of Control of the Company was reconstituted and as such the number of its members went up from four to six, out of which two members were necessarily to be from the British Council of Ministers. The main task of the Board of Control was to guide the Indian administration and also the Court of Directors. It was also specifically mentioned that no move of war and peace could be made without taking the Board of Control into the confidence. The control over the Company was further tightened when its Charter was renewed in 1793. A specific direction was given to the Company administration that it would have to draw a written code of law for India. Thus, a new tradition was set as the judicial courts could interpret these written laws and pure discretionary powers of the administration was bound to be curtailed. In 1813 the Company Charter was renewed with a proviso that the Company monopolistic hold over the Indian trade would end and a new era of free trade would be initiated. More importantly, under the new Charter, the chairman of the Board of Control was necessarily to be from among the Ministers of the government. The Charter of 1833 further tightened the control of the government over the Company. Besides, it provided for a law commission to facilitate the codification of law. Subsequently, both civil and criminal codes were prepared based on the recommendation of the law commission. However, the Charter Act of 1853 did not specify the period for the Company Raj. Rather it was made clear that the Company would be in control till the Parliament would make alternative arrangement. Moreover, the total number of members of the Executive Council of the Governor General was raised from six to twelve; out of which, six were to be the members of the British Council of Ministers. But 1857 rebellion brought about the end of the Company Raj as India came directly under the British Crown. The new dispensation also led to the creation of a new office of the Secretary of State who was also to be from the British Council of Ministers.

However, the rebellion of 1857 prompted the British Establishment to do some rethinking about the role of the Indian elite in running the colonial administration. It was felt that some kinds of the association of the Indians with colonial administration could help them in understanding the feelings of the Indian people. This led to the enactment of the Indian Council Act of 1861. According to the new Act, the membership of the Executive Council of the Governor General was further expanded. It was also provided that fifty percent of its members must be from non-official category. But in subsequent years the Council turned out to be weak and ineffectual. It could hardly take any major decision without the prior consultation with the Government. Besides, even the so called non-official members were found to be nothing more than the drum-beaters for the government. The Council Act of 1861 came under severe criticism of the nationalist leaders. On their persistent demand, the Indian Council Act of 1892 was passed. Under the new Act, the number of Council membership was further increased. The non-official members were to be elected from the institutions of local self-government viz. the district board, municipal corporations and municipalities. However, the 1892 Act did not materially change the situation. The government could easily retain its majority in the Council. Besides, the members had simply the right to debate the government budget. They did not enjoy the right to vote over the budget proposals. The nationalist leaders expressed its dissatisfaction with the Act of 1892 also. They believed that the government continued to be autocratic and the Council was hardly in a position to control and direct its activities. Despite their reservation about its powers, leaders like Gokhale and Pherozeshah Mehta used its forum to expose the misdeeds of the government and also the flaws in its policy formulations.

The first decade of the twentieth century saw a virtual earthquake in the politics of the country. The partition of Bengal and Swadeshi movement radically changed the temper and tenor of the Indian politics. There was a militant nationalist school led by Tilak, Bipin Chandra Pal and Lala Lajpat Rai. They started dominating the Indian political scene as it was evident both at Benaras (1905) and Calcutta (1906) Congress. The Moderate wing of the Congress was getting exasperated with the nationalist leadership which led to the Surat split of the Congress in 1907. Incidentally, the politics of England was also fast changing. The Liberal Party emerged as a big force in the British politics. The Indian Moderates had a lot of expectations from the British Liberal Party. There were informal contacts between these two groups. All this provided the political background for a new Act of 1909; also known as Morley Minto Reforms. This Act increased the number of the members of the Council both at central and provincial levels, though the government majority in the Supreme Council was retained. The number of the non-official members was also increased. At the level of the Provincial Council there was a provision for the majority of the non-official members, though in practical terms it did not mean much as even the non-official members more often than not sided with the government.

The Act of 1909 led to the enhancement of the powers of the Council and their members on a limited scale. Under the Act, the members could not only discuss the budgetary proposals but could also put forward counter proposals and even exercise their vote over them. The members did enjoy the right to ask questions and even the supplementary questions. But only those members could ask supplementary questions, who had raised the original questions. The members had also the right to discuss the issues of public importance. The system of indirect election was provided under the Act. Separate electorate system was provided for Muslims, Christians and chamber of commerce. District Boards and universities were taken as separate entities for the election purposes. In fact, there was no provision for territorial and general representation.

The most glaring weakness of this Act was the granting of the separate electorate system to the Muslims by the Government. However, in all categories, the franchise was limited based on property and educational qualifications. In actual practice, even the non-official members used to side with the government barring a few. They rarely used their own discretion. The non-official members who came from different background could rarely join hands to confront the government. In a word, the Act of 1909 was hardly adequate to tame the government in any meaningful way.

The Government of India Act, 1919

In the second decade of the twentieth century, there was another radical change in the politics of the country. The partition of Bengal was undone in 1911, which did create some kind of bad blood between the colonial administration and the Muslim community. Both in the Balkan conflict and the First World War. Turkey and Britain stood face to face as they were in opposite camps. On account of all these developments, Indian Muslims found themselves between the two horns of a dilemma. The Caliph of Turkey was their religious head and the Raj was their immediate ruler. As such, they wanted to retain the loyalties of both. But if they were forced to make a choice, they could prefer to be on the side of the Caliph. Sensing the strong feelings of the Indian Muslims for the Caliph, the colonial administration assured them that it would take care of the interests of Turkey and her Caliph. Such an assurance did assuage the feelings of the Indian Muslims who expressed their willingness to support the British in the First World War.

Another historical fact needs also to be mentioned as a background to the Act of 1919. Indian Muslims League and the Indian National Congress had joined hands at Lucknow (1916) and enter into a pact which came to be known as the Lucknow Pact. Mahatma Gandhi had also lent his support to the British war efforts after coming back to India in 1915. Besides, Russian Revolution (1917) had also aroused a lot of feeling for freedom among the people all over the world. Even the First World War was being fought to promote the principle of self-determination among the people of the world. As a result, the Indian people were expecting big steps towards constitutional development leading them to self-government. This feeling was further strengthened when on 20 August 1917, Montagu, the Secretary of State for India, made a declaration in the British Parliament that the government would soon take concrete measures to lead India on the road to self-governments. Subsequently, Montagu-Chelmsford jointly prepared a constitutional report which took the final shape of the Act of 1919. The major provisions of this Act were as follows:

(1) There was no major change so far the central government was concerned. The central government continued to remain unresponsive. The members of the Executive Council could not be removed by passing a resolution of the central legislature. They continued to remain responsible only to the Secretary of the State and ultimately to the British Parliament which had the last word in all these matters.

However, some minor changes were also brought about at the central level. The number of the members of the Executive Council was not fixed. The Central Legislature was made bicameral. The Central Assembly had altogether 103 elected members and 40 nominated ones. The upper house had 60 members out of which 34 were elected and 26 were nominated by the government. The election was held on the basis of the limited franchise which comprised only 10 per cent of the population. Only a part of the central expenditure of the government was to be approved by the Central Assembly. Its members did enjoy the right to ask questions and to move adjournment motions. The Assembly could even reject the proposal for the government expenditure. But the Governor General had the right to reject the resolution passed by the Central Assembly. Thus, though it could not be called as a responsible government, but certainly it has to take into account the feelings and aspirations of the people. Similarly, though the position and status of the Secretary of the State remained as strong as ever, but he could no longer ordinarily interfere in respect of the transferred subjects at the provincial level. But so far the reserved subjects at the provincial levels were concerned, he was as strong as ever. However, it was mentioned that if the Central government and Central Assembly were in agreement on a particulars issue, the Secretary of the State could not interfere in such matters. But the fact of the matter was that the Central government had to dance to the tune of the British government, hence this provision was hardly of any practical use.

The Act of 1919 and the Provincial Government

The most important provision under the Act of 1919 was in respect of the provincial government. Prior to this Act, the Provincial Government used to work as the agent of the central government as most of the powers were concentrated in the central government. But the Act of 1919 provided for a constitutional division of power between the central and Provincial Government. Defence, foreign affairs. Princely States, public debt, custom, post and telegraph, money, railway, communication were kept within the purview of the central government. Institution of local self-government, education, medicine, irrigation, land reforms, agriculture, police, jail and similar other subjects were kept within the purview of the Provincial Government. But all residual powers were to remain with the central government. Besides, it was also provided that with the prior consent of the Provincial Governor, the Central government would have powers to legislate on any of the items of the Provincial list. The Governor General had the authority to put any item from the central list under the purview of the Provincial Government.

The Provincial list was also divided in two parts–reserved subjects and transferred subjects. The underlying idea behind this division was that subject of local/provincial development nature were put in the category of the transferred subjects. But the subject which had connection with the wider public good were kept under the reserved category. However, it went without saying that the government wanted to retain the real powers in its hands in the name of public good.

Dyarchy under the Act of 1919

Dyarchy as a system of government was introduced at the provincial level under the Act of 1919. The simple meaning of dyarchy was two types of executives under the Act: (a) Ministers and (b) Councillors. The Ministers were responsible to the Provincial legislature whereas the councillors were, primarily responsible to the colonial government for their work. In other words, the transferred subjects were in the hands of the Ministers, whereas the reserved subjects were to be handled by the councillors. This system of double governance was called dyarchy.

Ministers: Ministers were to look after the administration of the transferred subjects. Only the members of the Provincial legislatures could be made ministers. If any minister at the time of his appointment did not happen to be a member of legislature, he would have to acquire it within a period of six months of his appointment. Legally speaking, the ministers were appointed by the Governor, but in actual practice, only those who did enjoy the confidence of the legislature could be made ministers. A minister could be removed if the legislature was to pass a vote of no confidence against him. In special circumstances, the Governor could discard/reject any recommendation made by the ministers.

Councillors: The councillors at the provincial level were appointed by the colonial government on the recommendation of the Governor. They were appointed for five years. However, they could be removed from their position by the Crown on his discretion. They were ex-officio members of the Provincial legislature. They had the authority to answer the questions in the Provincial legislatures. But they could not be removed by a resolution of no confidence passed by the Provincial legislatures.

After the election of 1920-21, dyarchy was introduced at the Provincial level. But the nationalist leaders were critical of it on several counts. Some of these points of criticism were as follows:

(i) Though the Provincial list was divided into two categories of transferred and reserved subjects, but no separate financial provision was made for each of them. In fact, adequate financial provisions were never made for the transferred subjects which greatly hampered their work.

(ii) The Ministers could not have an effective control over the bureaucrats, who were mostly of the British origins. More often than not, these bureaucrats ignored the recommendations of the ministers.

(iii) Dyarchy was basically an attempt to marry some kind of popular sovereignty with the autocracy of the colonial administration. It was virtually an impossible task like mixing of chalk and cheese.

(iv) The division of subjects between transferred and reserved subjects had no logical basis. Hence, the dividing line between the two was not clear and well-marked. For example, the agriculture minister had neither the responsibility of the forest department nor of irrigation. He did not have control over the agricultural loan or drought relief fund. Hence, ministers could not work in any effective way and deliver the goods.

(v) In provinces, the Governor enjoyed special powers and position. He had many trump cards with him. In very special circumstances, he could remove a minister. Besides, without his goodwill a minister could not get sufficient fund, nor could he depend on the support of the members nominated by the government. As a result, the ministers were most of the time looking up to him and also looking for his support. Ministers were not on a strong wicket, as the principle of collective responsibility was missing from their working.

Despite all these weaknesses, some scholars have underlined the positive side of dyarchy. One of the positive side was that the people did get a voting right though limited in nature. That led to some kind of political awareness among the people. Besides, the Indian leadership got an opportunity to experience the art of governance from very close quarters which proved to be of immense value in the subsequent years. Besides, despite their limitations, some of the ministers did good work and were able to deliver the goods to the people. Besides, it was during this period that some of the progressive legislations were passed. Some of these measures were: Bombay Local Board Act of 1923, Madras State Aid to Industry Act, 1923, Bombay Education Act, 1923 Bihar and Orrisa Village Administration Act, 1923. All these were the positive side of dyarchy. But even with all its weaknesses, it provided the guidelines for making both law-making and administration more people-oriented in the subsequent years.

The Government of India Act, 1935

The historical background for the Act of 1935 was provided by Gandhian movements like the non-co-operation and civil disobedience movement, on the one hand and constitutional reports like Nehru Report, Simon Commission Report and deliberations at the Round Table Conferences on the other. But in making of the Act, the Indian leadership had hardly any major hand. The actual work was primarily done by the British Government and the British Parliament.

Main Provisions of the Act of 1935

The Act provided for the Indian Union comprising British India and Princely States. To that end, the provisions for the division of power between the centre and provinces was made in a very specific way. Besides, the provision for federal court was also made so that in the case of dispute between the centre and provinces, judicial adjudication could help to resolve it. The powers were distributed on the basis of three lists: the Union List, the Provincial List and Concurrent List. Along with these provisions, the central legislature was made bicameral–the Federal Assembly and the Council of States.

In the Federal Assembly, the British India was to have 250 members and the Princely India 125 members. In the Council of States their number was 150 and 104 respectively out of its total membership of 260. Six member were to be nominated by the government. The system of election of both houses was also to be different. The members of the Council of States were to be elected by the people based on the limited franchise. But its members from the Princely India were to be nominated by the Princes. On the other hand, the members of the Faderal Assembly were to be elected indirectly. Its members from the British India were to be elected by the elected members of the provincial Assemblies. The Act had made it clear that the Union would come into being only if fifty percent of the Princely Indian States opted for it.

It needs to be mentioned that at the central level, the Act did not provide for the responsible government. There was to be kind of dyarchical system at the centre. Defence, foreign affairs, communication, Adivasis and some of the other subjects were to be administered by the Governor General and his Executive Council. They were not be responsible to the Central Legislature as it happens in the parliamentary system of the government. But the rest of the subjects were to be managed by the Ministers who were to be responsible to the Central Legislature. However, at the central level, the position of the Governor General was to be supreme. For the reserved subject, he was to be responsible only to the Secretary of the State and the British Parliament. In certain subjects such as finance, defence, minorities, Princely States and adivasis, he had the authority to take decisions in his own discretion. In fact, his powers were so vast that he could easily bypass the legislatures. He had the power to call and prorogue both the houses of the central legislature. He could also stop any discussion relating to Princely India in the House. He could refuse to give his consent to any Bill passed by the legislature or to send it back to the House for reconsideration or he could refer it to the British Crown for his/her consent. In special circumstances, he could veto a Bill. In brief, his power and position was unassailable.

We have to remember that the proposed Union under the Act of 1935 never came into being as Princely India did not evince much interest in it. Perhaps the Princes were scared of the Praja Mandal Movement. By joining the Union they could lose both their autonomy and autocracy. However, non-starting of the Union did not make much difference to the government. There was a provision in the Act that in case it is not fully implemented at the central level, it could act under the Act of 1919 by making suitable changes in its provisions.

The Act of 1935 and the Provincial Autonomy

The most significant part of the Act of 1935 related to the provision of the provincial autonomy with a responsible government at a provincial level. As such the dyarchical system provided under the Act of 1919 was abrogated. Instead, a fully responsible government was to be installed at the provincial level; of course with certain limitations. The simple meaning of provincial autonomy was that the provinces were to be the constitutional entity and as such they could enjoy the provincial autonomy. In other words, they were no longer dependent on the Central Government and on its whims and fancies. It also needs to be emphasised that though the proposed Union under the Act of 1935 did not come into being primarily because of the Princes indifference, but the provision relating to the provincial autonomy was implemented as provided under the Act.

However, the provision for provincial autonomy was hedged by many limitations. In the area of legislation, it was provided that the provincial legislature was competent to legislate on subjects drawn from both the provincial and the concurrent lists. But in case of any conflict between the central and provincial legislation regarding any subject of concurrent list, the former would prevail over the latter. At the same time, it was also provided in the Act that in case the Province had enacted a law in respect of a subject from the concurrent list with the prior consent of the Governor General, in that case the law made by the Province would prevail over the central legislation. On the other hand, it was also provided that if any legislation is enacted by the central legislature with the prior consent of the Governor General on any subject from the concurrent list, in that case the central law would prevail over the provincial legislation. Similarly, it was also provided that in case of conflict between the Centre and the Province, the final decision would rest either with the Federal Court or the Governor General. Moreover, in case of any emergency the central legislature enjoyed the power to enact laws on all subjects including those from the provincial list. Not only that, in many cases the prior consent of the Governor General was required even before introducing the Bill in the Provincial legislature.

The Act provided that the provincial government was free to act on all subjects on which the provincial legislature was competent to act. But the provincial government was to act in such a way that the legitimacy and acceptance of the central Government was enhanced. The Governor General could direct the provincial

Governor on any subject or could assign a special task to be performed by him. Moreover, the Governor General, could also direct the provincial Governor in respect all subject falling within his discretionary powers.

Apart from the above, even the pre-dominant position of the provincial Governor could adversely affect the extent and nature of provincial autonomy. In special circumstances, he was supposed to act as the agent of the central Government. In case of any constitutional crisis, the Governor could take over all the powers of the provincial government. Besides he also enjoyed the authority to act in his discretion on several subjects. He could withhold his consent to any Bill, send it back for reconsideration by the legislature, or could refer it to the Governor General for his consent. In a word, the pre-eminent position of the Governor in the provincial scheme of things put a great limitation on the provincial autonomy.

Under the Act of 1935, every province was to have a Council of Ministers. The Ministers were to be appointed by the Governor as per the provisions of the Act. However, in actual practice, only those who enjoyed the confidence of the provincial legislature could be appointed as Ministers. The Governor would administer oath to the leader of the largest party of the House who would be the Prime Minister. The other Ministers were to be appointed with his consent and consultation. They could continue to be in office for five years, provided they continued to enjoy the confidence of the House.

Provincial Autonomy at Work

Under the Act of 1935, elections were held in the early part of July 1937. Congress achieved majority of seats in Madras, Bihar, U.P., Orissa, Bombay and emerged as the largest party in Bengal, Assam and North West Frontier Province. Only in Punjab and Sindh its position was weak in terms of legislative seats. Congress wanted to be assured by the provincial Governors that they would not interfere in the working of the provincial government. It made it a condition for the formation of the government in the provinces. Ultimately, such an assurance came, and the Congress formed the government in six provinces it had won the majority seats.

Subsequently, the Congress led governments were installed even in Assam and the North West Frontier province. Jinnah and Muslim League tried to form a coalition Government with the Congress both in Bombay and U.P. But for various reasons the move failed. Enraged, Jinnah started playing the communal card after 1937, which ultimately led to the partition of the country. Subsequently, there were many tussels between the Governor and the Council of Ministers, particularly on the issue of the release of political prisoners. But ultimately the problem was solved. In the Congress ruled provinces, the provincial autonomy worked well. The government did good work in respect of prohibition, revenue laws, peasants rights, minimum wages for the working class and in many other areas. But in September 1939, the world was plunged into the Second World War. India was made a party to the War without any consultation with the nationalist leaders/organisations. The Congress asked the government to give specific assurance in respect of Indian freedom and also immediate installation of the responsible government. But the government refused to give any such assurance. Hence, in October 1937, the Congress governments resigned. Thus, this phase of provincial autonomy and responsible government came to an end.

We find that the provincial autonomy suffered from many limitations both from the overpowering position of the central Government and even that of the Provincial Governor. However, it did yield some positive results. One, it became absolutely clear that the Indian leadership was competent enough to run the government in an efficient and effective manner. The provincial Government put up good record. It also brought the Indian leadership closer to the people of India as it took several initiatives in different fields which relieved the people of their sufferings. The people were further drawn to the national movement which was amply demonstrated during the Quit India Movement by their massive participation.

13 *The Nature and Structure of the Indian Society: Different Stages of Colonial Enquiry*

So long as a regime of caste persists, it is difficult to see how the sentiment of unity and solidarity can perpetuate all classes of the community.

H.H. Risley

We have already seen that with the victories at Plassey and Buxar and acquisition of the Diwani rights, a new chapter was opened in the life, of the East India Company. As Tagore had observed that the Company got a sceptre in one hand and a weighing machine in the other and the latter could be turned and twisted in favour of the Company by using the former. History is a witness to the fact that through trade and commerce, as well as by clever political and strategic moves, it was fully successful in acquiring political power in India.

The Company was clever enough to understand that an adequate knowledge of India's culture, religion, history, language, social structure was necessary to keep India under its thumb. It was all the more necessary as the ruled (Indian) people were entirely different from their rulers (the British) in terms of culture, religion and history. It is true that the British did have some experience of imperial possession in respect of America and Ireland. But there was literally a sea of difference between those societies and the Indian society. For instance, the people of Ireland except that they were adherents of Catholicism, were quite akin to the British in terms of race and culture. On the other hand, the aboriginals of

America and other Carribean regions were not culturally as developed as the people of India. They could be easily driven out and their land could be captured. But India was an entirely different country. She was high on the scale of history, culture, religion, and history. It was nothing but a historically bizzare event that such a culturally developed country (India) had come under the tutelage of the British. Hence, it was quite clear to the British that they would have to acquire sufficient knowledge about the different aspects of the life of the Indian people for sheer permanency and stability of their rule in India. Let us clearly understand that acquiring such a knowledge was not out of their intellectual inquisitiveness, rather it was the need for the very stability of the rule. As the Company Raj started expanding, so started changing the need and method of acquiring these informations about India. In this chapter, we would delve into the evolution of the British changing colonial policy on this score. Primarily, there were three distinct phases – the age of the Orientalists, the age of the Reformists and Christian missionaries and last but not the least, the age of the policy of 'divide and rule'. In the following pages, we would be taking readers through all the above mentioned three phases of the British colonial policy.

The Orientalists and Their Thinking

By the Orientalist School, we refer to a galaxy of scholars who had deep interest in the history, culture and religion of the Indian people. They pinned their faith in the ancient books and scriptures of India as they looked upon them as the main source of Indian culture and civilization. They also believed in the golden period of the ancient Indian history. However, they did not concern themselves with the basic question as to what extent those old social and cultural values were relevant in their times and the level of their acceptance by the Indian people in the prevailing situation. The interest in the Orientalism received a big boost with the publication of Edward Said's book *Orientalism* in 1978. Said argues that the Orientalist scholars of the eighteenth and the nineteenth century pursued their studies in respect of the Eastern countries, particularly the middle

East on wrong hypotheses and intellectual formulations. According to Said these scholars were working in the interest of the Western countries and even their understanding of the people of Asia was based on prejudices. They were primarily promoting the colonial and the imperialist interests of the West. There is no dearth of critics of Said's major hypotheses and that of his basic approach. Our purpose here is not to go into the details of that controversy. Here our primary focus is how these Orientalist scholars in the early days of the Company Raj pursued their ideas and thought and in the process, how did they influence colonial policy of the Company Raj.

To fully grasp the efforts of the Orientalists, we have to remember that despite the Company getting Diwani rights in 1765, it was still concentrating more on trade and commerce than on administration. In fact, even for the collection of revenues, it was banking on the employees of the Nawab as it did not yet have a detailed and authentic information about the people of India. In this area of work, the first name that occurs is that of Alexander Dow, who wrote *History of Hindustan* during the period of 1768. Actually this work was based on a Persian book called *Tehrika Ferojshahi*. Dow gave a detailed description of the culture and religion of the Hindus. It was mentioned in that book that four *Varnas* of Hindu society have been created out of the different parts of the body of Brahma – which had been specifically mentioned in the *Purush – Shukta* of *Rigveda*. Besides, that book also contained descriptions about, all Hindu *sanskars* – religious rituals from birth to death.

But the first major initiative on the part of the government was taken when in 1772 Warren Hastings became the Governor of Bengal. He fully understood the need for detailed information about the people of India in the very beginning of his rule. He was also convinced that the colonial administration would have to fully grasp the nuances of the code of law of ancient India. He was equally aware that the codes of law for Hindu and Muslims were bound to be different. Hence, they would have to be viewed and studied differently. Further, that the code of law for Hindus was to be discerned from their scriptures and the ancient books. Similarly for Muslims, Koran and Hadith would work as the main source-books. On the initiative of Lord Hastings, a code of law was developed for Hindus with the help of pandits and old scriptures of India. It was published in 1776 by N.B. Halhed titled *A Code of Gentoo laws*. The main purpose of this work was to understand the tradition, culture and social behaviour of Hindus. A similar code of law was developed for Muslims based on Koran and Hadith. Hastings made it clear that in respect of inheritance, social behaviour and contracts, these codes would work as the main reference book. However, an eminent historian like Metcalf is of the opinion that despite the existence of various communities in India, such an over emphasis and focus only on two communities of Hindus and Muslims actually complicated the matter in the subsequent years.

Looking back, one could easily see that during that period, serious attempt was being made to decode and understand the nature and structure of the Indian society. It was during the same period that William Jones, the primus among the Orientalists, translated *Manusmriti* in English and got it published. Not only that, he was instrumental in founding an organization called Asiatic Society in 1784 in Calcutta. He also started an academic journal called the *Asiatic Researches* under the auspices of the same society. That journal became a chief medium for the publication of serious research work. Another major initiative in the same area came in the form of the establishment of Calcutta, Madrasa in 1781 and Benaras Sanskrit College in 1794.

Instead of going into further details, let us try to understand one basic question: How did these academic efforts of the Orientalists impact the colonial policy of the Company and with what results? It is interesting to note that during those days there was widespread impression among a section of the European scholars that there had been a long tradition of the 'Oriental Despotism' in the Eastern countries. The credit must go to the Orientalist scholars for removing such misunderstanding, as their work made it absolutely clear that there had never been such tradition in India. Rather through their studies it became clear that there had been rather a long tradition of the rule of law in the Indian context.

However, the major weakness of the Orientalists was that they were not interested in taking into consideration the deterioration in the old Indian cultural tradition, which is a natural process in the course of historical developments. Perhaps, they were not even concerned about it. Their thinking was that instead of directly confronting these issues, it would be much better if the problem could be tackled by introducing these codes in the judicial system. It is believed that William Jones had told Lord Cornwallis that, that was the best course open for the Company Raj. And even Halhed as early as in 1776 had made it clear that such a course of action was the best way for the imperialist rule in India. Metcalf, an eminent historian, believes that the basic flaw in the Orientalist way of looking at the Indian situation was that they had refused to consider and analyse the Indian historical developments that took place after the ancient India. Thus, they did not attach much importance to the historical experiences of the Indian people.

Another area in which the Orientalist scholars made significant contribution was their attempt to link up the history of India with that of Europe. They lay great emphasis on the common sources of the people of India with those of Europe. They even found a parallel between the Greek and Roman Gods with those of India. Besides, they also underlined the fact that Sanskrit was much closer to the European languages like Latin and Greek. William Jones was very much appreciative of culture, poetry, philosophy and religion of India. However, many scholars also believed that the Orientalists were not oblivious of the interests of the colonial rule. For they did not raise any big question mark against the European culture, civilisation and their epistemology and ontology. Nor did they pay much attention to the accumulated distortions and degenerations which had gathered in the process of the Indian historical developments.

Yet another area in which the Orientalists made significant contributions was in respect of the colonial understanding of the caste system in India. William Jones translated *Manusmriti* in 1784 – a religious text containing legal and social code for different castes. That text greatly impacted the colonial policy in the earlier stage of the Company Raj. *Manusmriti* supported *chaturvarna vyavastha* (four fold division of the society) and also *Varnashram dharma*. In this system the Brahmins occupied the top position on the social ladder and the Shudras were at the bottom–*Kshatriya* and *Vaishyas* occupying the second and the third position respectively. In the initial years of the colonial rule, the administrators believed that if the traditional code of law did not go against the colonial rule and those of social good, it should be adhered to. As such, no deliberate attempt should be made to discard and violate these religion sanctioned social code of law. Such an understanding led to a widespread acceptance of Brahminic tradition. Niccholus B. Dirks in his book *Castes in Mind: Colonialism and the Making of Modern India* is firmly of the opinion that the modern form and use of castes in India has a direct relationship with the colonial rule. He even blames the colonial policy for the presently prevailing caste based identity politics. He also underlines the fact that the present understanding of Hindu *dharma* and caste system has a lot to do with the Orientalist scholarly work which greatly impacted the earlier colonial policy.

Such an Orientalist understanding even inspired a number of colonial administrators to collect and collate a huge amount of research materials in respect of the Indian society and culture. For example, Thomas Munro in South India, Colin Mackenzie in central India, John Malcolm in Maharashtra and G. Duff in Rajasthan had collected valuable information pertaining to their respective areas. Based on their deep studies, they came to the conclusion that the colonial administration should not interfere much in the social and religious life of the people of India. Rather it should thrash out a policy in keeping with the traditions and social norms of the people. Though Max Muller came much after the Orientalists, but he virtually toed their line of thinking. He even wrote a paper on the caste system in India and 1857 rebellion. In that paper, he opined that the caste system should be viewed in the light of the provisions of the Indian scriptures. He did concede that the prevailing caste system is entirely different from one that prevailed in the Vedic age. But he made it clear that the Hindus should not be subjected to the use of force. Nor should there be a direct attack on their culture and faith.

In view of the above discussion, it could be safely concluded that the Orientalist school played a crucial role in the initial evolution of the colonial policy, which in turn gave stability and legitimacy to it. But it is equally true that the policy also strengthened the retrogressive forces of the Indian society.

Age of the Reformists: The Utilitarians and the Anglicists

Towards the end of the eighteenth century, the colonial policy went through a subtle but significant change. During the regime of Lord Cornwallis, the ideas like rule of law, institution of private property started being discussed in a meaningful way. Lord Cornwallis made a significant contribution in respect of the Permanent Settlement of Bengal. He also greatly expanded the powers and functions of the District judiciary. Subsequently, the colonial policy underwent even greater changes. Cornwallis policy of limited and impersonal rule was replaced by more active and personalised rule. Hence, the place which was earlier occupied by the District judge was taken over by the District Magistrate. He became a *Mai-Bap* in the eyes of the people. Some of the Company's new administrators like Thomas Munro, John Malcolm and Charles Metcalf became the ardent supporters of the new policy orientation. Their primary argument was that there had been a long tradition of personalised rule in India. Hence, the colonial policy must follow the same well-tried policy of personalised rule. The central role assigned to the District Magistrate symbolised such a paradigm shift in the colonial policy. The new policy also impacted the ways and means of acquiring information about the Indian society and culture. Now such informations were to be collected from the field, instead of scanning the scriptures. Francis Buchanan, Colins Mackenzie and Thomas Munro were the pioneers in this area. They did argue that the colonial policy should be based on the old tradition, but the tradition itself should be viewed in the light of the field experience rather than from scriptural point of view. They were of the opinion that rural India had an age-old tradition, which was hardly affected by the change of the government at the centre. Lord Cornwallis and Thomas Munro might have differed in respect of certain policy measures, but there was not much difference between their basic approach as both of them underlined the centrality of the Indian tradition.

But let us not forget that there was another school of thought in England which had entirely different perspectives on the Indian society. Their basic premise was that the Indian society was totally degenerated. In fact, it was in the grip of all kinds of social evils. Hence, it could be reformed and regenerated only by the governmental intervention. The Christian missionaries were in the forefront of such line of thinking. The most prominent name among them was that of Charles Grant. He was totally dedicated to the idea of spreading Christianity. He was also an employee of the Company. He prepared a report for the Chairman of the Board of Control for the Company in which he underlined the fact that the Indian society was corrupt and degenerated to the core. What was more, these people were also obstinate in their thinking and belief. His diagnosis for the Indian society was that the caste system was the chief villain of the piece. As this was based on religious belief; it was difficult to bring about any material change in the lives and thinking of the Indian people. The only viable way, he asserted, could be a joint effort by the government and the Christian missionaries. This line of thinking was further strengthened by a number of other Christian missionaries like William Carey and William Ward and others. Their primary emphasis was that the caste system would have to go lock, stock and barrel, if any meaningful regeneration of the Indian society was to take place. In fact, they were committed to the idea of spreading Christianity in India and they thought that the total destruction of the caste system was a prerequisite for such a venture.

However, one positive aspect of their thinking was that they were able to collect huge amount of material from the field. For instance, William Carey prepared a book on Bangla language, after interviewing a large number of people. Similarly, William Adams also collected huge amount of data on the traditional system of education in Bengal. Subsequently, Robert Caldwell did a similar work on South India, particularly in respect of Tamil grammar.

This tradition of delving into the empirical realities continued in the subsequent years. In this connection, the name of William Tennant is mentioned, who had collected a vast amount of material based on his in-depth interactions with the people. Thus by 1818, when the Marathas were badly beaten by the British, the colonial administration had collected detailed information on the different aspects of the Indian society. They had also come to the conclusion that all talks of cultural unity of India were imaginary, as there were vast differences and divergences in the different parts of the country.

At this stage, let us try to understand the basic difference between the perspective of the Christian missionaries with that of the Orientalists on the Indian society. The Orientalists were admirers of the Indian culture and religion, primarily based on Indian scriptures; though they did accept that the Indian society had fallen from that ancient golden age. They also thought that the ancient culture could be revived through introducing some of its codes in judicial courts and administration. On the other hand, the Christian missionaries were firmly of the opinion that the Indian society had always been of a degenerated nature–full of hypocrisy and double tongue. A scholar like Bernard S Cohn believed that such difference of perspective was linked up to the social background of these two groups. The Orientalists were from the higher strata of the British society, whereas the Christian missionaries were from lower social background.

However, this tradition of delving into the empirical realities of the Indian society did continue in the subsequent years. Based on these field studies the reformist idea started gathering momentum. In fact, even the British society was also going through an intellectual churning. Jeremy Bentham and Adam Smith were emerging new intellectual titans in the British society. They were impacting the mainstream thinking of the British society. Thus, by the time Lord William Bentinck came as Governor General of India in 1828, the colonial administration was developing a major reformist agenda for the Indian society. The basic idea behind such a reformist agenda was that human nature could be improved through legal and educational measures. He was also of the opinion that as a defeated people, Indians were not in a position to resist these reformist measures. The rank of these reformist group was joined by the Christian missionaries, supporters of free trade, educational reformers and the Utilitarians.

A big historical background was there behind these reformist programmes. In India, a group led by Raja Rammohun Roy and his Brahmo Samaj had emerged demanding socio-religious reforms in India. On the Company front, a number of prominent officials were spearheading these reforms. For instance, Charles Grant, a Christian missionary, James Mill, a prominent Utilitarian, and Macaulay, an educational reformer, were working for the Company at that point of time. All of them were committed to a reformist agenda for India. Hence, the old policy of non-interference in the Indian society was to be discarded, and a vigorous reformist agenda was to be pushed through. In fact, this new reformist age had been heralded by the publication of James Mill's book *The History of India* in 1818. Mill had presented a full picture of the degenerated Indian society. He even went to the extent of making a comment that Hindus were the most saleable people in the world. Hence, it was a sacred duty of the British to free them from such rotten tradition of culture and religion. He further argued that to that end, an effective and good government capable of enacting good laws was to be provided for the people of India. Only through all these measures, the people of India could be freed from Brahminic domination. His son John Stuart Mill further extended this line of thinking. But in certain respects, he differed from his father. According to him, educational programmes were to be more effective than mere legal remedies. He also favoured the idea of a representative government for the people of India. He believed that the real task of the British was to raise the Indian people on the scale of civilization. He was willing to hail the day when the Indians would be running their government based on the British pattern. There were other people who favoured reforms in different fields. Thus, reforms were carried both in educational field as well as in socio-religious ideas,

Educational Reforms

In the initial stages of the colonial rule, the policy of non-interference in the educational life of India was followed. However, by 1820 the voice for reforms in the educational field started gathering momentum. The demand for English education was raised from several quarters including from the urban elite of Bengal. Raja Rammohun Roy was its great supporter. Lord Macaulay and Lord William Bentinck were its great protagonists. There was a great debate between the Orientalists and the supporters of English education on the points of introduction of the Western education and English as the medium of instruction. By 1935 supporters of the English education had won the day. It was in 1935 that Western education and English as the medium of instruction was introduced. By 1845 a large number of the English medium schools had come up. With minor changes, the new system of education introduced by Macaulay continued till the end of the British rule.

Socio-religious Reforms

From the very beginning, the Christian missionaries were of the opinion that the only way to free the people of India from their outdated social system was to work for the spread of Christianity in India. But outside the Church there was not much support for that idea. There was another line of thinking that if and when English education was introduced, Christianity would automatically spread in its wake. A prominent name supporting such line of thinking was that of Travelin. When Macaulay and Bentinck opted for English education, they had implicitly accepted the Travelin line of thinking. They had rejected the Missionary idea of direct attack on the Hindu religion. Hence, they started with secular education in the schools. Bentinck's most notable reforms was the abolition of sati which was ardently supported by Raja Rammohun Roy.

His line of thinking was that all reforms which were not against the Hindu religion and were not against the human nature could be carried out. Lord Dalhousie took this line of thinking still further. In 1850 he got the law passed that all those who had converted to Christianity would be entitled to their ancestral property. He also provided for widow remarriage. His third important decision was to provide grants-in-aid for the missionary schools. When critical points were raised against his decision, he agreed that secular education would be provided even in these missionary schools. Besides, he also conceded that the schools run by the Indians would have the same facilities. Commenting on these measures undertaken by Bentinck and Dalhousie, Metcaff, a prominent historian, opines that these reforms were primarily meant to put an end to Hinduism. But the rebellion of 1857 changed the entire situation. It also led to a radical change in the colonial policy which we would be discussing in the next section.

1857 Rebellion and the Paradigm Shift in the Colonial Policy

The rebellion of 1857 greatly impacted the colonial policy. The scare of rebellion persisted for a long time and made the British to rethink and reorient their colonial policy in India. The British were confronted with several questions. How to ensure that such rebellion did not occur in future? How to deal with the different sections of the Indian society? How do we understand the feelings and frustrations of the Indian people in respect of our rule in general and any policy measure in particular? How all these queries and considerations are to be integrated in a new colonial policy? These were some of the questions which were being discussed in the wake of the 1857 rebellion inside the British Establishments. The most momentous decision taken by the British was to end the Company Raj and take India directly under the tutelage of the British Crown. Some of these concerns and assurances were reflected in the Royal proclamation of November 1858. Queen Victoria gave a solemn assurance to the people of India that in future there would be no interference in the culture and religion of the people of India. Besides, the Indian Princes were also assured that there would be no more takeover of their States. On the whole, the basic purpose of the Royal Proclamation was to assure the Indian people that no excesses would be committed against any section of the Indian society.

However, it remained an intriguing question for the British as to how the Indian people could launch a united struggle against them, crossing all the boundaries of caste, creed, religion and region. Consequently, they wanted to ensure that such eventuality did not occur again. Because the British were fully aware that in a case of any united assault by the Indian people, the colonial administration would not be able to withstand it. At the same time their success in suppressing the rebellion had also raised their level of self-confidence. They wanted to ensure that their rule was on a permanent basis. The subsequent colonial policy was guided by these two streams of colonial thinking. These considerations were reflected in their new policy in the various fields.

Reorganisation of the Army

The greatest worry of the British was the behaviour of the army during the 1857 rebellion. Hence, the first major task they undertook was the reorganisation of the Army. Based on the report of the Royal Commission for the reorganisation of the Army, a decision was taken that in Bengal the ratio of the European and the Indian forces would be 1 : 2, whereas in Bombay and Madras it could be 1 : 3. The ratio of the British forces was enhanced to rule out any kind of army rebellion in future. Thus, the Indian component of the army which had the strength of 2,38,000 in 1857, came down to 1,40,000 in 1863. But much more radical measures were taken to ensure internal composition of the different units of the army. Ample care was taken to ensure that no unit of the army was dominated by any single caste. Rather every unit must have a mixed character comprising different caste and religious groups. Another major decision was taken to bar the recruitment of people from certain areas and castes in the army. This was mostly done in respect of the Bengal Army comprising mostly from Awadh and Bhojpur areas and that too mostly from the Brahmin families, which had successfully revolted against the British. Simultaneously, it was decided that those sections of the Indian people who had helped the British to successfully suppress the rebellion, would be given preference in the army recruitment. In this category fell the people of Punjab and Nepal. They were declared as being of the martial races.

Ensuring the Support of the Indian Elite

The British were fully aware that they would not be able to rule over such a vast country like India, without the active support of the elite section of the Indian people. Hence, they tried to ensure the support of the Indian elites by making suitable changes in their policy stances. There was some restoration of rights to the Nawabs of Avadh areas. The other Princes were also being treated liberally. It was made clear that their adopted sons would enjoy all the rights of inheritance. The Princes were also assured that not only their dignity and rights would be ensured, but there would no more interference in their internal affairs.

The Indian Council Act of 1861

The 1857 rebellion had taught a hard lesson to the British that they must evolve an effective mechanism to feel the pulse of the people of India. To that end the Indian Council Act 1861 was enacted which provided that non-governmental members would be nominated for the Council membership. Through the nomination to the Council, the British wanted to ensure the support of the Indian elite for their rule. It is interesting to note that between 1862 and 1888 altogether 36 Indian were nominated for the Council's membership, out of which 23 were from the landed gentry and 6 were from the Princely India.

Census Policy and Its Impact on Indian Society

In the wake of the 1857 rebellion, the British initiated a policy of 'divide and rule' which continued till the end of their rule with various modifications. For such a policy of 'divide and rule', the Census policy turned out to be the most effective tool. It is true that some kind of Census was being carried out in different areas even before 1871. But 1871 was supposed to provide the base year for a comprehensive census recordings. It was also decided that while going through census, a comprehensive account of the Indian people must be recorded in terms of race, caste and religion. This was being done to stifle the feeling of emerging nationalism among the Indian people on the one hand, and to promote the feeling of separate identities among the different sections of our society on the other hand. To that end, arrangements were made to collect research material from the field on a large scale. The underlying motive of the British was that through such a census policy they would be able to promote the feelings of separateness particularly among the lower castes and minority religious groups. In this way, the upper caste Hindus, who were in the forefront of the emerging nationalist movement, would be isolated and weakened. Thus, arrangements were made to collect field data through district gazetteers, caste studies, studies on religious groups, so as to emphasise their separate identities. With focus on education, economic status, profession and their location in the ritual scale, there emerged a feeling of jealousy and competitiveness among the different sections of the Indian society, particularly among adivasis, backward classes and depressed classes. Thus, caste which was earlier an institution of social cooperation was being turned into that of competitiveness and separateness. In the census of 1871, a lot of data was collected in respect of different castes. The census of 1881 took it on a much higher level. The castes with larger population were being separately studied. In the census of 1891, a new perspective in respect of the study of the caste system was added: it started being viewed in terms of races of Arya and Anarya. The Census Commissioner made it clear that the feeling of nationalism would not grow in India as its inhabitants were from different castes, races, language groups and religions. It is interesting to note that the Census Commissioner was saying all this on the eve of 1891 census, when the Indian National Congress as an instrument of Indian nationalism had already been founded in 1885. This line was further pushed forward by Risley who worked as the Census Commissioner for the census of 1901. He was firmly of the opinion that by promoting religious and caste identities, the colonial rule could be put on a permanent basis. In 1907, Risley introduced a new element in the census: the ritual/

religious status of different castes started being recorded. Thus, different castes started competiting for higher ritual status. He also promoted the idea that in such a divided society there was always a lurking danger of anarchy and lawlessness. Hence, he advocated for a strong and even autocratic State. He also favoured political representation on community and religious basis. He was opposed to the principle of territorial representation. It was primarily because of him that separate electoral system was introduced in the Act of 1909. By 1911 some of the lower castes were put in the category of the depressed classes. An attempt was also made to arrange for their separate enumeration. The primary idea behind such an attempt was to reduce the strength of Hindus by separating the 'depressed classes' from the Hindu fold. It was also an attempt to create an unbridgeable gulf between caste Hindus and non-caste Hindus. But because of the stiff opposition from the nationalist leadership, ultimately such an attempt was abandoned. A similar attempt was made through Communal Award in 1932, which Mahatma Gandhi foiled by sitting on a fast unto death, which ultimately resulted in the Poona Pact.

Similar attempt was made in respect of different religious groups. The data collected about their education, caste, creed, food habit etc. helped in the consolidation of different religious groups. By identifying Hinduism with Brahminism an attempt was made to reduce the strength of the Hindus. Sikhs, Budhists, Jains were being enumerated separately since 1871. By the census of 1891, even Arya Samajies started being enumerated separately. The separate identity of the Indian Musalmans was underlined again and again which created bad blood between Hindus and Muslims. To promote such separateness, the provision for political representation was also used. This became very evident when under the Act of 1909 the system of a separate electorate was introduced. In fact, the census reports and constitutional reforms started supporting each other. Through census, separate identities were created and through constitutional reforms and politics of competitiveness, they were further strengthened. Thus, separatism was given an institutional form.

The above survey made it absolutely clear that the real purpose of the British behind collecting and collating all kinds of data and informations about the different sections of the Indian society was to seek and ensure the stability and permanence of the British rule. In the beginning when the Company Raj was weak and insecure, an attempt was made to collect data about the Indian society and culture from the ancient religious books and scriptures. A policy of non-interference was followed, so far the culture and religion of India was concerned. But in the subsequent years, when the Raj became more stable and reformist groups emerged in England, a policy of reform through State intervention into the Indian social life was followed. The ways and methods of understanding the Indian society also changed. Greater emphasis started being laid on the collection and collation of empirical data. After the rebellion of 1857, a new policy of 'divide and rule' became most pronounced. The breaking of the Indian unity by putting wedges among the different sections of our society became the primary aim of the British colonial policy. Separatism started being promoted by underlining caste and religious identities. Caste studies, district gazetteers and census enumeration became the major instruments of such policy. The politics of political representation also played a crucial role in this nefarious game of the British. The system of separate electorate was introduced for the different sections of our society. That may not have ensured the permanence of the British rule but it certainly led to the partition of the country.

If we look at the entire history of British colonial rule in India, we could easily dismiss their claim that their rule was meant to make the people of India more cultured and modernist. French colonialists called their colonial rule as a part of their civilising mission. Michael Mann is of the opinion that even though the British did not describe it as their 'civilising mission', but they hardly differed from the French in their claim. They claimed that they were working for raising the moral and material levels of the people of India, but in actual practice, their primary aim was to seek legitimacy and stability for their rule. To give legitimacy to their rule, at times, they claimed themselves as the successor to the Mughal Empire. But more often than not, they claimed legitimacy for their rule, on the basis of the progress and prosperity of the people of India. When their rule was weak and vulnerable, they underlined the fact that their rule would come to an end when the people of India would be civilised and modernised. But when their rule became more stabilized and secure they changed the track by saying that the people of India were incapable of being like them. Hence, there would be a need for benevolent but despotic rule. After the 1857 rebellion, when the Indian people put up a united fight, the British started promoting divisiveness and separatism in keeping with their general policy of divide and rule. Michael Mann raises a question, to what extent did the British succeed in their so called civilising mission in India? Perhaps according to their own understanding, they did not succeed, as the people of India would be never like them. But their rule brought in many kinds of distortions in the Indian society in its trails. The most devastating impact was that composite and united identity of the Indian people was broken off and their separate and divergent identities got promoted There could hardly be any doubt that real purpose of their occupation of India was to give legitimacy to their colonial rule. Their claim of making India a more civilised and modernized country was nothing more than their public claim, which could not be taken at its face value.

PART III

Indian Response to the British Challenge

Every nation secures precisely as good a government as it merits.

A.O. HUME

As the Bible say 'unto everyone that shall be given'. We must be strong in everyway ....So long as they (the British) look down upon us they can not fraternise with us. If we stand at their doors with palms over-stretched, we shall only be turned away, again and again.

RABINDRANATH TAGORE

Sons of Ind, why sit ye idle
Wait ye for some Deva's aid
Buckle to be up and doing
Nations by themselves are made.

POET UNKNOWN

14 Peasant and Tribal Rebellions During Colonial Period

Millions of peasants in India are struggling to live on half an acre. Their existence is a constant struggle with starvation, ending too often in defeat. Their difficulty is not to live human lives, .. but to live at all, and not do die.

W.S. LILLY

We have earlier seen that the foundation and consolidation of the British Raj had not gone unchallenged even in the initial period. Fierce resistance was offered both by different Princely States and even by the people in general in several parts of the country. Further consolidation of the Raj brought in its trail massive misery for the people of India in general and peasants and tribal groups in particular. Both handicraft industries and agriculture were ruined under the various ill-formulated policies of the Raj leading to the emergence of mass pauperization of the people. One of the ways in which the people of the country responded to the British challenge was through armed rebellion. Peasants and tribals were in the forefront of the armed resistance. These resistances were located in different areas and also in different times. We propose to study some of the major armed rebellions of peasants and tribals in this chapter. Ayodhya Singh has devoted an entire book *Bharat ka Mukti Sangram* to the study of a number of these rebellions. We propose to take up for our study only some of these major movements particularly those in which people's participation was massive. First of all, it would be in the fitness of things to underline some of the common causes for the eruption of these rebellions in different parts of the country. One of the major provocations for these rebellions came from the ruthless and autocratic administrative policy of the Raj. What gave added provocation was the faulty revenue policy and the introduction of a new policy making land a marketable commodity. Land revenue was being enhanced in geometrical progression and the system of its collection was becoming day by day more ruthless and autocratic. Peasants had to sell their land for paying the land revenue in cash. At the same time atrocities committed against peasants by landlords and zamindars were also becoming more or less a regular affair. The new judicial system based on legal quiblings further complicated the matter. More often than not, religious leaders worked as prime movers in these armed struggles. They organised and led the people against the foreign rule and local landlords. The members of the disbanded armies of the old *nawabs* also played their own role in these struggles. The cumulative impact of all these factors led to the eruption of these rebellions.

Peasant Rebellions

Peasants were one of the worst victims of the British Raj. Spiralling quantum of land revenue and the ruthless methods of its collection virtually broke the back of the Indian peasants. They rose in rebellion in several parts of the country. Some of them are being dealt with in the following pages.

Sanyasi-Faquir Rebellion

Sanyasi rebellion had engulfed parts of Bengal and Bihar during the period ranging from 1763 to 1800. The major groups involved in the process of that rebellion were ever impoverishing peasants and artisans, members of the disbanded armies of *nawabs* and that section of *sanyasis* who were engaged in agricultural work. Peasants provided the social base for the rebellion. Ex-armymen provided the leadership, and sanyasi and faquirs inspired and provided a religious fervour to the whole process of the struggle. They inspired these rebels to launch a fight to finish struggle. The leaders came both from Hindu and Islamic backgrounds. They attacked not only the offices of the Company Bahadur but also those of zamindars. The Company described them as looters and thugs. But they were challenging the Company with the support of the peasantry. They attacked the Dacca centre of the Company and raised the slogans of *Aum* and *Bande Mataram*. These rebels successfully captured the Company in Dacca and kept it under their control for some time. Similar attacks were launched against different centres viz. Patna, Hooghly, Cooch Bihar, Patna and Saran. Subsequently, North Bengal became the main centre of the rebellion. Majanu Shah was the main leader of this rebellion. He travelled from place to place both in Bihar and Bengal to inspire people to continue the struggle. But during December 1776 he was severely injured while leading the struggle from the front. Subsequently, he succumbed to his injuries. After his death, his brother Musa Shah took over the leadership and the rebellion continued for some time. But internal fissures appeared, which led to the weakening of the movement. The leadership went in the hands of Bhavani Pathak. But he was also killed while fighting. Stray incidents did continue for some time. But ultimately the rebellion was suppressed. Bankim Chandra Chattopadhyaya in his novel *Anandmath* had given a picturesque description of this rebellion and his song *Bande Mataram* continued to inspire the Indian freedom fighters in general and the Indian revolutionaries in particular for a long time during our freedom struggle.

Neel Rebellion (1859-67)

In the nineteenth century Bengal, peasants were cultivating indigo, but it was being processed and produced by the European Indigo planters and some of the local zamindars. These European indigo planters and local zamindars were committing all kinds of excesses and atrocities against the peasants engaged in indigo cultivation. The new Company Charter Act of 1933 made it easier for any and every Britisher to come and settle down in India with full freedom to own land. As a result, a number of Britishers bought zamindaries and settled down in India. During those days, production of indigo was a very lucrative business, as synthetic indigo was yet to be invented. These European indigo planters used to force the peasants to cultivate indigo for their use. Their modus operandi was that by making some advance payment to the indigo cultivators, they used to entere into an agreement with them. In the process, they had to sell their product at the minimum price. Subsequently, they forcibly made the cultivators to work for them and sell their production to them even at unrenumerative prices. Thus, whereas a peasant could have earned some profit by cultivating a piece of land with a crop of his choice, he was forced to grow indigo even when he could not receive even his cost of production. If he tried to resist, he was severely punished. Vishwnath Sardar was first to rise in rebellion against such atrocious practices. He was from Nadia district. In the first decade of the nineteenth century, he ignited rebellious fire among the indigo cultivators drawn from the different parts of Bengal. But ultimately he was caught by the police and hanged. Similar kinds of rebellions also occured in the Mymensingh district, in the third decade of the nineteenth century.

However, by 1858-60 the peasants really lost their patience. Excesses and atrocities committed against them went beyond all measures. Hence, anger erupted and took the form of an armed rebellion. In different parts, the people rose in rebellion. They started raiding the bungalows of the indigo planters. They started refusing to cultivate the indigo plants. The centre of rebellion was the village Govindpur of Nadia district. The peasants stopped cultivating indigo. When the indigo planters started sending their goons and *lathaits* to control the peasants, the latter started paying them in their own coins. Similar resistance spread in different parts of Bengal. According to the estimate of *Anand Bazar Patrika,* 50 lakhs peasants participated in such resistance. A situation of widespread anarchy prevailed in the villages. Thus, the government was forced to set up an Indigo Commission in March 1860. It submitted its report in August 1860.

Meanwhile the peasants launched a No Tax campign. They stopped paying rent to indigo planters and zamindars. Ultimately, peasants won the battle and forcible cultivation of indigo by peasants was stopped for good. In their struggles, the peasants got the support of a number of Bengali intellectuals. One of them was Deenbandhu Mitra, who wrote a drama called *Neel Darpan* which vividly depicted the plight of indigo-cultivating peasants. Even some Christian missionaries lent their support to the peasants. But the unity of the peasants and their determination to fight to finish turned out to be their greatest strength. *Neel* rebellion continues to occupy a distinct place in the annals of history of the peasant movements in India.

Pabna's Peasant Rebellion (1872-73)

Pabna Rebellion has a historic place in the history of the peasant's revolt in India. As per the section 10 of the 1859 declaration the peasants had been given occupancy right over the lands they have been cultivating for a long time. But zamindars were employing all kinds of tricks and instrumentalities to prevent the peasants from exercising their rights. Apart from dispossessing the peasants from lands, they were harassing them in several other ways.

At times, they would take away their cattle or they would lodge false court cases against them. All this made the peasants to lose their proverbial patience. Yusufshahi paragana was the main centre of the Pabna rebellion. Earlier this area was under the purview of the local zamindars. But as the zamindars could not deposit the required amount of the rent to the government, so it was auctioned. Thus, the area came under the purview of the new zamindars who enhanced the land revenue in an excessive manner. Peasants were not in a position to pay the enhanced rent. Consequently, they were being subjected to several kinds of harassment by the zamindars. Apart from enhanced land revenues, other types of taxes were also being imposed on them. Besides, the actual area under peasant's occupation was also manipulated to extract extra revenue from them. The peasants went to the court for the redressal of their grievances. Such a bold initiative on the part of the peasants virtually enraged the zamindars. One of the peasant leaders was kidnapped by the zamindar's henchmen. Peasants started resisting such sinister moves of the zamindars.

The peasants of Yusufshahi paragana founded peasant's organization in 1870. Their leaders went from village to village to enlist support for their cause and organisation. In the process, they also launched a No Tax campaign. Besides, they also lodged several court cases against the zamindars. The movement spread to other areas also. Peasants also started resisting armed attempts on the part of the zamindars to subdue the peasants. Several armed confrontation did take place which also led to several court cases launched against the peasants. In some of these court cases, the peasants also suffered imprisonment. But the peasants were determined to resist these atrocities at every level. What was more, peasants belonging to both Hindu and Muslim communities were united on this score. Initially, the government also supported the zamindars. But in the face of the relentless struggle on the part of the peasants, the government relented subsequently. As a result, the government was forced to make a solemn declaration in July 1872 that no one be allowed to indulge in any illegal work. Zamindars had to take back their decision for the enhanced rent. Thus, the primary cause of this revolt was ultimately settled. In this struggle, a number of Bengali intellectuals like Surendranath Banerjee, Dwarakanath Ganguli, Ananda Mohan Bose and others had extended their unstinted support to the peasants cause.

This rebellion led to a new Bengal Tenancy Act of 1885 which provided that a peasant's family cultivating a piece of land for 12 years or more would be entitled to have ownership right over it. It was a matter of great relief for the peasants. In all these peasants resistance movements, one could see a persistent common pattern and a lot of common ground. All these struggles were a reaction to excesses and atrocities committed by the zamindars and the officers of the Company. All these were localised movements as the problems faced by them were of localised nature. They could not be taken as organised movements launched at all India level to get rid of the Company Raj. There was another common factor in all these movements: they were mostly spontaneous in nature. They took an organisational form in the course of the movement and even their leadership was of a local nature. But all these movements made it clear that there was a limit to which the people could suffer. And once that limit is crossed, the people are bound to revolt. Through their resistance, the people forced the government to take effective steps for the redressal of their grievances. In a word, these movements made their own contributions towards the emergence of the rule of law in our country.

Tribal Rebellion

The tribal people of India were one of the worst victims of the colonial rule. For millenia they had led an isolated life from other groups. Over the ages they had evolved a lifestyle which was in keeping with their natural environment. Forest lands were their mainstay. They were used to enjoying the bounties of Nature while keeping their environment clean and intact. They had also enjoyed their own system of governance without much of external influences. In a word, they were used to leading a peaceful life away from the humdrum and tension ridden modern life.

The colonial rule adversely impacted their lives. Tribal chieftains started being treated as zamindars and through them the colonial administration extracted excessive land revenue from them. Gradually, they were being deprived of their forest resources which they had enjoyed freely for millenia. Not only that, through colonial administration and their henchmen, outsiders in the form of money lenders also started penetrating among them. Gradually they also started losing their land and they were being turned into a landless labour class. The government, officials started committing all kinds of atrocities against them. In the process, even the tribal chieftains were made victims of the system. All these led a deep sense of resentment among the tribal people, which ultimately resulted in several rebellions on their part. In the following pages, we would be taking only a few major tribal rebellions for our study.

Santhal Rebellion (1855-56)

The Santhals are located in Rajmahal hills and adjoining areas, now a part of Jharkhand State. Earlier they had their own independent State in the Champa area. They had fully enjoyed their autonomy and a lifestyle free from outside interference. With the coming of the Company Raj, they had lost their autonomous existence. All kinds of interferences were entering into every walk of their lives. With the entry of the money lenders in their areas, their life started being miserable. The money lenders were being supported by the government officials including the police. By 1855-56 the situation became unbearable for them. After 1793 with Permanent Settlement of Bengal, zamindari system had been introduced in the area. A kind of slavery system got introduced as a part of debt recovery system. Money lenders used to enter into an agreement with them through which the Santhals became bonded labour for generations. Once a Santhal family was snared into a money lenders net, it was almost impossible for him to free himself for generations. Not only that, even their women folk were being subjected to all kinds of sexual harassment. Even when a Santhal approached a law court, he could hardly get any relief. All this exasperated the Santhals and they had no other option except to revolt against such an oppressive system. There was also a long tradition of rebellion among the Santhal community which also inspired them for a big rebellion in 1855. On 30 June 1855, a big gathering of the Santhals took place in the Bhagnadih village of Santhal paragana. The Santhals from nearly 400 villages participated in that meeting. They took a solemn pledge that they would launch an armed rebellion against the Company Raj and also against all outsiders. They were fully convinced that through armed rebellion they would be able to establish a regime of religion and justice. In fact, they were hoping for the coming of the Satjug. The village Bhaganadih was the own village of Sidhu and Kano who were the real leaders of the movement. The government officials were told to leave the area within 15 days otherwise they would have to pay with their lives. It was also made clear that Santhals would have their own Raj. Thousands of Santhals armed with their traditional weapons launched the struggle. Zamindars, government officials and money lenders started being attacked. Police stations, railways and post offices, as being symbols of government authorities, were also under attack.

But the government soon took the counter measures. Martial law was imposed and army was given free hand to deal with the situation. In such a massive operation by the army 15 thousand Santhals lost their lives. A handsome prize was to be given to any one giving a clue for the capture of the leaders. In February 1956, Sidhu was captured and killed by the police. In similar manner Kano was also killed in the same year. Thus, the army was able to suppress the Santhal rebellion. A number of conspiracy cases were launched against the rebels and severe punishment was awarded to them. But one positive result of the rebellion was that Santhal *pargana* was soon recognised as a separate administrative unit. It goes without saying that Santhal rebellion occupies a unique place in the annals of resistance against the British.

Munda Rebellion (1899-1900)

Like Santhals another tribal group Munda, residing in Chhota Nagpur region also rose in rebellion during 1899-1900. Birsa was their leader. Hence, at times it is also described as Birsa-Munda rebellion. Munda were used to collective farming. But after coming of the British Raj, zamindars, money lenders and other outsiders started playing havoc with the lives of the Mundas. Their system of collective farming was totally destroyed. They started losing their land. That created a great sense of resentment among the Mundas. They started demanding that the land should be under their ownership and in no case under the zamindars. Mundas were also resenting against the spread of Christianity in the area. Many of the Mundas who had become Christians were not happy. They could see a lot of hypocrisy among the Christian missionaries. They were convinced that the spread of Christianity was also a part of the British stratagem to subdue the local people. All this convinced them that unless the British rule is done away with, there would be no relief for them. Hence, they wanted to replace the British Raj with Munda Raj.

Birsa, their leader, was born in 1874. He had been a Christian convert for a while. But soon he returned to his own creed. In 1895 Birsa declared himself as a messenger of God and Mundas started looking up to him as their liberator. Thousands of Mundas started reposing their faith in him. In a process, Birsa was turned into a political leader as well. On the eve of Christians in 1899, he gave a clarion call for Munda's rebellion. He made a declaration that the British Raj was going to be replaced by Munda Raj. He was convinced that *Satjug* is coming soon. Thousands of Mundas joined his armed movement. They attacked the government offices. The Army was called which ruthlessly suppressed the rebellion. Birsa also known as Birsa Bhagavan was captured during 1900 and died while being lodged in the Jail.

Bhil Rebellion (1818-1831)

Bhils constitute a tribal group who are located in the land between Vindhyachal in the North of the western ghats in the south. They had a prominent position in Khandesh province. Basically Bhils are agriculturists. They are located both in the hilly tracks as well as in the plains. After the coming of the British, all kinds of atrocities started being perpetrated against them. Money lenders and zamindars were indulging in all kinds of harassment against them. All this led to a feeling of strong resentment among the Bhils. After the defeat of the Marathas, Khandesh came under the purview of the British in 1818. They had a long tradition of rebellion. But after 1818 they had a confrontation with the British. But the British captured their leaders and some concessional measures were taken in their favour. But it did not mollify the common Bhils. They remained hostile to the British regime. In 1819 they attacked police stations and other centres of powers. But the government soon took counter military measures. But the rebellion could not be suppressed even with strong measures. They remained invincible. But the government became more oppressive and started handing over capital punishment to the leaders. One of the leaders Chil Nayak was hanged in 1820. But even that did not deter the Bhils. In 1821 one of the Bhil chieftain Dasarath organized a massive rebellion against the British. But the British succeeded in suppressing the rebellion. But in 1822 Bhils again challenged the British. There was a widespread anarchy in the area. But they could not withstand the strong counter measures by the government. In this way, the scattered and occasional revolts among the Bhils continued for sometime. But the climax was yet to come. In 1831 Bhils under the leadership of Uchet Singh laid their claim on the kingdom of Dhar. But the British again succeeded in pacifying the Bhils. Thus, the period between 1818-1831 saw many turbulent uprisings among the Bhils.

Apart from all these major rebellions, a number of other rebellions continued in different parts of the country on different occasions. Ayodhya Singh had presented a detailed study of hundreds of these rebellions in his book *Bharat Ka Mukti Sangram*. In view of the limitation of our space, we have referred to only a few of these major rebellions.

Indian historians have taken two diametrically opposite views while making an overall assessment of these rebellions. On the one hand, Bipan Chandra points out several limitations of these movements. According to him, their leadership lacked any comprehensive view on the political economy of colonialism. Besides, they also lacked ideological orientation. Nor did they have any socio-economic-political programmes. They did not try to rise above their age-old tradition. They did not have any concrete vision of an ideal society, nor any programme for the national liberation. Hence, the British succeeded in suppressing them at times through ruthless measures and at other times through sheer persuasion.

But a historian like Ranajit Guha holds an entirely different view about these movements. He believes that these were primarily political movements. Peasants political consciousness was raised through these movements. They could very well identify who were their friends and who were their enemies. And that is the first condition of any revolutionary movement. He further states that the leadership of these movements came from the victimised groups. Hence, they turned out to be very effective. Even religious sentiments helped them to gather widespread support for these movements. They virtually got charismatic leaders on all these counts.

We do not have to go into the details of these debates. For historians are trying to superimpose their own ideological perceptions on these movements. We believe, that such attempts do involve great injustice to these movements and their leadership.

They have to be viewed in their temporal-spatio context, and their contributions should be viewed in their context. These movements were an expression of human revulsion and revolt against all kinds of acts of injustice. They symbolized the deep human yearning and need for freedom and justice. Their contribution to human redemption should be judged on that count only.

15 The Great Rebellion of 1857

Therefore, it is incumbent on all to give up the hope of the continuation of the British sway, side with me . . . in promoting the common good, and thus attain their ends, otherwise if this golden opportunity slips away, they will have to repent their folly.

BAHADUR SHAH ZAFAR

The great rebellion of 1857 was the biggest armed revolt against the Company Raj, both in terms of territorial spread and the number of the people involved in it. It has also been one of the most controversial issues in the annals of our freedom struggle. Besides, it has generated a vast amount of literature full of fierce argumentation and counter-argumentation. Taking a synoptic view of the whole gamut of issues involved, one could easily identify a set of five questions which have been raised and dealt with by different scholars and historians in their own perspectives. These questions are:

1. What were the distant and proximate causes for the eruption of such an unprecedented rebellion?
2. What were the major highlights of the event and how they did they unfold ?
3. Why did it fail so abruptly?
4. Would it be correct to describe it as India's first war of independence or just a sepoy mutiny?
5. What were its impact on the subsequent developments in the country particularly on the colonial policy?

In this chapter, we propose to examine all these questions in a brief and precise way.

The Causes of the Rebellion

It goes without saying that there were both distant and proximate causes for the revolt of 1857. Let us first look at the distant causes. It needs to be mentioned that the period between the battle of Plassey (1757) and the great rebellion (1857) had been marked by a series of armed resistance both from the regional States as well as by the peasant and the tribal groups. Marathas, Sikhs, Jats, Santhals, Bhils and others were in the forefront of the struggle against the British. Similarly *nawabs* of Awadh, Bengal and Mysore had tried to resist the Company Raj to the best of their ability. However, the British succeeded in subduing all of them on account of various reasons including the vast resources at their disposal and a better organised and equiped armed forces. In other words, there was a strong and consistent tradition of armed resistance to the Raj much before the great rebellion erupted in 1857. Perhaps, the occupation of Awadh in 1856 turned out to be the last straw on the camel's back. It is not for nothing that the most severe resistance to the Company Raj came from the Awadh region.

Dalhousie's 'doctrine of the lapse' had added fuel to the fire. According to this doctrine, the adopted son of a Princely State was not entitled for the inheritance of the State. It was clear to the people that this was nothing less than clear ploy on the part of the Company Raj to grab and expand its hold over a vast swathe of the Indian territory. It was under such clever move that a number of States like Satara, Jhansi, Sambhalpur, Nagpur and a host of other States had been taken over and integrated into the Raj. Such an ever increasing greed of the British for territorial expansion had created the groundswell of resentment among the various sections of our society. It is not for nothing that the bulk of the leadership of the rebellion came from these dispossessed Princely States. Added to it was the ill treatment meted out to the seat of the Mughal throne located at Delhi. Bahadur Shah Zafar, the last Mughal Badshah, was nothing more than a symbolic ruler of Hindustan. The Company had stopped printing his name on its coins in 1835, and also refused to pay any *nazar* (tribute) to him after 1843. Such a humiliating status of their Emperor followed by the occupation of Awadh had greatly alienated the Muslim masses and psychologically prepared them for the revolt at the first available opportunity. It, needs to be further underlined that the Islamic revivalist movements in general and Wahabi movement in particular had generated a strong anti-British feeling among the Muslim populace. Wahabi movement had even established an all-India network and popularised the concept of jehad in the minds of the Muslim. Bhakt Khan, who took over the leadership of the rebel forces in Delhi, was an out and out a Wahabi. Not only that, as K.M. Asharaf in his paper, *Muslim Revivalists and the Revolt of 1857* has established that Wahabi played a very crucial role in the entire process of rebellion. In a word, Muslim's resentment arising, out of the loss of power and their ardent desire to re-establish a powerful, centralised State remained a major source of inspiration throughout the course of the rebellion. Prince Feroz Shah, the grandson of the Mughal Emperor, Farrukhsiyar, Maulavi Ahmadullah Shah, Sarfaraz Ali, Dr. Wazir Khan of Agra, Liaqat Ali of Allahabad and Maulavi Allaudin Khan of Hyderabad were important religious leaders behind the rebellion. Apart from Bahadur Shah Zafar, who became the main symbol of rebellion, political leadership was also provided by Khan Bahadur Khan of Rohilkhand, and Begam Hazrat Mahal of Lucknow, who led the rebellion from the front.

No less important was the role of the deteriorating economic condition of the people in preparing the background for the rebellion. As noted earlier, the British rule virtually ruined both Indian handicrafts industry as well as Indian agriculture by adopting different policy measures to protect and promote its own interests. Millions of artisans were rendered jobless and the army of landless labour swelled on an unprecedented scale. Famines and drought like situations had become regular visitors to the country. High incidence of land revenue and its forcible extractions had alienated virtually the entire peasantry. Besides, the deliberate attempt of the British to destroy the Indian handicrafts, to promote their own industrial products, had left millions of artisans unemployed. Even a section of zamindars were unhappy as they had lost their zamindari on account of the non-payment of their dues at appointed times. All these measures had led to the mass pauperization of our people resulting in general discontent against the British rule. This was more true of the land around Awadh and Bhojpur, which resulted in the massive participation of the people of these areas in the rebellion.

Another causal factor responsible for the rebellion was the fear of the people of losing their religion and caste distinctions in view of the socio-religious reforms being carried out by the Company Raj. Even the reforms like banning sati, legal sanction for widow re-marriage and similar other moves were seen as a sinister plan on the part of the government towards religious conversion. What gave greater credence to such fear was the freedom given to the Christian missionaries under the Company's renewed Charter of 1813. Christian missionaries appeared determined to get the entire populace of India converted to Christianity. A number of schools had been opened by them, which were being used for religious propagation. There were instances of similar attempts being made from the other platforms as well. Introduction of the English education system in 1835 by Maucalay was also taken, at least by more orthodox sections of our people, as a step towards the final goal of religious conversion. In subsequent years, the Christian converts were allowed to inherit their ancestral property. All these moves had created a fear psychosis among the people for religious conversion. Thus, the threat to their religion had prepared a strong ground for the kind of rebellion that erupted in 1857.

Changes in the organisational and disciplinary matters of the Army had also generated a latent but deep sense of resentment among the sepoys of the Bengal Army. We have to bear in mind that it was the Bengal Army which was the mainstay of the British rule. In fact, it was on the strength of the Bengal Army that the bulk of the Indian territory including Punjab had come under the British occupation. In the beginning of their rule, the British took a lot of care to give due deference to the caste and religious sensibility of the sepoys. It also needs to be underlined that the Bengal Army was primarily manned by the upper caste Hindus, mostly comprising Brahmins, Rajputs and Bhumihars of Awadh and Bhojpur regions. They were quite sensitive to their caste and religious identities. However, after 1840 an attempt was made to re-organise the army on more professional basis. On the other hand, these sepoys were convinced that but for their support, the British rule would not sustain for a long time. At the same time, they were not only low paid but they had hardly any opportunities of being promoted. They were also very resentful to the contemptuous arrogence of the officers of the British origins. Besides, they were also unhappy with the prevailing evangelical attitude in the high echelons of the army officials. What was more, the British occupation of Punjab in 1849 and Awadh in 1856 had deprived them of foreign allowances which they used to receive while being posted in these areas. All these factors contributed to a subterranean current of resentment among the sepoys of the Bengal Army. Besides, during 1856 it was made legally incumbent on the armymen not to refuse foreign postings – which patently violated the Hindu's religious view of not crossing the sea as it might pollute them Syed Ahmed Khan, who had spent twenty years in the Company's service listed a number of causes for the rebellion viz. faulty nature of the British cultural and agrarian polices, humiliation of the Princes and landlords at the hands of the British and insolence and contempt shown to the Indians by the British officials. He strongly pleaded for a consultative mechanism and for a constructive dialogue between the British and the Indian leadership. The real significance of Syed Ahmad's opinion was that he was loyalist of the British and yet he listed several of the infirmities and inadeguacies of their policy.

Precipitating Cause of the Rebellion

Immediate provocation for the rebellion was caused by the introduction of the new Lee Enfield rifle. There was a widespread rumour that the cartridges for these rifles were greased with a combination of beef and pig fat. The fact that the catridges had to be bitten off before loading gave credence to their suspicion. The news spread like wild fire. It enraged both the Hindu and Muslim sepoys. They were fully convinced that the Company Raj was making allout efforts to despoil their religion. The rumour had travelled to a large number of army cantonments, spread over different parts under Bengal Presidency. What was more, the government found the rumour to be true after making field investigations. It hastened to withdraw the said grease. But the damage had already been done. Sepoys had lost faith in the government and they were not willing to take it on its words. It was more than a communication gap between the government and the sepoys of the Bengal Army. It was a real crisis of confidence and trust.

The Course of the Rebellion

The first shot of the rebellion was fired by Mangal Pandey a sepoy of Bengal Army, posted at Barrackpur in Bengal. He not only refused to use these greased catridges, but also shot dead his Sargent Major – a military official of the British origin. He was arrested and hanged. The daring act of Mangal Pandey soon reached most of the cantonments. It created a strong reaction among the sepoys of the Merut cantonment. On 24 April 1857, eighty-five sepoys of Merut cantonmens refused to use hese catridges. On 10 May 1857 they were placed in iron chains and were awarded ten years imprisonment. That led to a much bigger rebellion at Merut cantonment. The rebellious sepoys killed their British officers and on 11 May they marched to Delhi – the seat of the Mughal Empire. On reaching Delhi, they persuaded and pressured Bahadur Shah Zafar, the last Mughal Emperor, to accept the leadership of the rebellion. He reluctantly accepted their offer. With the capture of Delhi, the rebellion spread in North-Western Province and in Awadh. The bulk of the British contingents were mostly posted either in Calcutta or in Punjab. Hence, rebellion did not face much resistance from the British forces in the initial stages. Bahadur Shah Zafar was proclaimed as the Emperor of Hindustan and he became the symbol of resistance to the British rule. A large number of sepoys stationed at Banaras, Allahabad, Bareilly, Jhansi, Danapur and Jagdishpur joined the rebellion. At certain places particularly in Awadh areas, local chieftains, zamindars and talukdars, persuaded by the rebellious sepoys, assumed leadership, as they had their own grievances against the Company Raj. In fact, in the wake of the British occupation of Awadh, most of the talukdars had been divested of their fiefs. Naturally, they were an unhappy lot. Another section comprising the Priencely States were also full of resentment. Thus Begum Hazrat Mahal of Lucknow, Kunwar Singh of Jagdishpur, Nana Saheb of Bithoor, Khan Bahadur Khan of Bareilly and Rani Lakshmi Bai of Jhansi soon started leading the rebellion from the front. They had joined the rebellion partly out of their own grievances against the Company and partly under the pressure and persuasion of the sepoys. However, South India, Punjab and the bulk of Bengal remained untouched by the rebellion. Intensity of the rebellion was mostly confined to Central India, Awadh, Bhojpur and North-Western Province.

However, in the north, particularly in Awadh and Bhojpur, Rohilkhand and Bundelkhand areas, it assumed the form of a popular revolt. In these areas the civilian population joined the rebellion in a big way. As we have seen earlier, the bulk of the Bengal Army comprised the sepoys of these areas. They had strong social and religious roots. Hence, popular mobilisation was quite easy for the rebellious sepoys as the people belonging to different sections of the society participated in it. But by the middle of 1858, the rebellion virtually collapsed. Kunwar Singh died in May 1858, Rani of Jhansi died fighting in June 1858, Nana Saheb along with a number of rebels fled to Nepal and Tantia Tope was captured and executed in April 1859. Thus by the beginning of the year 1859 the rebellion was ruthlessly suppressed by the British.

Reasons for its Failure

The reasons for the collapse of the rebellion were not far to seek. The most important reason for its sudden collapse, despite popular support, could be found in its uneven spread in the territorial terms of the country. It was mostly confined to the parts of North India and Central India. Large sections of India, including the elites of Punjab and Bengal refused to support it. A number of the Princely States stood by the British. South India remained aloof. Had there been a simultanecus spread of the rebellion all over the country, the British might not had been able to suppress it so soon and so successfully. The second reason lay in the nature and structure of the armed forces posited against each other. The rebels did not have a central or national command system. For a while, it appeared that the days of the Company Raj were numbered. However, the government soon took strong countermeasures and succeeded in suppressing the rebellion in a very short period. What helped was the fact that both Punjab and major parts of Bengal had remained untouched by the rebellion. Besides, there was a concentration of the British forces both in Punjab and Calcutta. Bengal Bhadralok, who had benifitted from the Company Raj and the Sikhs who had suffered at the hands of the Bengal Army in the Anglo-Sikh wars were for all practical purposes hostile to the rebellion. Sikhs were also apprehensive of the restoration of the Mughal Empire at whose hands their religious *gurus* had suffered immensely. By 20 September 1857 the British forces supported by Gorakhas and Sikhs succeeded in capturing Delhi. Bahadur Shah's children and grand children were captured and killed and he himself was deported to Burma where he died subsequently.

However, the fall of Delhi did not mark the end of the rebellion. It continued in the areas like Kanpur, Banaras, Allahabad, Lucknow, Bareilly and a host of other places. In most of these areas, it had assumed the form of a popular rebellion. But they were not fighting under a single command under the leadership of a single general. The rebel forces were fighting under different leaderships scattered in different areas. There was not much co-ordination and much less co-operation among them. They were facing the British Army which had a better command system, was more disciplined and had better weaponaries at its disposal. In view of the above, it was not surprising that the British, despite initial setbacks, did manage to suppress the rebellion, more so when they had followed a no-holds bar policy in letting loose their entire repressive machinary. Thousands of people including a large number of innocent people were either blown out of the cannons or hanged from the nearest trees and murdered in various ruthless ways. The will and determination of the British, to pay any price in terms of men and materials, to hold on to the their Indian Empire was also a major factor in their ultimate victory. The rebels also committed some strategic mistakes. Instead of concentrating on Delhi, if they could have captured Calcutta in the initial stages, the British rule could have hardly got a chance to survive. They could have prevented the arrival of more British forces from the sea route which certainly could have sealed the fate of the British. Since the various uprisings remained un-cordinated and under different leadership, the British forces were able to defeat them one by one. All said and done, it was more of a spontaneous rather than a well-planned rebellion. Perhaps only organised ideological group behind the rebellion was that of Wahabis who did contribute substantially to the cause of the rebellion.

The Character of the Rebellion

Once the rebellion was over, a fierce debate was initiated about its true nature and character. Even inside the British Establishment, two dominant and diametrically opposite views emerged regarding the nature of the rebellion. Participating in the Parliamentary debate as early as in 1857, Premier Palmerston described it as being nothing more than 'sepoy mutiny'. However, Disraeli, the opposition leader, characterised it as 'national revolt'. Subsequently, a number of the British scholars and even some of the army personnel toed the Parlmerston line. Some of the Indian nationalist leaders looked upon the rebellion as a part of our freedom struggle. However, even among the Indian scholars, there is no unanimity about the nature of the rebellion. Savarkar described it as India's first war of independence, as it was fought for the sake of Swaraj and Swadharma. However, even an eminent historian like R. C. Majumdar refused to take it as a 'national revolt'. According to him, the rebellion was confined to only a part of India and major parts of India's remained totally untouched by it. Besides, there was no sense of united nationalism behind the rebellion. Most of the rebels were fighting their own battle. Hence it could not be described as a popular rebellion. On the other hand, historians like S. N. Sen and S. B. Chaudhury looked upon it as the first major national united effort to challenge the alien rule. They also argue that there was a popular involvement in the rebellion. And therefore, there is nothing wrong in describing it as an integral part of our national struggle. The debate on the nature of the rebellion is still on. Those who do not accept it as a part of our national struggle, argue in the following manner:

1. There was nothing like the united national feeling during the period when the rebellion took place. Indian society was divided on caste, community, region and religion basis.
2. It was the support of a section of the Indian people to the British which led to the survival of the British Empire during the rebellion.
3. More than half of the territory of India was untouched by the rebellion.

On account of all these reasons, they argue that the rebellion of 1857 does not be deserve to described as a struggle for India's independence.

On the others hand, there are scholars who assert that the rebellion involved mass participation of the people and they were determined to throw out the British rule for good. Bahadur Shah Zafar, the last Mughal Emperor, became the symbol of such national resistance. Besides, there was a rare communal harmony between the Hindus and Muslims in the course of the rebellion. At many Muslim dominated places, a ban was imposed on cow slaughter to assuage the religious sensitivity of the Hindus. Thus the rebellion was nothing short of a national upsurge against the British rule. In fact, this has become a matter of an endless debate. But the general view among the Indian historians is that the rebellion should be viewed as a part of our national liberation movement, as both Hindus and Muslims fought shoulder to shoulder against the British rulers. Besides, there was a large involvement of people in the entire process and their ultimate goal was to throw out the British regime from the Indian soil. In this debate, historian Metcalf has added a new angle in his book, *The Aftermath of Revolt*. According to him, the rebellion of 1857 was more than a mere sepoy mutiny but less than a national revolt. A related question which is also under debate is: what was the ultimate goal of the rebels? There is also a wide divergence of views on this point. Some scholars believe that the restoration of the Mughal Empire was their final destination. And that is why they had declared Bahadur Shah Zafar as the Emperor of Hindustan (India). But there are other scholars who assert that they favoured a decentralised regional authority with the Mughal Emperor just a symbol of the central authority. On this point too, Metcalf asserts that had the rebels succeeded in their effort, they would have been at each others throats.

Impact of the Rebellion

The last question that the rebellion has raised is regarding its impact on the British colonial policy at large. The most concrete result of the rebellion was the end of both the Company Raj and the Mughal empire. The Crown took over the reign of India on 2 August 1958. Under the government of India Act passed by the British Parliament a new office of the Secretary of the State for India was created. The designation of the Governor-General was changed to that of 'Viceroy' who assumed the supreme authority in India as per the Proclamation made by Queen Victoria in November 1858. The Viceroy was to be advised by an Executive Council now comprising twelve members out of which six were to be non-official members. This was provided under the Indian Council Act of 1861 – which was passed to meet the rising demands of the Indians like Syed Ahmad Khan, who wanted a regular forum for consultation between the British and the Indian people. Another important change was in respect of the British attitude towards the Indian feudal elite. Queen Victoria's Proclamation made it clear that the rights, dignity, honour and titles of the Princes would henceforth be guaranteed. In practical terms, it meant that virtually one third of India's territory comprising more that 500 Princely States would remain under the indirect rule of the British. The Proclamation also promised steps towards the promotion of the peaceful industries and works of public utility and improvement. It was also made clear that henceforth, there would be no interference in the social religious and cultural life of the people of India. To assure the feudal elements, Awadh talukdars were invested with honours and titles. All these measures strengthened the feudal elements of the Indian society who were supposed to provide the support for the British rule.

A more important change took place in the British assessment about the nature and structure of the Indian society. To seek stability and permanence for the British rule, India started being looked upon as a conglomeration of caste, community, region and religion. Concrete steps also started being taken to promote all these divisive tendencies.

In the wake of the rebellion of 1857, serious attempts were made to lodge new wedges in the divisive nature of the Indian society. A change of fundamental nature was carried out in respect of the reorganisation and recruitment of the army. As the people of Hindi heartland along with the major elements of the Bengal Army had revolted, a new recruitment policy for the army was adopted. The new policy shifted the catchment areas for the recruitment for the army personnel from Hindi heartland to Punjab and adjoining areas. A new concept of martial races covering Sikhs, Rajputs, Jats, Dogras, Gorakhas and others was introduced and they were recruited on a mass scale. The people from the Awadh and Bhojpur, who had earlier comprised the bulk of the Bengal Army, were virtually left out. The strength of the British elements in the army was increased, so as to have better control over the native sepoys. The army units started being organised on mixed caste basis. The idea was to rule out any possibility of the united opposition to the British rule on the part of army. It is entirely a different thing that towards the end of the British rule (1946-47) there did emerge a distinct possibility of an army rebellion in the wake of the INA trial and the Royal Indian Navy revolt. Perhaps, that was also one of the factors which was responsible for the British decision to transfer power in the Indian hands.

A far more important impact of the rebellion was a new policy of 'divide and rule' which was also more specifically reflected in the census policy. Starting with the census enumeration of 1871, a lot of emphasis was laid on the collection of material in respect of different caste, community and religious groups. This policy was further intensified in the subsequent census recordings. A concerted attempt was made to promote separate identities among the different groups of our people. This was also being done to isolate the Hindu upper caste people, who had became the mainstay of our national movement. It led to the rivalry and animosities between Hindus and Muslims which ultimately led to the partition of the country. Besides such a divisive policy also led to the emergence of identity politics which has become a bane of our post-independent politics.

In sum, the rebellion of 1857 was a great dividing line in the history of our people. It not only led to the ending the Company Raj as well as the Mughal empire, but more importantly, it opened a new phase of the British rule which promoted politics of caste and religious identities creating a lot of problems for our people, including partition of the country. However, it needs to be underlined that the great rebellion of 1857 also became a major source of inspiration for our national struggle, including the need for the Hindu-Muslim unity.

16 Socio-Religious Reform Movements During Nineteenth Century

If God is good and gracious, why then do millions of people die for want of a few morsels of food?

Ishwar Chandra Vidyasagar

Apart from the armed resistance, India also offered a strong socio-cultural resistance to the British all through the nineteenth century. In fact, India has always tried to counter any serious trans-national cultural encounter in her own creative and innovative way. Historically, she has always attempted to imbibe and integrate the best elements from the other contesting parties, while retaining her own basic cultural moorings. Such a creative approach has endowed her with a unique resilience, which helps her to stick to her own basic culture without taking resort to revivalism. This is how India has been able to renew and revivify her tradition in changing times. When Mohammad Iqbal asked the question why India has always survived culturally, whereas the cultures of Rome, Greece and Egypt had been extinct in the course of historical developments. Perhaps it is this cultural resilience of India he had in mind. In sharp contrast to it, Indian social structure was marked by holism and hierarchy. Islam came to India with a message of universal brotherhood and monotheism. India responded in cultural terms through Bhakti movements which put up relentless battles against all kinds of caste hierachy by underlining the essential unity of all beings. The British occupation of India posed a far more serious cultural challenge, as it had come with a message of modernity and scientific innovations based on human ingenuity and rationality. India once again responded to the British challenge by attempting to put her social life in order, through a number of socio-cultural reform movements during the nineteenth century. It is these movements which constitute the subject matter of the present chapter.

For a proper understanding of these movements, it would be in the fitness of things to have a bird's-eye view of then prevailing situation. As stated earlier, initially the British had adopted an attitude of indifference to socio-cultural problems of India. Lord Warren Hastings backed by the Orientalist scholars like William Jones and others favoured such an approach to the Indian situation. It is true that even during those days a number of Christian missionaries were of the opinion that only through the spread of Christianity, the degenerataed Indian society could be put on the rails. However, there was not much support from the British Establishment to this line of thinking during those days. But those who pursued such an approach got a God send opportunity when the Company's Charter came for renewal in 1813. With a renewed Charter, a sum of one lakh was put at its disposal to be spent on the spread of scientific education in India. By that time the chorus for intervention in the Indian social order was joined by free traders, the Utilitarians, Anglicists and the Christian missionaries. They reached a decisive phase when William Bentinck came as the Governor General in 1828. He is known for two major decisions – abolition of sati in (1829) and the introduction of the English education with the support of Lord Macaulay. This trend continued till the outbreak of the 1857 mutiny, when a new orientation was given to the British policy which came to be known as divide and rule. But throughout this period the British continued to give a critical look to the Indian society, which the Indian elite could not but respond. They responded by launching a number of socio-religious reform movements to meet the situation in their own way.

The second set of factors which also provided a historical background to these movements was provided by the emergence of a new class of English educated Indian elite. They had to strike a balance between the two extremes of thought. One extreme was provided by the young Bengal movement and the others by the traditional Hindu orthodoxy. The main inspiration behind the young Bengal movement was the cult figure of Vivian Dorzia, who was a teacher in Hindu College, Calcutta. His students in their first flush of modernity were adopting the Western way of lifestyle including beef-eating in public. On the other extreme was the bulk of the traditional elite which was sticking to its old orthodox way. The new English educated elite had to walk cautiously to strike a balance between these two extremes. Some small steps were being taken to work out a balanced approach. For example, Calcutta Book Society was set up in 1819 to make available new literature to the people. Similarly, for translating European scientfic literature a society was set up in 1825. This was followed by another organisation called Society for Regulations of General Knowledge. Thus there was a general awareness among the new elite that some measures would have to be taken to meet the new challenge facing the Indian society. All this provided a background to these new socio-religious reform movements.

In the third place, the prevailing situation in the socio-cultural field of India also prompted the new elite to take some concrete measures to put their house in order. The Hindu society was full of ritualism. The spirit of real religion was missing and idolatry, and other social evils were the order of the day. The status of Shudras and woman had gone exceptionally low. Brahminism was ruling the roost and untouchability was prevailing in every walk of social life. Child marriage, forced widowhood, sati and other social evils were widely prevalent. The Indian elite was aware of all these problems, as the British were highlighting them at every available opportunity. In brief, all these factors provided the historical background for the emergence of the socio-religious reform movements of the nineteenth century.

For a better understanding of these movements, two general comments are called for at this stage. One, that these movements were more of social than religious in nature. In any case, they were not purely religious movements, as they were primarily concerned with the prevailing social evils like oppression of the Shudras, child marriage, sati and enforced widowhood. In fact, humanism was the the primary source of their inspiration. Hence, most of the leaders of these movements favoured State intervention for the eradication of these evils. For example, Raja Rammohun Roy sought State intervention for the abolition of sati. Even Vivekananda made it clear that he did not care much about what was provided in the scriptures. For him the real issue was the upliftment of the people by getting rid of all these prevailing social evils.

The second issue which these leaders were grappling with, was the challenge of modernity and scientific temper, which the West had brought in its trail. It is true that there were some points of differences among these leaders and their organisations about the real content and direction of these reforms. But there was a general agreement that our socio-cultural tradition would have to be brought into the tune with the modern times. They perceived the Western challenge at two levels. At one level, they could not have ignored the critical points made by the different sections of the critics, including the Christan missionaries and the Utilitarians. Even the entire British Establishment was backing these critics to the hilt. Besides, some of the empirical evidences were supportive of these critical points. Hence, it was incumbent upon these leaders to give a fresh look at our cultural heritage. They were aware that the British wanted to inject a deep sense of inferiority among our people on account of some of these weaknesses. They were also aware that the British were doing all this more for justifying their rule rather than out of genuine concern for our people. But these leaders were also convinced that in the course of historical development, some decay and degeneration had accumulated in our socio-religious life. Hence, they could not have taken recourse to revivalist line of thought. On the other hand, they were also aware of the soundness of the basic contours of our cultural tradition. Hence, they could not have joined hands with the British to reject our entire cultural heritage. That would have virtually amounted to throwing the baby with the bath water. Hence, they had to take a very nuanced and balanced stand. To that end, they adopted a two pronged strategy. They made a deep study of our cultural heritage and came out with the theory that our basic mooring are not against modernisation and scientific challenge. Hence, our people need not have any sense of inferiority on that count. In fact, our people should have a sense of self-confidence. They also pointed out that there was no contradiction between reason and revelation in our cultural heritage. Besides, it is also marked by a deep sense of universalism. They did admit that certain excrescences had gathered in the course of historical developments, which could be tackled by resorting to a reformist agenda. It was this basic approach which virtually marked all these reformist movements. With these general comments, let us give a brief look at some of these movements and their basic orientations.

Brahmo Samaj: Brahmo Samaj was founded by Raja Rammohun Roy. It was one of the oldest socio-religious reform movements in the early part of the nineteenth century. Roy was well versed in Arabic, Persian, Sanskrit, English and Bangla. He was well-read in Indian religious scriptures as well as those of Semitic religious tradition including Islam and Christianity. He was deeply concerned about the Indian state of affairs of his times, particularly in respect of women – their status as well as their other problems like sati, enforced widowhood, child marriage etc. He was greatly influenced by the Western idea. But he was willing to challenge the *pandits* as well as the Christian missionaries. He also favoured the introduction of English education in India. In 1815 he founded Atmiya Sabha to propagate some of his ideas. Towards the end of his life in 1828 he founded Brahmo Samaj. The Samaj was primarily committed to the propagation of his view of Hinduism purged of all social evils, including Brahminic ritualism and idol worship. Brahmo Samaj started a new tradition of reformed Hinduism which gathered momentum in subsequent years, inspiring a number of other reform movements. Roy's greatest achievements was efforts towards the abolition of sati. It was with Roy's support that William Bentinck was able to legally abolish sati in 1829.

After Roy's death in 1833, the leadership of the Samaj went in the hands of Devendranath Tagore, Vijay Krishna Goswami and Keshav Chandra Sen. Subsequently, fundamental difference of opinion emerged between Tagore and Sen. Tagore wanted to keep a live contact with the Hindu society, while Sen wanted to keep the organisation independent with a view to go whole hog for reforms. In 1867 there was a split in the Samaj and supporters of Tagore founded Adi Brahmo Samaj. This was followed by another split in 1878, which again resulted in the formation of Sadharan Brahmo Samaj. On account of internal schism and with emergence of other reform movements, Brahmo Samaj got weakened and came to be virtually confined among the Bhadrolok of Bengal.

Arya Samaj: Swami Dayanand (1824-1883) was the founder of Arya Samaj. A Gujarati Brahmin by birth, he turned out to be a great scholar of Vedic studies and wrote his own commentary on the Vedas. His interpretation of the Vedas gave a new vision of Hinduism, free from ritualism, superstitious belief and social evils. He was fully convinced that the Vedas are the real repository of all knowledge, both of secular and sacred nature. He was totally against the prevailing caste system which greatly discriminated against the Shudras. He was equally against the low status assigned to women in the existing social order. He supported the right of every one including women and Shudras for Vedic knowledge and other educational facilities. He launched a relentless battle against all kinds of superstious beliefs prevailing in the Hindu Society. He founded Arya Samaj in 1875 and wrote his classsic work *Satyarth Prakash*. He was also a great supporter of Hindi. After his death in 1883, there was a difference of opinion among the leaders of Arya Samaj. Mahatma Hans Raj and Lala Lajpat Rai favoured English education while the old system of a Gurukul was favoured by Swami Shraddhanand. Swami Shraddhanand founded Gurukul in Kankhel, Haridwar in 1902.

Arya Samaj made several seminal contributions in social, educational and cultural fields. One of its major contributions was the spread of militant nationalism. Arya Samaj played a crucial role in the freedom struggle. Some of its leaders made supreme sacrifices in the cause of the nation. Another contribution was the spread of education particularly among the lower strata of the society. It also tried to rid the Hindu society off the blind faith and put it on the path of scientific and rational thinking. Dayanand's criticism of other religions did create bad blood among the followers of different religions. But he was not a revivalist, despite his faith in the Vedas as the repository of all knowledge. He had a heavy reformist agenda for his vision of new Indian society.

Prarthana Samaj: Prarthana Samaj was founded in 1867 by Atmaram Pandurang, M.G. Ranade, R.G. Bhamdarkar, K.T. Telang and others. Prarthana Samaj was mostly active in Maharashtra. Earlier in Maharashtra region organizations like Manav Dharma (1844) and Paramhansa Mandali (1849) were active and they could be very well taken as the predecessors of the Prarthana Samaj. They were also opposed to the idol worship and Brahminic domination under the caste system. But they failed to get much of the popular support. They were mostly secret organisations and by 1860 they were virtually non-existent.

Prarthana Samaj was also concerned about the decline and degeneration of the Hindu society. It was also opposed to idol worship and caste system. It stood for spreadiing education among all classes of people including lower castes and women. It also favoured widow re-marriage. But there was a basic difference between the approach of Brahmo Samaj and the Prarthana Samaj. The leaders of the Prarthana Samaj wanted to reform the Hindu society as insiders whereas Brahmo Samaj was keen to maintain its separate entity. Subsequently, Ranade, one of the prominent leaders of the Prarthana Samaj, founded the Social Conference to work out his agenda of social reforms.

However, Tilak was opposed to the social reforms to be imposed by the alien government. That was the stand on which he opposed the age of the Consent Bill in 1891, which he tried to raise the marriageable age of the Hindus from 10 to 12. Ranade and Gokhle were supporters of the Bill. With the nationalist movement gathering momentum in the early parts of twentieth century, the organisations like Prarthana Samaj went into the background and virtually lost their sheen.

Ramakrishna Mission

Ramakrishna Mission was founded by Swami Vivekanada, an ardent disciple of Ramakrishna Paramahansa. The ideological foundation of the Mission was based on the thoughts of Ramakrishna Paramahansa. Ramakrishna was born in 1835, a period which was marked by a strong currernt of atheism and attack on Hinduism. Western culture and Western lifestyle were gathering popularity among the youth of Bengal. Those were the days of the young Bengal movements. There was a strong feeling going around that the country would have to reorientate its cultural scales according to the Western wind. True, the Brahmo Samaj was active, but it was not in a position to thwart the coming onlaught of the Western cultural juggernaut. Ramakrishana's life was full of spriritual awakening from the very beginning of his life. Though married, he never got caught in the snares of his worldly life. He was a devotee of Kali of Dakshineshwar. But a *triveni* of Gyan, Karma and Bhakti was freely flowing in his personality. He believed that service to His creation is real devotion and service to God. Another fundamental belief of his system was his faith in Sarva Dharma Sambhava. He himself realised God by practising and pursuing different religions paths.

Vivekananda was one of the most ardents disciples of Ramakrishna. He founded the Mission which shifted to Belur Math in 1897. He created a big impression while attending the World Parliament of religions in 1893, at Chicago, USA. He underlined the centrality of service to Daridranarayan He was responsible for spreading a feeling of strong nationalism among the people of India. He spread the message of Vedanta all over the world. Ramakrishna Mission has a unique place in the field of service to humanity.

Theosophical Society: Theosophical Society was founded by Madam H.P. Blavatsky, Colonel H.S. Olcott and others. Theosophists firmly believe that all religions are basically derived from one source. Hence, none of them could provide an exclusive road to human salvation. In fact, each of them had a distinct place and role in the great plan for human salvation. Further, they believe that all human beings carry a spec of divinity in them and, therefore, universal brotherhood is divinely sanctioned. They also have strong faith in the idea of life after death. They also have equally strong faith in the existence of divine wisdom. They also believe that it is through the human agency that divine plan for human salvation could be implemented. They had strong faith in all kinds of occultism. In India, Madam Annie Besant was primarily responsible for the spread of theosophical ideas. She came to India in 1893 and the headquarter of Theosophical Society was set up in Adyar, in Madras. She also plunged into the Indian freedom struggle and launched her own Home Rule Movement in 1916. She also occupied the position of the Congress president. She played a crucial role in spreading the basic principles of Hinduism all over the world.

Islamic Reformist Movement

It was during the same historical era that religious awakening started taking place among the Muslims. There were two types of Muslim religious awakenings: revivalist and reformist. Syed Ahmed Barelwi stood for puritanism and wanted to work for the revival of the original spirit of Islam. There were other religious leaders like Maulana Quadir of Delhi, Maulavi Karamat Ali of Jaunpur who mostly worked among the Muslim community of East Bengal. Chirag Ali of U.P. was another reformer who tried to reform the prevailing Islamic practices. He wanted to find a reconciliation between Western civilization and Islamic belief system. Another notable Islamic reformer was Ghulam Ahmad who started his movement in Gurdaspur district of Punjab in 1889. He was greatly influenced by the reformist movements of Hinduism and Western liberal ideas. He was all for religious tolerance and openly opposed to the idea of jehad against non-Muslims. In 1891 he claimed himself as the second Ahmad and also as the promised messiah under Islamic theology. Ahmadiyas had a bitter contest with the traditional Islam and are still being treated as falling beyond the purview of Islam. They have done good educational and social work.

Sir Syed Ahmad Khan and the Aligarh School

It was Sir Syed Ahmad Khan (1817-1898), who did the most effective work among the Muslim community. He was vehemently opposed to the system of Pir and Murid as it was being practised in India. He was also against slavery. He stood for the emanicipation of woman and favoured liberal interpretation of Koran.

But his most significant work was in the field of education. He favoured the spread of English education among the Muslim community. He worked incessantly for a new reconciliation between the Muslims and the Britishers. In 1875, he founded the Aligarh School which was turned into a Mohammedan Anglo Oriental College of Aligarth. Today it is known as the Aligarh Muslim University. He was opposed to the ideas of Indian National Congress and strongly pleaded with the Muslim community to keep away from it. In 1886 he set up the Anglo Mohammedan Educational Conference as a rival body to the Indian National Congress. He also preached against polygamy and fatalism quite widespread among the Muslim community. He died in 1898. Afterwards, Aligarh movement went in the hands of Ali brothers who headed Khilafat movements in subsequent years.

Critical Appreciation

Historians have raised a number of critical points against the socio-religious movements of the nineteenth century. One major critical point against them is that the ideas were greatly influenced by colonial thinking. In other words, they did not put up their agenda of reforms on their own. In fact, they were following what the British reformers were saying. For instance, one of the basic colonial thinking was that the religious scriptures had tremendous grip over the thought processes of the Indians. Hence, support for any socio-religious reform must be sought from religious scriptures. Our reformers taking a clue from the colonial thinking also sought support from religious scriptures for their reformist agenda. As Latamani has shown in her study that the colonial administration decided to ban sati only when they were convinced that there is no religious sanction for it.

Let us consider this line of thinking a little more closely. In our country, continuity (tradition) and change (modernity) have never been irreconciliably opposed to each other. This is what has been called modernity of tradition by some scholars. For example, seers of Upanishads brought the knowledge of the Vedas in tune with their own times. Buddha and Mahavira added new dimensions to the reformist agenda by attacking Brahminism and the caste system. Adi Sankarcharya brought about a new reconciliation between Buddhism and Hinduism so much so that he was called a Buddhist in disguise. Similarly, the poets and thinkers of Bhakti Movement brought about our cultural tradition in tune with their times in the face of the Islamic challenge. Hence, the socio-religious reform movement of the nineteenth century should be taken as a link in the great chain of our long tradition. Therefore, to find out their roots only in colonial thinking will do a great deal of injustice to them.

A second critical point is that the leaders of these movements looked up to the colonial administration and sought its support for their reformist agenda. It is true that they sought the support of the State for legal sanction for their reforms. But they primarily worked in the civil society in the attempt to raise the social consciousness of the people. In fact, they never rejected their own tradition nor did they dilute their national identity. Most of their ideas and items of reforms were derived from our own tradition. Hence, it would be unfair to them if they are to be blamed for seeking support from the State for legal sanction.

A third point that has been raised is that their work could not be described as constituting an era of Indian rennaissance. However, historians are divided on this point. A section of the scholars are not inclined to accept the period of these movements as an era of Indian renaissance. Their primary argument is that these movements did not have much of direct link with the common masses of India. They were mostly confined among the elite section of our society. Besides, they did not lay down any great school of philosophical thoughts. Hence, they stood nowhere in comparision with the European rennaissance. But another section of the Indian scholars find no fault with the idea of these movement constituting an era of Indian rennaissance. They argue that these movements virtually laid the foundation of modern India. To that end, they made deep studies of the ancient Indian tradition and tried to bring its basic tenets in tune with their times. They were not revivalists, rather they were modernisers and pro-changers. Not only that, their work resulted in new tradition in many areas of art and culture including music, painting, dancing and various kinds of literary works. Hence, there is nothing wrong in accepting that period as an era of Indian rennaissance.

It goes without saying that they did release strong currents of nationalism in India. Vivekananda, Dayanand and others inspired many generations of freedom fighters. Secondly, they infused a new sense of self-confidence among our people without which nationalism could not have grown in our country. Thirdly, they also laid out a path of socio-cultural salvation of our people. By any standard, these were not small achievements for the leaders of these movements.

17 Gender Issues in Nineteenth Century Colonial Era

Therefore, I charge you, restore to your women their ancients rights. ...Educate your women and the nation will take care of itself; for it is true today as it was yesterday, and will be to the end of human life. The hand that rocks the cradle is the power that rules the world.

Sarojini Naidu

The colonial rule went through several distinct phases so far the gender issues were concerned. In this chapter, an attempt would be made to take stock of the attitude and consequent action adopted by the colonial administration towards the gender issues during the nineteenth century. This period is important as some of the radical measures like the banning of sati, widow-remarriage and similar other measures were taken during this period. There is another reason why this period is important, so far as the gender issues are concerned. It was during the same period that socio-religious reformist movements were active and the gender issue was one of their major concerns. In the early part of the nineteenth century, at times the colonial administration and the reformist movements joined hands to tackle some of the social problems including those relating to the Indian women. This period is important for another reason; towards the end of the nineteenth century, with the emergence of nationalism, surprisingly the gender issues were put on the back burner. Lastly, feminst scholars like Kumkum Sangari and Sudesh Vaid have come out with a new thesis that the measures taken both by the colonial administration and the reformist movement virtually strengthened the system of patriarchy.

For all these reasons, the gender issues during the nineteenth century India call for an investigation.

I

In the initial stages, the colonial rule tried to attempt an attitude of non-interference in the socio-religious life of the Indian people. During those days the colonial rule was so fragile and insecure that a discreet policy of non-interference appeared to be the better part of the valour. For example, Warren Hastings, who was the Governor-General of India during 1772-1784, tried to pursue such a policy in a full-fledged form. He was firmly of the opinion that the colonial administration should be run on the basis of the codes provided in the ancient scriptures of the Hindus and the Muslims. Perhaps another reason of such a policy of non-interference was the non-availability of detailed information about Indian culture, society, language etc. This was a major handicap for the colonial administration more so as there was a huge cultural gap between the ruler (the Britishers) and the ruled (the Indian people). The policy of non-interference appeared to be the best option under such circumstances.

What strengthened the hands of Warren Hastings was the support to such policy given by the scholars of the Orientalist school. The Orientalists were deeply interested in the Indian culture and the ancient Indian history. They looked at the Indian scriptures as the primary source of Indian religion and culture. The first attempt in this areas was made by Alexandar Dow who wrote the *History of Hindustan* during 1768-71. Subsequently, *A Code of Gentoo* was penned by Halhed at the initiative of Warren Hastings. William Jones, perhaps the best representative of the Orientalist school, translated *Manusmriti* and set up the Asiatic Society in Calcutta during 1884. For a better understanding of Hindu and Muslim ways of life and thought, Banaras Sanskrit College was set up in 1794 and Calcutta Madarasa in 1781. It needs to be mentioned that the Orientatists were talking about the golden age of the ancient India. However, they did not specifically talk about the gender issue. It was H.T. Celebroke who made some specific reference to the gender issue. It was he who wrote a piece *On the Duties of the Faithful*

Hindu Widow in which he presented the textual position of sati. He also wrote a piece on the Vedas and made specific reference to Gargi and Matreyi. The real significance of the work of the Orientalists was that the Indian intelligentia felt that they were the inheritors of the great culture, though it was on the decline during their own times. Hence, they felt the need for its revitalization and revivification.

In the subsequent period, the policy of non-interference was replaced by that of a reformist agenda. Advocates of such a new policy comprised Anglicists, Utilitarians, Free traders and similar other groups. They were firmly of the opinion that the Indian society has been in a state of moral degeneration since time immemorial particularly in respect of women and shudras. Hence, they pleaded for State intervention both in socio-cultural life as well as in the education field. It was the thrust of such a policy which led to the abolition of sati and the introduction of English education during this period.

It is interesting to note that during the early part of the nineteenth century, the new policy of the colonial administration had all the support of a section of the Indian elite led by Raja Rammohun Roy, the founder of the Brahmo Samaj. It was with an open support of Roy that Lord Bentinck succeeded in abolishing the system of sati. Roy also supported the introduction of English education in India which he thought would have great modernising impact on the Indian society. Roy had also introduced a new argument for raising the status of women in the Indian society. He rejected the then prevailing social norm that the highest goal of women's life was to became a *pativrata*. He asserted that like Hindu men, her highest goal was to seek final salvation (*mukti*). This is so because in spiritual realm, woman is in no way inferior to man. He also used this argument while pleading for the abolution of sati system. In the subsequent period, the issue of raising the status of women in the Indian society became one of the major programmes of all the socio-religious reform movements like Prarthana Samaj, Arya Samaj, Ramakrishna Mission and others. An attempt was made to assert that the status of women was very high in ancient India. R.C. Dutt came out with the thesis that Vedic women were highly educated, chose their own life-partners and even went in for second marriage. Not only that, Bankim Chandra even asserted that women had played an activist role and fought shoulder to shoulder along with their men against their enemies. He illustrated it by delineating the life-pattern of Shanti – one of the main characters in his novel, *Anandmath*.

It needs to be mentoned that the coloinial administration was using the argument of the degenerated status of the Indian society to justify the British subjugation of Indian people and even their intervention in their socio-religious life. This was the true implication of Mill's *History of India* which tried to assert that moral degeneration particularly in respect of women, and shudras had been the hallmark of the Indian society since the ancient times. Hence, it was only through legal and educational intervention that the Indian society could be brought on the rails. Reacting to such assertion, early social reformers like Roy and Vidyasagar, while disageeing with such general condemmation of the Indian society, tried to take concrete measures in respect of sati, child marriage, widow remarriage.

II

In the field of women studies Kumkum Sangari and Sudesh Vaid have edited a book entitled *Recasting Women: Essays in Colonial History*. In a rather lengthy introduction to the book, they argue that all said and done, it was the age old institution of patriarchy which had been strengthened both by the working of colonial administration as well as by the socio-religious reform movements. In support of their main thesis they make a distinction between 'modernising movements' and 'democratising' movement. They argue that a 'modernising movement' could work for social improvement without fundmentally bridging the steep gap between two sexes – man and woman. At their best these movements could work for the betterment of the middle class women leaving behind the bulk of the women of dispossessed sections of the society. On the other hand, any democratising movement would primarily work for the betterment of the women of the dispossessed section; thus truly working for the basic change in respect of gender. According to them, the nineteenth century socio-religious reform movements really belonged to the modernising category. Hence, while apparently working for the modernisation of the Indian society, they inadvertently strengthened the institution of 'patriarchy'. In the similar vein, the colonial administration also strengthened the institution of patriarchy, particularly through land revenue settlements. One of the steps taken by the colonial administration was to grant individual ownership to the landholders which strenthened their position. It also resulted in impoverishment of the working class and their woman-folks as property rights were given to their men-folks of the landed class only. Replacing the power of the village Panchayat by the District Magistrate also weakened the position of women in the society.

These agrarian changes also affected the nature and structure of the working classes. Besides, such changes were also necessitated by recurrent famines, the decline of handicrafts production and emergence of modern industrial sector. As a result, women were pushed out of traditional village occupation. But they did not have much opportunities in the new industrial sector. Thus, they were pushed to the domestic sphere.

The middle classes, which emerged during this period comprising urban and professional trading classes, village literate classes, land holding classes actually built up the ideologies of Hindu/Indian womanhood. Subsequently, it is their movement which took the form of cultural nationalism. According to Sangari and Vaid the kind of identity of womanhood which the reformist and the nationalist leaders built up thoroughout the nineteenth century though opposed to the colonial view, did not strike at the root of the gender inequality. Besides, that identity of womanhood had a marked difference from that of the lower classes women.

III

In the book edited by Sangari and Vaid there is a major contribution of Partha Chatterjee. In his paper *The Nationalist Resolutions of the Women Question* Partha raises an important question as to why the gender issue was put on the back burner towards the end of the nineteenth century, the phase of the early nationalism. In other words, the vehemence with which the leaders of the Bengal renaissance like Raja Rammohun Roy, Ishwar Chandra Vidyasagar, Keshav Chandra Sen, Devendranath Tagore and others raised the women issues was missing from the discourse of the early nationalist leaders. Partha Chatterjee tries to unravel this historical riddle in his paper. He assests that these issues were not amicably settled earlier and yet early nationalists did not put them up high in their agenda. He also rejects Ghulam Murshid's argument that during early.and middle years of the nineteenth century, the women issue was raised and highlighted under the impact of the Western liberal ideas. But in the subsequent period, an attempt was made to highlight the glorious nature of the Indian culture and the high status of women in ancient India. Besides, the nationalist issue came to the forefront and gender issue was pushed in the background. Partha finds faults with Murshid's basic argument that early radicalism on the gender issue had its roots in the Western liberal value system. Sumit Sarkar has also rejected Murshid's formulation as according to him early renaissance leaders were not that radical as at times it is made out to be by scholars like Murshid. This is so because these leaders supported the Shastras and did not oppose patriarchal nature of the family system. In fact, they favoured symbolic rather than substantive social change. Thus, Sarkar argues that their attempts at reforms in respect of women were not totally inspired and derived from the acceptance of the liberal and the rationalist idea from the West. Rather they were results of finding solutions for their interpersonal relationship for surviving in a hostile world. Sarkar's main argument is that the fault lies with our concept of modernity itself. Sarkar's regards the social reform movements as being a failure. Hence, according to him the early nationalist leaders could not be taken as being retrogressive as scholars like Murshid tend to believe. Partha while ageeing with Sarkar's basic formulation is unwilling to accept that the problem of personal adjustment could provide the full explanation. Rather Partha believes that the nationalist leaders did try to tackle the gender issues within their own ideological perspective. He argues that the gender issues were not put on the back burner because it was overtaken by the nationalist issues.

Rather, the gender issues were not specially highlighted by the nationalist leaders, because they had solved them within their own ideological perspective. Partha's main argument is that the nationalist leaders solved the gender issues by separating the material aspect of life from the spiritual aspect. Their main contention was that the West was ahead of them in the material field, but India excelled them in spiritual field. It was such a separation which was primarily responsible for the women issues not being articulated by them in any conspicuous manner. Hence, their primary stand was that while the material aspects of life of the West needs to be cultivated, but equally important was retaining the spititual essence of our cultural life. Thus, they opted for the selective appropriation of the Western modernity. Hence, they could not have gone whole hog in embracing the Western liberal ideas, as they were determined to retain the spiritual essence of the Indian culture. Thus, debate about material and spiritual side of life led to dividing its 'outer' and 'inner' aspects. Compromises, would have to be made in the outer side of life, but the inner side, the (*ghar*), must remain protected. Outside world (*Bahir*) represents material side, inner side (*ghar*) is the repository of spiritual values. Men had to interact in the outer world, which did involve all kinds of compromises. But women hold the fortress of home protecting its spiritual values. According to Partha the nationalist looked at the whole issue in this way: the West must be challenged in the material field by imbibing their values, but it should not be allowed to enter into our spiritual world represented by our home. As such, the role of woman became exceptionelly important as she symbolises the inner world, where Indians stand head and shoulder over the West. As Partha observes:

The nationalist paradigm in fact supplied an ideological principle of selection: It was not dismissal of modernity; the attempt was rather to make modernity consistent with the nationalist project.

IV

According to Sangari and Vaid, even the so-called progressive social regulation turned out to be counter productive. For instance, the

Regulations of 1812 introduced in the Bengal Presidency was meant to curb the widows immolation. However, the regulations had provided for 'legal' and illegal category based on voluntary or coercive immolation. Thus immolation was taken to have some kind of the government approval. Hence, it failed to prevent sati in any significant manner. Even after the abolition of sati in 1829, a category of voluntary sati was re-introduced in the subsequent period. Or take the example of the widow remarriage act of 1856. Some of the provisions of the Act debarred widows after remarriage from inheriting her share in her husband's property. Besides, she had also to give up her claim over her children. Hence, only a few women could opt for remarriage in the light of all these limitations. Similarly, women were denied employment in coal mines on the ground that it was hazardous to their health. But no better opportunities for work were offered to them. Hence, they had to fend for themselves by taking up petty employment elsewhere.

On all these grounds, these writers make a fervent plea of tackling the issue of patriarchy. They conclude by saying, that these anti-woman practices are not feudal remnants which would vanish in time. Rather they are the products of sustained reformulation of the concept of patriachy.

Emphasising the exclusion of large sections of women, particularly of the lower classes, who were hardly covered by Matreyi-Gargi, Sita-Savitri syndrome, Uma Chakravarti observes:

"Vast sections of women did not exist for the nineteenth century nationalists. No one tried to read the text what rights the Vedic Dasi and others like her had in the Vedic golden age. Recognising her existence would have been an embarrassment to the nationalists. The twentieth century had continued to reproduce in all essentials the same kind of womanhood that the nineteenth century had so carefully and so successfully constructed as an enduring legacy for us".

V

In subsequent years particularly in the Gandhian era, women came to the freedom struggle in a big way. They played an exceptionally active role during the salt satyagraha and the civil disobedience movement. Earlier they had also participated in the Swadeshi Movement and even in the revolutionary movements. A large number of women left the cosy corners of their homes and participated in the national movement. They made sacrifices and underwent all kinds of sufferings. Kasturba Gandhi, Mani Behan Patel, Raj Kumari Amrit Kaur, Sarojini Naidu, Durgabai Deshmukh, Kamla Nehru, Vijayalakshmi Pandit, Swarup Rani and a host of other women led the national movement from the front. Thousands of others who suffered and sacrificed in the cause of the people remained unknown and unsung. During the Quit India Movement, Aruna Asaf Ali and Sucheta Kripalani virtually became household names. Earlier Annie Besant, Muthu Luxmi, Sarala Devi, Kalpana Joshi, to name just a few women, had made their own contributions towards the freedom of the country. It was the saintly personality of Mahatma Gandhi which brought thousands of women workers to the mainstream of the national movement.

VI

The points which Sangari and Vaid have raised in respect of the role of the socio-religious movement on gender issues need to be critically examined. Their primary grudge is that the age-old social institution of patriarchy was never challenged by them. In fact, it got strengthened by the kind of identity of womenhood that was projected by these movements. Their second critical point is that the kind of modernisation of social system that was sought by these movements remained confined to Bhadralok Mahila and did not touch the women lower strata. In other words, it benefitted only the middle class women folks.

A number of counter-points could be raised against their critical observations. First, it goes without saying that the nineteenth century movement led the foundation for women activism which was greatly reflected in the subsequent movements. They participated in the revolutionary movement as well as in the Gandhian movement. Besides, they also made their own contributions by quietly suffering, when their menfolks were in jails or they were running as fugitive revolutionaries. What is more, as sisters and mothers and even as comrades they remained the constant source of inspiration to their men who were fighting for Indian independence. One could hardly ignore the contributions of earlier women awakening which got intensified in the subsequent period. As Tilak once observed: The extremists of today will be the moderates of tomorrow, just as the moderates of today were the extremists of yesterday.

However, it must be said that the kind of issues which the feminists like Sangari and Vaid are raising were not there either on the agenda of the leaders of the Bengal rennaissance or that of the early nationalists. If the issue of the women liberation could not be put on the national agenda during those days, it would be unfair to blame those leaders. In the kind of socio-cultural milieus they were working, it was not possible for them to put it on the centre stage. Besides, they were fighting on several fronts and they had to present and fight for an overall agenda of social and national regeneration. Hence, they could not have taken up any sectional issues with the same vehemence with which today sectional leaders including the feminists are raising. Besides, it is also unfair to judge them on the basis of the issues which have become prominent only during recent decades and that too only on the agenda of the concerned group leaders. For example, the issues like the relative role of patriarchy and matriarchy are being raised only recently. They could not be transported to the age when they did nor exist. The nature of any social act would have to be judged in the light of the context that it was being undertaken. It has got to be context-specific and it should not be taken as being context-free. Hence an issue like patriarchy could not be taken as a measuring rod to pass judgement on the action or inaction of the leaders of the bygone era when they did not exist. For them, participation of women in public life was itself an act of liberation. These leaders did lay the foundation for woman-liberation on which the succeeding generations could weave a new agenda. It is a different matter that a lot remains to be done for the woman's causes even today.

18 Emergence of Indian Nationalism: The Historical Backdrop

The very discontent and impatience it (Congress) has evoked against itself as slow and non-progressive among the rising generation are among its best results or fruits. The real task is to evolve the required revolution whether it could be peaceful or violent, the character of the revolution will depend upon the wisdom or unwisdom of the British Government and action of the British people.

DADABHAI NAOROJI

Apart from these two responses, i.e. armed rebellion and socio-cultural reformism, the third response came in the form of Indian nationalism. It underlined the greater unity of the Indian people and provided a new forum for the ventilation of their grievances. This process, ultimately, culminated in the formation of the Indian National Congress (INC) in 1885. However, that momentous event was preceded by a number of other developments. And it is to them that we focus our attention in this section. These background developments leading to the formation of the Indian National Congress could be put into two categories: distant causes and proximate or precipitating causes. We can even study the distant causes under the following sub-categories:

1. Rise of Modern Intelligentsia

As we have seen earlier, the traditional elite comprising *nawabs*, talukdars and zamindars backed by peasants and other sections of the society, had tried and failed in their attempt to oust the British from the Indian soil during the 1857 rebellion. Thereafter, they went into disarray: some of them compromised and worked as collaborators with the British, others were destroyed and still others were left to fend for themselves. Thus, a vacuum was created at the traditional elite level, which was filled up by the newly educated elite, thrown up by the Macaulay System of Education. These new elites were well-versed in discourses on democracy, rule of law, liberty and equality among men, which was emerging as the reigning ideology of the West. Above all, they were becoming victims of discrimination even at their own personal levels. Moreover, being the product of a new educational system based on English medium instruction, they had developed a pan-India character which enabled them to formulate and articulate the new themes of discourses at an all-India level. All this provided them with a new opportunity to plan an all-India organisation with more pronounced political and economic programmes. It is not surprising at all that they actually founded the Indian National Congress (INC) in 1885.

2. Deteriorating Economic Conditions

The deteriorating economic condition of people, which had assumed a gigantic form in the last quarter of the nineteenth century, created a psychological base for the emergence of the Indian nationalism. In the process of their mass pauperisation, the people came to identify the British colonial rule as the chief villain of the piece. What gave greater credence to their general perception was the solid intellectual work undertaken by the early nationalists like Dadabhai Naoroji, M. G. Ranade, R. C. Dutt and others, who dug out facts and figures to prove beyond any reasonable doubt, that the British rule was definitely contributing to the mass impoverishment of our people. Of particular interest was the Drain Theory which came to be associated with Dadabhai Naoroji. The quintessence of this theory was that the Indian wealth was being drained out to Britain in various ways, viz. salaries and pensions of the British civil and military officials, payment of interest on the loan taken by the Government of India, ploughing back of the profit proceeds to Britain arising from the British capital investments in India, and home charges (expenses) on the Indian Government establishment in England. They even identified the actual channel through which the drain of Indian wealth to Britain was taking place: it took the form of an excess of Indian exports over its imports for which India received nothing in economic and material terms. Naoroji even calculated that this drain of Indian wealth amounted to one-third of its total savings. Thus, Naoroji succeeded in establishing a direct correlation between the British colonial rule and the mass poverty in India. It is true that Naoroji and others did not push their findings to their logical conclusions as they did not demand the end of the British rule. But by focusing on the ugly face of the British rule they greatly contributed to the emergence of Indian nationalism.

3. Contributions of Social-Religious Reform Movements

No discussion on the causes leading to the emergence of Indian nationalism would be complete without taking into account the contributions of socio-religious movements in this regard. It is true that they became ardent critics of the decadent aspects of the Indian social system, viz. caste system, idolatry, polygamy, child-marriage, widow-burning sati, etc. But at the same time they underlined the significance of some of the key components of the ancient Indian heritage, viz. its universalism, rationalism and monotheism, etc. Thus they were working to bring about renaissance, reformation and enlightenment in India at one go. This created a new sense of self-confidence among our people and released a tremendous source of energy. They charted a new path for our people and impressed upon them that some of the key concepts of modern times, like equality, nationalism and universalism are not alien to our real cultural heritage. All these greatly contributed to the emergence of the new nationalism in the country.

4. Role of Earlier Political Associations

The formation of the Indian National Congress was preceded by the emergence of a number of secular political organisations which prepared the soil in which the Congress could be planted subsequently. Bengal was the first place where such organisations came up initially. Bengal British India Society, was founded in 1843 which had been preceded by the Landholders Society of 1837. In 1851, both these organisations merged, and thus came into being the British Indian Association. This was followed by the Madras Native Association and the Bombay Association, both of which came into being in 1852. All these organisations were raising secular issues like excessive land revenue and other related issues. They had a narrow social base and their work was marked by great caution and circumspection, but as pioneers, their role could not be minimised. Dadabhai Naoroji organised one such organisation in London in 1860, which was called the East Indian Association. This was followed by the foundation of the Indian Association by Surendranath Banerjee in 1876. The other presidencies soon followed suit. Poona Sarvajanik Sabha organised by Ranade and others and Satya Shodhak Samaj founded by Jyotiba Phule also played a critical role in this regard. In the similar manner a number of associations also come into being in other places, viz. Bombay Presidency Association, Madras Mahajan Sabha, Allahabad People's Association and Indian Association of Lahore. All these associations raised issues concerning the people and actually prepared the congenial background for the formation of the Indian National Congress in 1885.

5. Role of the Indian Press and Literature

The protests against the unjust and exploitative nature of the British rule did not end with the failure of the 1857 rebellion. Some of the leading lights of the rebellion of 1857 like Kunwar Singh and Rani Lakshmi Bai were soon turned into icons and a number of patriotic songs were composed praising their heroic deeds. Patriotic songs and dramas started being circulated through fairs and *melas* and this kept the lamp of nationalism burning. The vernacular press also played a leading role in raising the political consciousness of the people. *Bharat Mitra* (Hindi) and *Jam-e-Jahan Numa* (Urdu) are worth mentioning in this regard. The English Press did not lag behind either. *Amrita Bazar Patrika* and *Som Prakash* from Calcutta, *Indu Prakash* and *Native Opinion* from Bombay, and *the Hindu* from Madras played a leading role in building up nationalistic feelings in the country. Litterateurs also lent a helping hand to that venture. Dinabandhu Mitra, the writer of a drama *Neel Darpan* vividly described the atrocities committed on the indigo growers. Perhaps more than any other writer of his time, Bankim Chandra Chattopadhyaya played a critical role in building up the nationalistic feelings in the country. His song *Bande Mataram* which he later on incorporated in his historic novel *Anandmath* depicted the daring acts of Sanyasi revolts. *Bande Mataram* soon became the battle cry of Indian nationalism. In the Hindi region, Bhartendu Harishchandra played a similar role in arousing and sustaining patriotic feelings among the people of the Hindi heartland.

Proximate or Precipitating Causes for the Emergence of Indian Nationalism

Apart from these distant causes, there were a number of precipitating causes which also contributed to the emergence of Indian nationalism. The most important was Lord Lytton's (the Viceroy of India from 1876–80) new anti-India policy. In the four years of his rule he imposed two draconian acts – Vernacular Press Act (1878) and Arms Act (1877). The Press Act tried to censure, control and dominate the Vernacular Press which had emerged as the strongest medium for the ventilation of the people's grievances. Through the Arms Act he sought to disarm the people of India once for all and, thus, rule out any future possibility of armed resistance to the British. Not only that, he removed import duty on cotton clothes for facilitating greater entry of British textile goods into the Indian market. The lowering of age from 21 to 19 as the maximum age for Indian candidates for ICS examination which further alienated the educated Indian middle class: it was seen as an attempt on the part of the government to prevent Indians from the ICS competition.

All this infuriated the Indian middle classes and a plethora of protest movements were launched, in which the Indian Association

VANDE MATARAM

HAIL to thee, Mother! Thy proud sons greet thee,
  Fair as the moon and clear as the sun;
Terrible fair as a bannered army;
  Patient and strong till the day be won;
Calling thy sons to the high endeavour;
  Sealing them true to the task begun.

Others will fight with hatred and slaying,
  Wade to a kingdom through blood outpoured.
We will conquer with God's own armour;
  We will slay with the Spirit's sword;
Vanquish by Love that can meekly suffer;
  Die and arise in the name of the Lord.

Prophet souls that have watched for the dawning,—
  Patient hope in your sleepless eyes,—
Cry and exult! for the flags of morning
  Flame on the face of the eastern skies!
Welcome the end of your night's long travail!
  See your sun in his strength arise!

India, my India! Mother beloved!
  Shatter the chains of thy thraldom past!
Ransom thy captives and raise thy fallen!
  Fold to thy bosom thy sons outcast!
Rise in the might of thine ancient splendour!
  Shout for thy great Release at last!

J.C.W.

led by Surendranath Banerjee played a crucial role. Lord Ripon who had replaced Lord Lytton in 1880, virtually stirred up a hornet's nest when he sought an amendment in the Criminal Procedure Act, so as to empower the Indian Judges of *muffasil* towns to try the European accused involved in criminal cases without jury. He introduced a Bill to that effect, which came to be known as Ilbert's Bill. This infuriated the Anglo-Indian community and they rose virtually in rebellion. The government was forced to withdraw the

Bill in the face of a powerful protest from the Anglo-Indian community. This was an eye-opening experience for the Indian political elite: they were now convinced more than ever that a properly organised protest movement could force the government to make a retreat on any important issue. The Ilbert Bill controversy gave a new urgency for floating an all-India organisation. At the behest of the Indian Association, a national conference was held in Calcutta from 28 to 31 December 1883, which was largely attended, drawing people from all quarters of the country. This experience further encouraged our leaders to call another conference, which ultimately resulted in the foundation of the Indian National Congress in December 1885.

To sum up, India responded to the British challenge in several ways including the armed rebellion. But ultimately she opted for a new national movement that led our people to their independence in 1947. Thus, the first step on the long road to independence was taken in the form of the foundation of the Indian National Congress in 1885 which become a symbol of our nationhood.

19 British Colonial Rule in India: An Evaluation

The British connection has made India more helpless than she was before, politically and economically.

MAHATMA GANDHI

In the preceding chapters we have already surveyed and critically examined various aspects of the British colonial policy at different stages of their colonial rule. In this chapter we seek to present an overall assessment of the British rule in India, which impacted the different walks of our national life. There are two schools of thought on the question of an overall impact of the British rule on the Indian society. The protagonists of the Raj believe that it played a positive and constructive role in India. On the other hand, the majority of the Indian leaders have been of the opinion that the British rule was primarily responsible for the ruination of our economic-cultural and political life. The scholars of both the groups have their own facts and arguments to support their respective contentions. We propose to make fairly an objective study of the claims of both the schools of thought. To that end, we would consider the impact of the British rule primarily in political, economic, social and cultural/educational fields.

Political Impact

Many scholars look at the impact of the British on the political side of our national life in positive terms. They are of the considered opinion that the British rule promoted the political unity of the country. Their primary contention is that India was never united in territorial terms, as it did under the British rule. Even the partition of the country did not materially change the situation as a vast swathe of the land still remained within the purview of India–more land than it ever came under any single Indian ruler. Not only that, these scholars also argue that the kind of Indian nationalism, which emerged in the last quarter of the nineteenth century, was also a by-product of the British rule. The imperialist school of scholars were in the forefront of such formulation. They assert that India was never a nation–it was nothing more than a conglomeration of castes, communities and religious and linguistic groups. Hence, the emergence of India as a powerful and united State could be legitimately attributed to the British rule.

On the other end of the scale is the nationalist school. It claims that India has ever remained a nation from time immemorial. They further assert that our concept of nationalism has been different from the European concept of nationalism. Our emphasis has been on the cultural unity of the people rather than on political unity based on the administration of a centralised State. Mahatma Gandhi in *Hind Swaraj* underscores the fact that India had remained a nation since the ancient days. He asserts that our four pilgrimages located at the four corners of the country have ever remained the symbol of our nationhood. Hence, according to Mahatma Gandhi, it is a travesty of truth to say that our nationalism is a by-product of the British rule.

In the political realm, a second major contribution of the British rule is taken to be the foundation of the rule of law and an independent judicial system. Besides, freedom of Press was also ensured and a limited democratisation of polity was also introduced. But the fact of the matter was that all these measures were being taken to ensure stability and legitimacy of the British regime. This is so because in normal and peaceful times, the system did look somewhat democratic, but in the case of any real or imaginary challenge to the British rule, its democratic veneer at once disappeared and its ugly, autocratic face automatically used to come into being. Thus, even a small provocative move was dealt with in a most authoritarian way–all kinds of undemocratic ordinances were brought in and the rule of law was suddenly replaced by the rule of men. The democratic mask was suddenly taken off and even the freedom of Press used to be stifled as if it never existed.

The British are supposed to have made significant contribution in the democratisation of our polity through various constitutional development measures. On this score, it is submitted that the constitutional Acts of 1861, 1892, 1909, 1919 and 1935 did lead the Indian people on the path of democratisation. They gave them an opportunity to be trained in running and administering the democratic institutions. Such an experience with democratic institutions turned out to be of great help even in the post-independent India. A similar argument is given in respect of civil services. Through I.C.S. a system of strong governance was established which played a crucial role in the administrative unification of India.

As a counter-point, so do many scholars assert, it could be said that the real motive behind all these measures was to stabilise their rule in India and not to take Indian people on the road to democracy. It is also argued in favour of the British that the British established a strong tradition of army and police under civilian control. Such a tradition of the army under the civilian control turned out to be of great help even in the post-independent India.

But let us not forget that all these institutions were raised to control and pacify the rising wave of the Indian nationalism. Besides, army and police were frequently used to meet any threat to their rule in India.

Economic Field

As stated earlier, the British Raj led to the ruination of both Indian agriculture and Indian industries, leading to the problem of mass pauperization of the Indian people. Our early nationalist leaders like Dadabhai Naoroji, R.C. Dutt and others squarely blamed the British for mass poverty in India. In fact, such an understanding was also behind the emergence of the Indian national movement. But many Marxist scholars do believe that the destruction of the autarkic village system was a necessary precondition for the introduction of the capitalist system in India. Karl Marx, in a series of articles, had put forward such a thesis in which he underlined both the destructive and constructive aspects of the British rule in India. The destructive aspect was obvious, as the people suffered in a massive way, as their system of production and the way of life were adversely affected by the British rule. But the positive side of the British rule was that a firm foundation for the introduction of the capitalist system of production was introduced in India. Marxist scholars like R.P. Dutt and A.R. Desai have been giving these arguments at ad nauseam. On this point of the debate, one could safely assert that slavery could never open the floodgate of human liberation. If this was so, then thousands of people all over the world would not have sacrificed their lives in the cause of national liberation. Hence, one could very well agree with Mahatma Gandhi when he asserted that the British connections have ruined India, economically, politically and even culturally.

There is another debate in respect of the impact of the British rule on the economic life of India: whether India went through a process of de-industrialization or was it more than compensated in the subsequent years in the process of re-industrialization? Sumit Sarkar has put forward two diametrically opposite views of two scholars on this point. American scholar Maurice D'Maurice contests the Indian nationalist opinion that India went through the process of de-industrilization in the initial years of the British rule. He is of the opinion that such a claim of the Indian nationalist leadership is a myth, as they tried to prove their thesis only on the basis of import export data. His primary contention is that there are not enough data to reach at such a conclusion. He also argues that with the destruction of the traditional Indian elite, it was quite natural that the production of luxury goods would go down. Besides, it is possible that in the eastern part of India the handicraft industry might have been destroyed. But on that basis alone it would not be right to claim that during the Company Raj the handicrafts had been destroyed in the entire country. An entirely opposite view on this score has been presented by an Indian economist– A.K. Bagchi. He quotes from 1901 census data to contend that the working population engaged in industrial production went down from 18 per cent to 8 per cent. Even if one accepts Maurice's basic contention that sufficient data is not available to reach at such a conclusion, poverty and large-scale sufferings of our people might have spoken more loudly than any set of lifeless data.

The nature and motive of the British when they initiated the process of industrialization in the later period of their rule constitutes the third issue of the debate. Did they wish India to be turned into a highly industrialized country or was their purpose just to make maximum profit by investing their capital in India? Most of the scholars believe that the British started making investments in India only when it became most profitable. Hence, profit motive and not industrilization was their primary concern. A number of arguments are advanced in the support of such contention. First, since the days of the foundation of the Congress in 1885 the Indian nationalist leadership was demanding the protection of Indian industries. But the Government did not pay any attention to it. Hence, it is quite clear that they did not want to promote Indian industries. The second argument is that the British invested their capital in certain areas in which the possibility of maximising their profit was there. They did not invest in heavy industries which always constitute the backbone of the rapid industrilization. The fact of the matter was that the slow and tardy pace of industrilization which they started after 1860, did not even fully compensate the loss in industrial terms, which India had suffered during the initial years of the British rule. Thus, by the time the British rule ended, India had remained a poor and backward country. One could safely conclude that the economic policy for India was never formulated on the basis of what suited most to India, but what promoted the British interests. Dadabhai Naoroji's drain theory conclusively proved that much of the wealth of India was taken to England through fraud and force which provided the basic capital for the initiation of the industrial revolution in England.

Social Field

British rule also impacted the social life in India. On account of its economic policy, a number of new classes like landlord, landless labour, zamindar, industrial worker, and educational elite emerged in India's social life. All this created an environment of domination, exploitation and inequality. Besides, by relentlessly pursuing the policy of 'divide and rule' they promoted a feeling of divisiveness among our people based on caste, religion, creed, region and language, Census policy and constitutional provisions also promoted separatism and identity politics. They also created various kinds of divides among our people–Hindu-Muslim, adivasies, non-adivasis, caste Hindus-non-caste Hindus, Arya-Anarya and similar other divides. Separate electorate system for various communities further promoted such divisiveness among our people. The cumulative impact of all these measures was that the Indian social life was broken to pieces. One of the pernicious results of such policy was the partition of the country. However, that did not solve the Hindu-Muslim divide which continues to persist even today. Besides, the identity politics which was initiated as a result of the British policy is posing a serious threat to the unity of India even in our own times.

Educational and Cultural Field

We have already seen that Raj's educational policy greatly affected our social and cultural life. Its most striking impact was to be seen in the emergence of a new English educated middle class elite. It is this class which was the mainstay of the Indian national movement. There is a school of thought even in India which takes it to be the greatest contribution of the Raj. It is argued that it is through this class that scientific knowledge of the West was mediated to India. It is further said that if today India has emerged as big knowledge power in the world, due credit must be given to the introduction of English education in India.

But we must also look at the other side of the picture. Let us not forget that the basic motive of Macaulay, who was instrumental in introducing English education in India, was to create a class of people who might look like Indians but must think, feel and act like the British. In a way, Macaulay's prophecy had come true. It has created a big gulf between the common people and the English-Indian elite. It has led to the creation of the two Indias–Bharat and

India–Bharat of the common people and India of the elite. They differ in their thinking process, in food, dress, life style and the world view. Introduction of globalisation and liberalization has further widened the gulf between the rich and the poor. But the fact that initially this gulf was created by the British rule could not be wished away. Let us end up this part of our study by making a general comment. Whenever an assessment of the impact of the British rule on Indian polity, economy and social and cultural life is made, one compares the end result of the British rule with the state of affairs in which India was on the eve of the British arrival. Often many people forget that India would not have stood still at the point of time of the British arrival. Every society changes in a natural way. Indian society would not have stagnated on that level either. To say that but for the British occupation, the Indian society would not have changed is nothing but a direct assault on the human ingenuity and dignity. Therefore, to attribute all dynamic changes in the Indian society to the British rule is neither fair nor just. On the other hand, many people including Mahatma Gandhi believed that but for the British intergennum, India might have developed on the basis of the genius of her own people. In the age of globalization, the colonial and slavish mentality is growing among the elite section of our society. A number of our leaders like Vivekananda, Aurobindo, Raman Maharshi, Dayanand and Mahatma Gandhi and others tried to hold up the tide of Westernisation in their own way. They revived the Indian spirit in a big way. A similar challenge of Westernisation is facing us today.

Chronology of Major Events from AD *1600 to 1947*

1600	Royal Charter for the English East India Company
1612	First English factory at Surat in western India
1613	Mughal Emperor Jahangir grants trading rights to the English company
1639	Foundation of Fort St. George in Madras
1651	English factory at Hugli in eastern India
1698	The English obtain zamindari (landowning) rights in Kolikata, Sutanuti and Gobindapur in eastern India
1707	Death of Aurangzeb
1717	Mughal Emperor Farrukhsiyar grants duty-free trading rights to the English company
1745-49	First Anglo-French War
1751-54	Second Anglo-French War
1756-63	Seven Years' War in Europe Third Anglo-French War in India resulting in the elimination of French competition.
1756	Nawab of Bengal captures Calcutta from the English, leading to confrontation between the two
1757	Battle of Plassey
1761	Third Battle of Panipat
1764	Battle of Buxar
1765	Grant of *Diwani* (revenue collecting rights) for Bengal, Bihar and Orissa to the English company
1767-69	First Anglo-Mysore War
1773	The Regulating Act
1775-82	First Anglo-Maratha War and Treaty of Salbai by which the British Government acquired control of Salsette
1780-84	Second Anglo-Mysore War
1784	The Pitt's India Act
1790-92	Third Anglo-Mysore War

1793	The Permanent Settlement of land revenue in Bengal
1799	Fourth Anglo-Mysore War
1802	Peshwa Baji Rao II seeks British protection and accepts a subsidiary alliance by the Treaty of Bassein
1803-05	Second Anglo-Maratha War resulting in defeat of the Maratha chieftains forcing them to accept subsidiary force
1817-18	Third Anglo-Maratha War resulting in the abolition of the office of Peshwa and annexation of his territory by the English
1829	Prohibition of *sati* (self-immolation by widows)
1833	Renewal of the Company's Charter Abolition of the Company's monopoly trading rights
1835	Lord Macaulay's Minute on Indian Education
1845-46	First Anglo-Sikh War
1848-49	Second Anglo-Sikh War and Annexation of Punjab
1853	Railways opened from Bombay to Thana
1856	Annexation of Awadh
1857-58	Mutiny and the Revolt: India's First War of Independence
1858	Establishment of Crown rule in British India
1861	Indian Councils Act
1883	The Ilbert bill controversy
1885	Foundation of the Indian National Congress
1892	Indian Council's Act of 1892
1905	Partition of Bengal and Swadeshi Movement
1906	Foundation of the All India Muslim League
1908	Tilak's trial and six years' imprisonment
1909	Morley-Minto Reforms
1911	Partition of Bengal annulled
1912	Imperial capital moves from Calcutta to Delhi
1914	The First World War begins
1916	Lucknow Pact between Indian National Congress and the Muslim League, the formation of the Home Rule League by Tilak and Annie Besant
1917	Russian Revolution, Champaran Satyagraha of Mahatma Gandhi
1919	Montagu-Chelmsford Reforms; Massacre of Jallianwala Bagh
1920-21	Gandhiji takes over leadership of the Indian National Congress; Khilafat and Non-Cooperation Movements under the leadership of Mahatma Gandhi
1922	Non-Cooperation Movement withdrawn after Chauri-Chaura

	violence; Gandhiji's trial and imprisonment
1923	The formation of the Swaraj Party: its candidates enter the Legislative Councils
1925	First Conference of the Communist Party of India held at Kanpur
1928	Visit of the Simon (Indian Statutory) Commission
	All Parties conference held in Calcutta; Motilal Nehru Report on the future constitution of India presented; rejection of Jinnah's amendments to the Nehru Report
1929	Lahore Congress and the resolution on Purna Swaraj
1930	Civil Disobedience Movement under Gandhiji's leadership
1931	Gandhi–Irwin Pact
	The Karachi Congress and its Resolutions on the Fundamental Rights
1932	Second phase of the Civil Disobedience Movement, The Communal Award and the Poona Pact
1934	Civil Disobedience Movement called off, The Formation of the Congress Socialist Party
1935	Government of India Act
1937	Inauguration of provincial autonomy
	Elections under the new Act
	Congress ministries in eight provinces
1939	The Second World War begins, resignation of the Congress Ministries
1940	The Muslim League Pakistan resolution; Lord Linglithgow's August offer of dominion status
1942	Cripps Mission ends in a failure
	Quit India Movement
1943	Mahatma Gandhi's Fast in Aga Khan Palace, Formation of the Azad Hind Fauz (INA) by Subhas Chandra Bose
1944	Gandhi–Jinnah talks
1946	Cabinet Mission to India, Interim Government, The Muslim League' Direct Action
1947	Mountbatten Plan and Indian Independence Act of 1947; Partition of India and the creation of Pakistan as an Independent State; India attains Freedom on 15 August 1947

Select Bibliography

General

Chand, Tara, History of the Freedom Movement in India, Vol. 1-4 Delhi, 1961

Chandra, Bipan. India's Struggle for Independence, New Delhi, 1987.

Desai, A.R., Social Background of Indian Nationalism, Bombay, 2005 (Reprint)

Dutt, R.P., India Today, Bombay, 1940

Majumdar R.C., History of the Freedom Movement in India, Vol. 1-3 Calcutta, 1963

Nanda, B.R. Mahatma Gandhi: A Biography, London, 1958.

Nehru, Jawaharlal, The Discovery of India, New Delhi, 1981.

Pandey, B.N. (ed.) A Centenary History of the Indian National Congress, Vol. 1-3, New Delhi, 1885.

Ram, M.S. (ed.) Freedom of India, In the Words of Its Architects, Chennai, 2003.

Sarkar, Sumit, Modern India 1885-1947, Delhi, 1999.

Sitaramanya, P., History of the Indian National Congress, Vol. 1-2, Bombay 1946.

Spear, Percival, Oxford History of Modern India, 1740-1947, London, 1965.

Part - I

Ahmad, Aijaz, In Theory, Classes, Nations, Literatures, London and New York, 1992.

———, "Between Orientalism and Historicism: Anthropological Knowledge of India", Studies in History, 7(1), January-June 1991.

Baber, Zaheer, The Science of Empire: Scientific Knowledge, Civilization, and Colonial Rule in India, Delhi, 1998.

Brydon (ed.), Post Colonialism, Vol. 1. New York. 2005.

Brydon (ed.), Post Colonialism, Vol. 4. New York. 2005.

Brydon, Diana, (ed.), Postcolonialism, Critical Concepts in Literary and Cultural Studies, London and New York, 2000, Vol. 2.

Carol A. Breckenbridge and Peter van der Veer (eds.), Orientalism and Postcolonial Predicament, Philadelphia, 1993.

Chakrabarty, Dipesh, Provincializing Europe: Postcolonial Thought and Historical Difference, New Delhi, 2001.

Chakravorty, Gayatri, Spivak, A Critique of Postcolonial Reason: Toward a History of the Vanishing Present, Calcutta, 1990.

Daniel R. Headrick, The Tentacles of Progress: Technology Transfer in the Age of Imperialism, 1850-1940, New York, 1988.

Didur, Jill and Hefferman, Teresa, "Revisiting the Sublatern in the New Empire", Cultural Studies, 17(1), January 2003.

Ferro, Marc, Colonization: A Global History, London, 1997.

Hobson, J.A. Imperialism. A Study: London, 1930.

Inden, Ronald, Imagining India, Oxford, 1990.

King, Richard, Oriental Enlightenment: The Encounter between Asian and Western Thought, London and New York, 1999.

Lenin, V.I. Imperialism. The Highest Stage of Capitalism, Moscow, 1966

Loomba, Ania, Colonialism/Postcolonialism, London and New York, 1998.

Ludden, David, (ed.), Reading Subaltern Studies: Critical History, Contested Meaning and the Globalization of South Asia, New Delhi, 2001.

Luxemburg, R, Accumulation of Capital, New York, 1951.

Marx and Engles, On Colonialism, Moscow, 1968.

Mommsen, Wlfgang and Osterhammel, Juergen P. (eds.), Imperialism and After, Continuities and Discontinuities, The German Historical Institute, London, 1986.

Mongia, Padmini (ed.), Contemporary Postcolonial Theory: NewYork. 1996.

Patel, Sujata, et al. (ed.), Thinking Social Science in India: Essays in Honour of Alice Thorner, New Delhi, 2002.

Patrick,. Williams and Chrisman, Laura (eds.), Colonial Discourse and Post-Colonial Theory: A Reader, Essex, Harlow, 1993.

Prakash, Gyan, "Writing Post-Orientalist Histories of the Third World: Perspectives from India Historiography", Comparative Studies in Society and History, 32(2), 1990.

———, Another Reason: Science and the Imagination of Modern India, New Delhi, 2000.

Said, Edward W. Culture and Imperialism, London, 1994.

Schumpeter, J.A., Imperialism and Social Classes, New York, 1951.

Schwartz, Henry and Roy, Sangeeta (ed.), A Companion to Postcolonial Studies. Oxford. 2000.

Schwartz, Henry and Roy, Sangeeta (eds.), A Companion to Postcolonial Studies, Oxford, Massachusetts, 2000.

Sen, Amartya, Reason before Identity. The Romanes Lecture. 1998.

Singh, Lata, "Sublatern Historiographic Critique of Colonialist and Nationalist Discourses", The Indian Historical Review, 21(1-2), July 1994-January 1995.

Sweezy, Paul, Modern Capitalism and Other Essays, New York, 1972.

Szymansky, Albert, The Logic of Imperialism, New York, 1981.

Young, Robert J.C. Postcolonialism: An Historical Introduction, Oxford, 2001.

Part II

Anderson, Benedict, Imagined Communities, London, 1983.

Argov, Daniel, Moderates and Extremists in the Indian National Movement, Bombay, 1967.

Barrier, N.G(ed). Cenus in British India, New Perspective. Delhi, 1981.

Basu, Aparna, Essays in the History of Indian Education, Delhi, 1982.

Bhagwan, Vishnoo, Constibutional History of India and National Movement, Lucknow 1974,

Chandra, Bipan. Nationalism and Colonialism in India, New Delhi, 1979.

Chandra, Bipan. The Rise and Growth of Economic Nationalism in India. New Delhi, 1966.

Chatterjee, Partha and Gyan Pandey (eds.), Subaltern Studies, VII. New Delhi, 1994.

Chatterjee, Partha. The Nation and Its Fragments, Princeton,1993.

———, Nationalist Thought and the Colonial World, London, 1986.

Cohn, Bernard S., An Anthropologist among the Historians and Other Essays, Delhi, 1987.

Das, Durga, India from Curzon to Nehru and After, London, 1969.

Desai, T.B., Economic History of India, 1757-1947, Bombay, 1972.

Desika, C. Readings in the Constitutional History of India, Madras, 1983.

Dutt, R.C. Economic History of India in the Victorian Age, Delhi, 1960 (Reprint)

Dutt, R.C. Economic History of India Under Early British Rule.

Gellner, Ernest. Nations and Nationalism, Oxford, 1983.

Greenfeld, Liah. Nationalism, Five Roads to Modernity, Cambridge, 1992.

Guha, R. and Gadgil, M. Past and Present: A Journal of Historical Studies. May, 1989.

Hiemsath, C., Indian Nationalism and Hindu Social Reform, Princeton, 1964.

Jaffrelot, Christophe. The Hindu Nationalist Movement in India, New York, 1996.
Majumdar, B.B., Militant Nationalism of India, Calcutta, 1966.
Majumdar, R.C., British paramountcy and Indian Renaissance, Bombay, 1966.
Mann, M. and Fischer T. H. (eds.), Colonialism as Civilizing Mission: Cultural Ideology in British India, London, 1968.
Mehrottra, S.R. The Emergence of the Indian National Congress, Delhi, 1971.
Metcalf and Metcalf. A Concise History of India, Cambridge, 2002.
Metcalf, Thomas. Ideology of the Raj, Cambridge, 1995.
Mishra, B.B. Administrative History of India Bombay 1970.
Mishra, B.B. Indian Middle Class, New Delhi, 1961.
Naoroji, Dadabhai, Poverty and un British Rule in India, London, 1903.
Philips, C.H., The East India Company, 1784-1834, Bombay, 1961.
Raychaudhuri, Tapan and Habib, Irfan, the Cambridge Economic History of India, Vol. 1.
Seal, Anil, The Emergence of India National Congress, Competition and Collaboration in Later Nineteenth Century, Cambridge, 1968.
Sen, S.N. Eighteen Fifty Seven, Delhi, 1957.
Singh, V.B. Economic History of India 1857, 1956, Delhi.
Stokes, Eric Peasants and the Raj; Cambridge, 1978.
Thompson E.J. & Garranet, G.T., Rise and Fulfillment of the British Rule in India, Allahabad, 1958.
Wolpert, Stanley. A. Tilak and Gokhale : Revolution and Reform in the making of Modern India, Delhi, 1991.

Part - III

Anil Seal, Emergence of Indian Nationalism, Cambridge, 1968.
Bipin Chandra, India's struggle for Independence, Delhi, 1989.
D. Rottermund, the phases of Indian Nationalism, Bombay, 1970.
Desai A.R. Social Background to Indian Nationalism Bombay, 1973.
Dutt. R.P. India Today, Calcutta, 1970.
Guha, Ranjit, Subaltarn studies vol. 1. Delhi
JJ. Broomfield, Elite conflict in a plural society Twentieth century Bengal, Los Angeles, 1968.
Nanda, B.R. Essays in Modern India, Delhi 1980
Pannikar, K.M. A survey of Indian history, Delhi, 1957.
Sarkar, Sumit, Modern Indian, 1885-1947, Delhi, 1999.
Tapan Raychaudhary, Indian Nationalism Animal Politics, Historical Journal, 2, 1979.
Valentine Chirol, India unrest, London, 1910.

Index

□□□